NO ORDINARY MAN 2

NO ORDINARY MAN 2

Resources for reflective worship on the person of Jesus

NICK FAWCETT

Kevin
Mayhew

First published in 2000 by
KEVIN MAYHEW LTD
Buxhall
Stowmarket
Suffolk IP14 3BW

0 1 2 3 4 5 6 7 8 9

ISBN 1 84003 567 6
Catalogue No 1500362

Cover illustration by Gabrielle Stoddart
Cover design by Jaquetta Sergeant
Typesetting by Louise Selfe

Printed in Great Britain

*To all my friends at Leigh Baptist Church in Lancashire,
where I spent my first years in ministry –
remembered with sincere thanks and affection.*

ABOUT THE AUTHOR

Nick Fawcett was born in 1957. He studied Theology at Bristol University and Regent's Park College, Oxford. His early years of ministry were spent in Somerset and Lancashire, and from 1989 to 1996 he was Minister of Gas Green Baptist Church, Cheltenham. From November 1996 to June 1999 he served as Toc H Chaplain and Development Officer for Wales and the West of England.

He is now concentrating full time on his career as a writer, proof-reader and indexer. His books to date are *No Ordinary Man* (1997), *Prayers For All Seasons* (1998), *Are You Listening?* (1998), *Getting It Across* (1999) and *Grappling With God*, Books 1-4 (2000), all published by Kevin Mayhew. He has also written the texts for the *Best Loved Choral Melodies Choral Collection* (1999) and had four hymns chosen for inclusion in the Churches Together Millennium Hymn Book *New Start Hymns and Songs* (1999), both also published by Kevin Mayhew.

He lives with his wife, Deborah, and their two young children, Samuel and Katie, in Wellington, Somerset.

ACKNOWLEDGEMENTS

I am indebted once again in the writing of this book to my wife, Deborah, for all the practical support she has so willingly offered; to Katherine Laidler for her much-valued work in editing the manuscript; to Peter Dainty for his typically perceptive comments and criticisms; and to Kevin Mayhew Publishers for the opportunity to put this and other material into print.

CONTENTS

INTRODUCTION

You will conceive in your womb and bear a son,
and you will name him Jesus.

He took a loaf of bread, and after blessing it he broke it,
gave it to them, and said, 'Take; this is my body.'

At three o'clock Jesus cried out with a loud voice,
'Eloi, Eloi, lema sabachthani?', which means,
'My God, my God, why have you forsaken me?'

Jesus himself stood among them and said,
'Peace be with you.'

Words of Scripture which testify to some of the great events surrounding the life and death of Jesus of Nazareth, the man executed as a criminal nearly two thousand years ago, but revered by countless generations since as the Son of God, the promised Messiah, the King of kings and Lord of lords. A man whose life from the beginning touched the lives of others, bringing a new dimension to their experience – a new understanding of life itself. A man whose coming was anticipated for centuries before his birth, and who has shaped the lives of millions since his death. A man who has won such love and devotion, such loyalty and commitment, that many of his followers have willingly endured all manner of ridicule and suffering, even death itself, in support of his cause. And a man who, according to Scripture, is alive now, wanting us to know the reality of his love and his message for ourselves.

So who was Jesus? Why did he come? How has he changed the lives of his followers? And what does he mean for us today? It is questions such as these which prompted the writing of my first book, *No Ordinary Man,* and which have similarly inspired this second collection of meditations, for it is my firm belief that those who encountered Jesus during his ministry must have asked very similar questions themselves. Imagine, for example, what it must have felt like to be one of the shepherds beside the manger, or one of the wise men at last coming to the end of your journey in Bethlehem; one of the apostles sharing in the Last Supper, or one of the women standing at the foot of the cross; one of those to whom Jesus appeared after his death, or one of those who felt the power of his Spirit at work in the early days of the Christian Church. How would you have come to terms with your experience? What would you have made of it all? In what way would it have shaped your understanding of Jesus? And, most important of all, how would it have changed your life?

This is what these meditations attempt to explore. Designed to put ourselves into the shoes of those who knew Jesus best, each is written from the standpoint of an individual whose life was influenced by Jesus – his parents, his disciples, his friends, his enemies; those who were healed, challenged, troubled or inspired by him. The events underlying each meditation are not described as if they are happening then and there, but as though the character in question is looking back, trying to make sense of the events which he or she was part of. And always the underlying question is the same: What does this man Jesus mean for me?

While there is inevitably some poetic licence in the interpretation of events, all the meditations in this book are rooted in a passage of Scripture, and I would urge that the two are used together.

There is a variety of ways in which these meditations can be used to complement passages of Scriptures and events from the life of Jesus which have perhaps become so familiar that they fail to speak as powerfully as they used to. They may be used in public worship, house groups, quiet days, or other reflective events. They can be employed individually to supplement the reading and preaching of the Word, or put together into a series focusing on a particular season such as Advent, Christmas, or Holy Week. Their presentation can be enhanced through the use of slides and music.

With the one hundred meditations in Section One I have included an appropriate Scripture passage (from the *New Revised Standard Version*) and a prayer. In Section Two there are suggested service outlines from Advent through to Trinity, together with ideas for quiet days. Suggestions for audiovisual material are listed in Appendices 1 and 2.

Of course, all of the meditations in this book finally say more about my understanding of Jesus than anyone else's. You may agree with what you read, you may disagree. Sometimes you may find new light shed on a passage of a Scripture, other times you may feel I have completely missed the point. My hope though is that at least something in this book will prompt you to think more deeply about what Jesus means to you and to our world today. If it does that then it will have served its purpose.

NICK FAWCETT

HOW TO USE THIS BOOK

This book is intended to offer a new dimension to worship. Just how you use it is up to you. You may wish to use a single meditation to reinforce the accompanying Scripture reading. You may take one of the suggested orders and use it as it stands. You may want to select parts of several orders and adapt them to your requirements. Or you may prefer to pick and mix, making use of some of the suggestions but using other ideas of your own. The book is designed to be flexible.

Should you wish to use slides and music, there are obviously certain basic requirements. A good hi-fi system, slide projector and screen are essential. You will also find the services of an assistant invaluable when it comes to presenting the material – ideally somebody to control the slide projector, and maybe as well someone to fade in and out the music. Remember, too, to ensure that those reading the meditations are given proper time to prepare beforehand, and that they are instructed to read slowly and clearly, beginning by announcing the title of the meditation.

Much of the recommended music can probably be borrowed from your local library if not from a friend. Should you wish to buy it, much is available on budget CD sets, namely: *The Voices of Angels (100 Heavenly Classics)*, *100 Romantic Classics*, *100 Relaxing Classics* and *100 Popular Classics*, all compiled by Castle Communications; *Discovering the Classics* (three volume double CD set), *Renaissance Choral Treasures* and *Classical Favourites for Relaxing and Dreaming* compiled by Naxos. Other works extensively used are Handel's *Messiah*, Mozart's *Requiem*, *Mass in C minor* and *Coronation Mass*, and a recent composition, *Fountain of Life*, by Margaret Rizza, available from Kevin Mayhew Publishers.

Slide collections can be bought from Rickett Educational Media Ltd (formerly The Slide Centre) (see Appendix 2), but again can probably be borrowed through your local Diocesan Resource Centre if you have one. Failing that, you might once more try your local library.

The way I have used music and slides is as backing for the suggested biblical readings. You might of course like to do things differently, perhaps, for example, as backing for the meditations instead. Once again this is a matter for personal choice. If you use music for backing though, make sure you have a reasonable voice-amplification system so that whoever is reading can be heard above it.

One final point, when using slides always run through them beforehand making sure they are the right way up and in the correct order. A picture of Jesus hanging upside down on the cross can destroy the atmosphere built up during a service – believe me, I know! Make sure also that you have a spare bulb in case one should blow, and arrange all electrical leads so that no one can inadvertently fall over them.

The more media you use in a service the more can go wrong, but equally the more powerful the final presentation can be.

SECTION ONE

MEDITATIONS

ADVENT

1

'THE PEOPLE WHO WALKED IN DARKNESS'

Resident of Jerusalem

Reading: Isaiah 9:2, 6-7

The people who walked in darkness have seen a great light; those who lived in a land of deep darkness – on them light has shined. For a child has been born for us, a son given to us; authority rests upon his shoulders; and he is named Wonderful Counsellor, Mighty God, Everlasting Father, Prince of Peace. His authority shall grow continually, and there shall be endless peace for the throne of David and his kingdom. He will establish and uphold it with justice and with righteousness from this time onward and for evermore. The zeal of the Lord of hosts will do this.

Meditation

'The people who walked in darkness have seen a great light.'
Do you remember those words?
Of course you do – it's hard not to, isn't it?
But do you think they mean anything?
Do you actually believe that things will change,
    that the Messiah will come
    and finally establish his kingdom?
I used to, once.
I used to read that passage time and again,
    a warm glow stealing over me
    until I tingled with anticipation,
    convinced that God would soon transform this world of ours.
Any day now, I thought,
    it can't be long –
    surely.
But another day, another month, another year came and went,
    and, with each one, faith lost a little of its sparkle,
    until finally the lustre is just about gone,
    no more than a dull gleam left
    where once that confidence shone so brightly.
What happened?

Did I misunderstand something,
     or did the prophet get it wrong,
     his vision not the glorious promise I thought it was
     but an empty illusory dream?
Believe me, I want to think otherwise,
     my spirit still crying out to be proved wrong,
     but just look around you –
     at the sin,
     the suffering,
     the sorrow,
     the squalor –
     and then tell me honestly
     where God is in all this.
Can you see that light he promised?
I can't.
I've waited, as so many have waited before me,
     telling myself that evil can't have the last word,
     that good must finally triumph,
     but there's still no sign,
     nothing to give grounds for optimism,
     and it's all I can do not to lose heart completely.
Yet I must hope;
     somehow, despite it all, I must keep faith,
     for if there's really nothing else in this world than what you see,
     then God help us!
I may have my doubts,
     and it may not be easy,
     but so long as there's even the merest spark of faith left,
     the tiniest, faintest flicker,
     I'm going to go on hoping,
     and go on praying:
     come, Lord,
     come!

Prayer

Gracious God,
> we talk of light shining in the darkness,
> yet sometimes the reality appears very different.

There is so much injustice and oppression in our world;
> so much greed and envy,
> pride, prejudice, hatred and evil.

We are besieged each day
> by stories of poverty, sickness, sorrow and suffering –
> some far afield,
> some on our very own doorstep.

Lord, we try to trust in your purpose,
> but there is so much that seems to belie your love
> and contradict our faith.

Reach out, we ask, wherever there is darkness,
> bringing help and healing, hope and wholeness.

Come again to our world,
> and may the light of your love shine in our hearts
> and in the hearts of all,
> to the glory of your name.

Amen.

2

THE MESSIAH – NOT COMING?

A Zealot

Reading: Psalm 24:7-10

Lift up your heads, O gates!
   and be lifted up, O ancient doors!
   that the King of glory may come in.
Who is the King of glory?
   The Lord, strong and mighty,
   the Lord, mighty in battle.
Lift up your heads, O gates!
   and be lifted up, O ancient doors!
   that the King of glory may come in.
Who is this King of glory?
   The Lord of hosts,
   he is the King of glory.

Meditation

The Messiah – not coming?
Don't make me laugh!
He's coming, all right,
   and it won't be much longer, you take it from me,
   any day now, I shouldn't be surprised.
How do I know?
Well, it's obvious, isn't it?
Just look around you at the world we're living in –
   the state of our society,
   the corruption,
   greed,
   self-interest;
   so much contrary to God's will –
   do you really think he's going to sit back
   and let that carry on for ever?
I can't see it, somehow.

No, he may be taking his time,
    and the delay may be hard to understand,
    but sooner rather than later
    the day of the Lord will be here,
    and what a day it will be,
    what a moment for us all!
At last we'll be free,
    a light rather than laughing stock to the nations,
    a sovereign people instead of subject state,
    for surely when he *does* come
    the call to arms won't be far behind,
    the sound of trumpets summoning us into battle
    and onwards to victory.
That's what God's promised us, isn't it? –
    a new kingdom,
    a fresh start,
    deliverance from slavery –
    and I can hardly wait for it to begin.
Just imagine the scene if you can,
    Jesus and Pilate head to head,
    Roman governor versus King of the Jews –
    that should be worth watching!
I could almost feel sorry for Pilate if I didn't hate him so much,
    for he won't know what's hit him,
    the might of his army powerless against the Lord's hand.
What will he do?
Oh, no doubt he'll wriggle and squirm a bit,
    even wash his hands of all responsibility,
    pretending it was all in the line of duty,
    but there'll be no escape,
    no way of avoiding final judgement,
    for, remember, it's God's anointed we're talking about here,
    the one who will come to establish justice and righteousness,
    to drive out evil,
    and finally, when the enemy is defeated, to bring us peace.
I know it's not been easy this time of waiting,
    hoping against hope for some sign of the Messiah,
    but God has promised that deliverance will come,
    and what he says we know he will do.
So don't tell me he's not coming.
It's just a matter of time, nothing more,
    the dawn of his kingdom round the corner,

here before you know it.
I only hope I'm still around when it arrives, able to see it for myself,
    for it will have been worth waiting for, no doubt about that –
    quite simply, out of this world!

Prayer

Lord Jesus Christ,
    we claim to serve you
    but all too easily we slip into serving ourselves.
Instead of listening to *your* voice
    we tell ourselves what *we* want to hear.
Instead of seeking *your* will
    we prefer our *own*,
    expecting you to conform to *our* expectations.
Forgive us all the ways, consciously and unconsciously,
    that we shut our minds to your living presence;
    to anything we would rather not see or hear.
Break through our narrow vision
    and help us to encounter you as you really are.
So may we truly know you,
    genuinely love you
    and faithfully serve you
    today and every day,
    to the glory of your name.
Amen.

3
'WHERE DID IT ALL START?'

John the Apostle

Reading: John 1:1-5, 10-14

In the beginning was the Word, and the Word was with God, and the Word was God. He was in the beginning with God. All things came into being through him, and without him not one thing came into being. What has come into being in him was life, and the life was the light of all people. The light shines in the darkness, and the darkness did not overcome it.

He was in the world, and the world came into being through him; yet the world did not know him. He came to what was his own, and his own people did not accept him. But to all who received him, who believed in his name, he gave power to become children of God, who were born, not of blood or of the will of the flesh or of the will of man, but of God.

And the Word became flesh and lived among us, and we have seen his glory, the glory as of a father's only son, full of grace and truth.

Meditation

'Where did it all start?' they ask me.
'Tell us the story again.'
And I know just what they want to hear –
    about the inn and the stable,
    the baby lying in a manger,
    shepherds out in the fields by night,
    and wise men travelling from afar.
I know why they ask, of course I do,
    for which of us hasn't thrilled to those marvellous events,
    that astonishing day when the Word became flesh,
    dwelling here on earth amongst us?
Yet wonderful though that all is, it's not where it started,
    and if we stop there, then we see only a fraction of the picture,
    the merest glimpse of everything God has done for us in Christ.
We have got to go right back to see more –
    before Bethlehem,

before the prophets
before the Law,
before time itself, would you believe? –
for that's where it started:
literally 'in the beginning'.
Yes, even there the saving purpose of God was at work,
his creating, redeeming Word
bringing light and love into the world,
shaping not just the heavens and the earth
but the lives of all,
every man, woman and child.
That's the mind-boggling wonder of it –
the fact not just that God made us,
but that through Christ he was determined from the outset
to share our lives,
to take on our flesh,
to identify himself totally with the joys and sorrows,
the beauty and the ugliness of humankind.
It defies belief, doesn't it?
Yet it's true –
God wanting us to know him not as his creatures
but as his children,
not as puppets forced to dance to his tune
but as people responding freely to his love,
and to achieve that he patiently and painstakingly prepared the way,
revealing year after year a little more of his purpose,
a glimpse more of his kingdom,
until at last,
in the fullness of time,
the Word became flesh and lived among us,
full of grace and truth.
It wasn't an afterthought, the incarnation,
a last-ditch attempt to make the best of a bad job –
it was planned from the dawn of time.
So next time you hear the story of the stable and the manger,
of the shepherds gazing in wonder
and the magi kneeling in homage,
stop for a moment
and reflect on everything which made it all possible,
the eternal purpose which so carefully prepared the way of Christ,
and then ask yourself this:
are you prepared to respond to his coming?

Prayer

Gracious God,
    despite our repeated disobedience
    your love continues undiminished,
    reaching out to us every moment of every day.
Despite the rejection of the world
    still you go on seeking to draw it to yourself,
    until every broken relationship with you is mended.
So it is now and so it has always been,
    from the beginning of time your nature always to have mercy.
Help us to appreciate the enormity of your faithfulness,
    and to use this season of Advent
    to open our hearts more fully to your grace;
    through Jesus Christ our Lord.
Amen.

4
I WANTED TO BELIEVE IT, HONESTLY!

Zechariah

Reading: Luke 1:5-20

In the days of King Herod of Judea, there was a priest named Zechariah, who belonged to the priestly order of Abijah. His wife was a descendant of Aaron, and her name was Elizabeth. Both of them were righteous before God, living blamelessly according to all the commandments and regulations of the Lord. But they had no children, because Elizabeth was barren, and both were getting on in years.

Once when he was serving as priest before God and his section was on duty, he was chosen by lot, according to the custom of the priesthood, to enter the sanctuary of the Lord and offer incense. Now at the time of the incense offering, the whole assembly of the people was praying out-side. Then there appeared to him an angel of the Lord, standing at the right side of the altar of incense. When Zechariah saw him, he was terrified; and fear overwhelmed him. But the angel said to him, 'Do not be afraid, Zechariah, for your prayer has been heard. Your wife Elizabeth will bear you a son, and you will name him John. You will have joy and gladness, and many will rejoice at his birth, for he will be great in the sight of the Lord. He must never drink wine or strong drink; even before his birth he will be filled with the Holy Spirit. He will turn many of the people of Israel to the Lord their God. With the spirit and power of Elijah he will go before him, to turn the hearts of parents to their children, and the disobedient to the wisdom of the righteous, to make ready a people prepared for the Lord.' Zechariah said to the angel, 'How will I know that this is so? For I am an old man, and my wife is getting on in years.' The angel replied, 'I am Gabriel. I stand in the presence of God, and I have been sent to speak to you and to bring you this good news. But now, because you did not believe my words, which will be fulfilled in their time, you will become mute, unable to speak until the day these things occur.'

Meditation

I wanted to believe it, honestly!
After all those years trying,
    all those false hopes and crushing disappointments,
    there was nothing I wanted to believe more.
A child!
A son!
At our time of life!
Wonderful!
But that was the trouble –
    we were too old,
    not just *over* the hill but well down the other side,
    and we'd both accepted we just weren't meant to be parents.
It hurt, of course it did,
    but little by little we'd come to terms with it,
    the pain easing as we threw ourselves into what was left us.
So why suddenly this strange vision,
    this sense of God speaking to me
    in a way so real and powerful
    it was as though an angel was there in person,
    spelling out the message word for word?
To be frank I felt we could do without it, both of us,
    and, whatever else, there was no way I intended
    to go running back to Elizabeth,
    opening up old wounds.
So I just laughed it off,
    shrugged my shoulders and carried on
    as though nothing had happened.
Let's face it, I reasoned,
    a few more years and we'd be pushing up the daisies,
    an end to life's mysteries once and for all.
Well, I couldn't have been more wrong, could I?
For it happened,
    every last word of it,
    down to the final detail!
How did I feel?
Well, you can imagine.
Ecstatic!
Just about beside myself with joy!
It was the proudest and most wonderful moment of my life,
    and for a time after the birth I could think of nothing else,

every moment too precious to waste.
Yet I've been thinking recently
    about those words spoken by the angel,
    for when he spoke of John's coming,
    he talked also of the role he was destined to fulfil:
    'He will turn many of the people of Israel to the Lord their God.
    With the spirit and power of Elijah he will go before him,
    to make ready a people prepared for the Lord.'
I forgot that afterwards in all the excitement,
    too much else going on to give it a second thought.
But do you think it could possibly mean what I think it does?
God's promised Messiah, coming at last?
A child, born to *me*, *that* was wonderful!
But for us *all*,
    a child to change the world –
    could that really be?

Prayer

Loving God,
    for all our faith
    there are some things we consider beyond us
    and beyond you.
Belief says one thing but realism another,
    and in consequence we set limits
    to the way you are able to work in our lives.
Yet time and again you have overturned human expectations,
    demonstrating that all things are possible
    for those who love you.
Teach us, then,
    to look beyond the obvious and immediate,
    and to live rather in the light of your sovereign grace
    which is able to do far more
    than we can ever ask or imagine;
    through Jesus Christ our Lord.
Amen.

5
WAS IT JUST A COINCIDENCE?

Elizabeth

Reading: Luke 1:24-25, 39-45

After those days his wife Elizabeth conceived, and for five months she remained in seclusion. She said, 'This is what the Lord has done for me when he looked favourably on me and took away the disgrace I have endured among my people.'

In those days Mary set out and went with haste to a Judean town in the hill country, where she entered the house of Zechariah and greeted Elizabeth. When Elizabeth heard Mary's greeting, the child leaped in her womb. And Elizabeth was filled with the Holy Spirit and exclaimed with a loud cry, 'Blessed are you among women, and blessed is the fruit of your womb. And why has this happened to me, that the mother of my Lord comes to me? For as soon as I heard the sound of your greeting, the child in my womb leaped for joy. And blessed is she who believed that there would be a fulfilment of what was spoken to her by the Lord.'

Meditation

Was it just a coincidence,
　　my cousin Mary conceiving like that so soon after I did?
There were some who thought so, certainly –
　　but not me,
　　and I'll tell you why.
For one thing, I'd given up hoping for a child –
　　at my time of life it seemed out of the question.
We'd tried, goodness knows,
　　hoping and praying that the miracle might happen,
　　but as the years had flown by
　　we'd reluctantly accepted it wasn't to be.
To be honest, such thoughts were long past,
　　the two of us content by then simply to grow old gracefully,
　　so you can imagine our feelings
　　when, out of the blue, the miracle happened after all –
　　even now I can't fully take it in.

Yet if you think that was strange, how about Mary,
    suddenly being told that she too was to have a baby,
    before she'd even slept with Joseph?!
Oh, I know what some people said about her –
    the cheap jokes,
    the sly innuendoes –
    but, take it from me, it was nonsense,
    that girl as innocent as the day is long,
    honest, sometimes almost to a fault –
    there's no way she'd have lied about anything like that.
So there we were,
    the two of us expecting together,
    only what a difference in the way we felt –
    on the one hand, me, scarcely able to contain my excitement
    and, on the other, Mary, unsure whether to laugh or cry,
    my mood of exultation, that day she came to me,
    matched by her sense of bewilderment.
It was that, I think, which brought home to me
    the special way God was working in our lives,
    for I was able to be to her the friend she so badly needed.
While all around raised their eyebrows at her story –
    even Joseph for a time –
    I understood,
    knowing God had touched her life as he'd touched mine –
    and that meant so much to her,
    a source of strength and inspiration
    during the testing months that followed.
It helped us both to realise that God was preparing the way
    for the child that Mary bore,
    everything which was happening to us
    part of his sovereign purpose,
    and, as if to confirm it, I felt my baby stir within me,
    seeming almost to leap up in joyful greeting.
Coincidence?
You call it that, if you want to –
    we knew better,
    the two of us aware that God was supremely at work,
    not just *our* lives destined to be changed
    by the children we carried within us,
    but the world itself,
    the very course of history,
    transformed for ever.

Prayer

Loving God,
> there are times when our prayers do not seem to be answered
> and the events of life are a complex riddle.

We look for your hand but do not see it.
We ask for your help but it does not seem to come.
Yet, later, we look back and recognise
> that you were at work all along,
> what was hidden from us at the time suddenly crystal clear.

Teach us, then, to trust
> even when we do not understand where you are leading,
> confident that though *we* may not know the way, *you* do.

Amen.

6

How did we feel about him?

Zechariah

Reading: Luke 1:57-58, 67-80

Now the time came for Elizabeth to give birth, and she bore a son. Her neighbours and relatives heard that the Lord had shown his great mercy to her, and they rejoiced with her.

Then his father Zechariah was filled with the Holy Spirit and spoke this prophecy: 'Blessed be the Lord God of Israel, for he has looked favourably on his people and redeemed them. He has raised up a mighty saviour for us in the house of his servant David, as he spoke through the mouth of his holy prophets of old, that we would be saved from our enemies and from the hand of all who hate us. Thus he has shown the mercy promised to our ancestors, and has remembered his holy covenant, the oath that he swore to our ancestor Abraham, to grant us that we, being rescued from the hands of our enemies, might serve him without fear, in holiness and righteousness before him all our days. And you, child, will be called the prophet of the Most High; for you will go before the Lord to prepare his ways, to give knowledge of salvation to his people by the forgiveness of their sins. By the tender mercy of our God, the dawn from on high will break upon us, to give light to those who sit in darkness and in the shadow of death, to guide our feet into the way of peace.'

The child grew and became strong in spirit, and he was in the wilderness until the day he appeared publicly to Israel.

Meditation

How did we feel about him?
Well, you don't really need to ask, do you?
We were more proud than words can say.
To think that our lad, John,
    should be the one spoken of by the prophet,
    chosen to proclaim the coming of the Messiah,
    to announce the dawn of his kingdom.
What an honour!

What a privilege!
The very thought of it still takes our breath away!
To tell the truth, we've had to be careful sometimes
    not to get carried away,
    not to put our son on a pedestal
    as though *he* was the one God had promised;
    heaven knows he's special enough to us.
Yet if ever we fell into that trap, he soon put us right,
    reminding us, in no uncertain terms,
    just what his role is in the great scheme of things.
It's funny how he knows,
    for we've never spelt it out to him,
    never had any need to –
    he seems to have understood from the very beginning
    what God expects from him.
You only had to see him as a boy to recognise that;
    the way he acted towards Jesus, especially –
    it was as though he had a special responsibility towards him,
    and I swear sometimes there was a hint of admiration in his eyes,
    even awe as they played together!
If anything, it's become more apparent as the years have passed;
    a special bond developing between them,
    but there's always been an element of distance too,
    a sense, on John's part anyway,
    of getting this close and no further,
    as though there's a gulf in status between them
    which he would never presume to cross.
Not everyone could do that, could they? –
    accept a supporting role rather than a position centre-stage –
    but there's never been a hint of resentment,
    still less any desire to thrust himself forward.
A voice in the wilderness, that's how he describes himself,
    sent to prepare the way of the Lord,
    to make straight his path in readiness for his kingdom –
    and he's shown since exactly what that means.
Not that he's the only one who longs for that day –
    we've all prayed for it for as long as I can remember.
The difference is that John doesn't simply talk about it,
    he's helping to make it happen,
    his actions as well as his words,
    his whole life, in fact,
    a daily witness to the change God requires of us –

a foretaste, if you like, of that transformation he holds in store.
You think you're ready for his coming,
    ready to welcome the Messiah?
Well, maybe you are,
    but before you get too complacent
    just ask yourself this:
    what are you doing to bring his kingdom closer?
For until you can answer that, take it from me,
    you're nowhere near ready at all.

Prayer

Lord Jesus Christ,
    you came as the servant of all,
    willing to take on our human flesh,
    to give of yourself freely,
    even to humble yourself in death on the cross.
You showed us that to find out what life truly means
    we must be ready to offer it to others.
And in John the Baptist
    we see a model of the response such love deserves;
    a readiness to serve in turn,
    to point away from self
    and to seek your glory rather than our own.
Forgive us that we find it so hard to follow,
    preferring instead the way of self-service,
    our own interests put before those of anyone else.
Help us to recognise that it is in giving that we receive,
    and so may we commit our lives to you
    and bring glory to your name.
Amen.

7
IT WAS THE STRANGEST OF DREAMS

Joseph

Reading: Matthew 1:18-25

Now the birth of Jesus the Messiah took place in this way. When his mother Mary had been engaged to Joseph, but before they lived together, she was found to be with child from the Holy Spirit. Her husband Joseph, being a righteous man and unwilling to expose her to public disgrace, planned to dismiss her quietly. But just when he had resolved to do this, an angel of the Lord appeared to him in a dream and said, 'Joseph, son of David, do not be afraid to take Mary as your wife, for the child conceived in her is from the Holy Spirit. She will bear a son, and you are to name him Jesus, for he will save his people from their sins.' All this took place to fulfil what had been spoken by the Lord through the prophet: 'Look, the virgin shall conceive and bear a son, and they shall name him Emmanuel', which means, 'God is with us'. When Joseph awoke from sleep, he did as the angel of the Lord commanded him; he took her as his wife, but had no marital relations with her until she had borne a son; and he named him Jesus.

Meditation

It was the strangest of dreams,
　　ludicrous really,
　　yet I just can't get it out of my mind.
You see, I dreamt God was speaking to me.
No, not face to face, I don't mean that,
　　but through this angel,
　　claiming to be his special messenger.
And do you know what he told me?
Take Mary to be your wife, that's what.
Just when I'd decided to put her quietly aside,
　　hush up the scandal as best I could,
　　this character was telling me to think again.
And why?
Because apparently it was nothing to do with her,

the baby she's carrying not the result of some fleeting passion,
   but conceived of the Holy Spirit,
   ordained by God himself.
Well, I've heard a few excuses in my time
   but that one really takes the biscuit!
I mean, who did the fellow think I was –
   some fool born yesterday?
It was laughable,
   and I'd usually have dismissed it without a second thought.
Yet I didn't –
   not then,
   not now.
A dream it may have been,
   but it's lived with me,
   as vivid today as when I first dreamt it.
I can't say why exactly –
   it was a mixture of things, I suppose.
There was Mary for a start,
   the way she looked at me as she broke the news –
   so trusting,
   so innocent,
   almost as though she too had met with God
   and was confident I would understand.
Then there was Elizabeth and Zechariah –
   heaven knows what got into them,
   but they were simply delighted,
   no hint of suspicion, let alone scandal, so far as they saw it –
   I suppose that boy of theirs, after so many disappointments,
   was enough to turn anyone's mind.
But what really swung it was this feeling deep within
   that somehow God had touched me;
   that, like it or not, life was changed for ever.
I was right in that, wasn't I? –
   for we're on the road to Bethlehem as I speak,
   my wife heavy with child,
   wincing with pain,
   praying it's not much further.
Did I do right, standing by her?
I still have my doubts, even now,
   still find it hard to meet her eye,
   for it takes some getting used to, a child you had no part in.
But despite the questions, I've done my bit,

taking her for my wife, just as I was told.
Now it's God's turn, isn't it? –
    over to him for the Saviour to be born,
    God with us!
Was it a dream, a figment of my imagination?
We'll soon see, won't we?

Prayer

Gracious God,
    you act in ways we do not expect,
    you speak in ways we do not always understand,
    you come at times and in places we least imagine,
    and all too easily we fail to recognise your presence amongst us.
Teach us to be awake to your prompting,
    however unlikely it may seem,
    and help us to respond whenever you call
    even though we have no idea where it all might lead.
Equip us to walk in faith,
    through Jesus Christ our Lord.
Amen.

8

'YOU'VE GOT IT WRONG,' I TOLD HIM

Mary

Reading: Luke 1:26-34

In the sixth month the angel Gabriel was sent by God to a town in Galilee called Nazareth, to a virgin engaged to a man whose name was Joseph, of the house of David. The virgin's name was Mary. And he came to her and said, 'Greetings, favoured one! The Lord is with you.' But she was much perplexed by his words and pondered what sort of greeting this might be. The angel said to her, 'Do not be afraid, Mary, for you have found favour with God. And now, you will conceive in your womb and bear a son, and you will name him Jesus. He will be great, and will be called the Son of the Most High, and the Lord God will give to him the throne of his ancestor David. He will reign over the house of Jacob for ever, and of his kingdom there will be no end.' Mary said to the angel, 'How can this be, since I am a virgin?'

Meditation

'You've got it wrong,' I told him.
'You can't mean me,
   no way!
Someone else perhaps,
   more worthy,
   more important,
   but not me!'
Honestly, what did I have to commend me?
No connections or special qualities,
   nothing –
   just an ordinary girl from Nazareth,
   so what could God see in me?
But it was academic anyway, for I wasn't even married yet,
   and there was no way I'd sleep with Joseph until I was.

So I came out with it straight,
   'Sorry, but you're wrong!'
Only he wouldn't take no for an answer.
Just stood there smiling,
   unruffled;
   and before I knew it he was off again –
   the message even more fantastic than before:
   God's power overshadowing me,
   a child born of the Holy Spirit,
   the Son of God!
It was way over the top,
   and I should have turned him out there and then,
   but I was flummoxed,
   too amazed to reply.
Even when I found my tongue it wasn't much use to me –
   my mind so befuddled with questions
   that I ended up saying, of all things,
   'Here am I, the servant of the Lord,
   let it be with me according to your word.'
Oh, it sounded good, granted –
   the epitome of humility –
   but if you only knew what I was thinking,
   you'd have a different picture then.
So what got into me, you ask?
How could I be so meek and accepting?
Well, what choice did I have, let's be honest,
   for as the angel said, 'With God, nothing will be impossible.'
How could I argue with that?
There was no way out, was there?
But it's one thing to accept that in principle,
   another when it turns your life upside down.
Do I believe it?
Well, I didn't at the time,
   but I do now,
   for I've just discovered I'm pregnant,
   and I say this perfectly reverently, God knows how!
It's astonishing and terrifying,
   exciting yet mystifying,
   my mind in turmoil, not quite sure what to think any more.
But one thing is plain now,
   beyond all question –
   with God, quite clearly, *nothing* is impossible!

Prayer

Gracious God,
  you may not ask of us what you asked of Mary,
  but nonetheless your challenge invariably comes,
  calling us to avenues of service
  which we would never imagine possible.
Whoever we are, we all have a part to play in your purposes,
  a unique role in making real the love of Christ
  here on earth, here and now.
Help us never to underestimate your sovereign power.
Grant us the humility we need to hear your voice
  and the faith we need to respond.
Like Mary, let us be ready to answer when you call:
  'Here am I, the servant of the Lord;
  let it be to me according to your word.'
All this we ask, through Jesus Christ our Lord.
Amen.

9

WAS IT ALL A DREAM?

Mary

Reading: Luke 1:26-38

In the sixth month the angel Gabriel was sent by God to a town in Galilee called Nazareth, to a virgin engaged to a man whose name was Joseph, of the house of David. The virgin's name was Mary. And he came to her and said, 'Greetings, favoured one! The Lord is with you.' But she was much perplexed by his words and pondered what sort of greeting this might be. The angel said to her, 'Do not be afraid, Mary, for you have found favour with God. And now, you will conceive in your womb and bear a son, and you will name him Jesus. He will be great, and will be called the Son of the Most High, and the Lord God will give to him the throne of his ancestor David. He will reign over the house of Jacob for ever, and of his kingdom there will be no end.' Mary said to the angel, 'How can this be, since I am a virgin?' The angel said to her, 'The Holy Spirit will come upon you, and the power of the Most High will overshadow you; therefore the child to be born will be holy; he will be called Son of God. And now, your relative Elizabeth in her old age has also conceived a son; and this is the sixth month for her who was said to be barren. For nothing will be impossible with God.' Then Mary said, 'Here am I, the servant of the Lord; let it be with me according to your word.' Then the angel departed from her.

Meditation

Was it all a dream,
    a figment of my imagination?
It feels like it now, I have to say,
    but at the time it was all too real –
    wonderful, exhilarating,
    yet at the same time terrifying.
'Blessed are you, Mary, for you have found favour with God.'
My heart leapt when I heard that –
    me, Mary, singled out for special blessing,
    chosen by God himself.

But then the angel spoke again,
    'You will conceive, and bear a son, and call him Jesus.'
Well, that took some getting used to, believe me
    the last thing I was expecting!
And yet, strangely, I didn't put up much resistance –
    just the one token query: 'How can this be?' –
    and then meek, docile submission.
I marvel now, looking back,
    yet at the time it seemed perfectly natural,
    as though no other response would do.
Why?
Well, to be honest, I suppose I never really believed it anyway.
I wondered, of course I did,
    and half accepted,
    yet if you'd pressed me hard enough
    there was always a little doubt at the back of my mind,
    the questions I couldn't dismiss –
    had I misread the signs,
    imagined the whole thing,
    or simply been listening to too many old wives' tales?
But that wasn't the whole reason,
    for to tell the truth, despite everything,
    I wanted to believe it more than you'll ever know.
Wouldn't you have with a promise like I was given? –
    'He will be great, and will be called the Son of the Most High,
    and the Lord God will give to him
    the throne of his ancestor David.
    He will reign over the house of Jacob for ever,
    and of his kingdom there will be no end.'
Need I say more?
If a child was unexpected, that was mind-boggling –
    a ruler over Israel,
    God's promised deliverer,
    born of my womb,
    flesh of my flesh.
It was too much,
    beyond anything I could bring myself to imagine,
    and yet too wonderful to dismiss altogether.
Was it all a dream?
Well, *you* might still think so,
    but *I* don't,
    not any more,

for as I speak these words I am sitting in a stable,
   looking down into a manger,
   and there gazing up at me is my little boy,
   Jesus.
It happened, you see,
   exactly as I was promised,
   just as the angel said it would,
   and if God was right in that,
   then why not the rest too?
How can I not believe?

Prayer

Gracious God,
   you promised Abraham that through his seed
   all the world would be blessed,
   and through Jesus
   you have reached out to the ends of the earth.
You promised your people
   that you would deliver them through the Messiah,
   and in the fullness of time that pledge was fulfilled.
You promised Mary that she would give birth to a son
   who would be the saviour of humankind,
   and the child was born, in a stable in Bethlehem.
Always you have been faithful,
   everything you have promised accomplished
   just as you said it would be.
Inspire us through that knowledge
   to trust you more completely,
   knowing that whatever life may bring
   your word will never fail us.
In Christ's name we pray.
Amen.

CHRISTMAS

10
HE LOOKED SO TINY LYING THERE

Mary

Reading: Luke 2:1-7

In those days a decree went out from Emperor Augustus that all the world should be registered. This was the first registration and was taken while Quirinius was governor of Syria. All went to their own towns to be registered. Joseph also went from the town of Nazareth in Galilee to Judea, to the city of David called Bethlehem, because he was descended from the house and family of David. He went to be registered with Mary, to whom he was engaged and who was expecting a child. While they were there, the time came for her to deliver her child. And she gave birth to her firstborn son and wrapped him in bands of cloth, and laid him in a manger, because there was no place for them in the inn.

Meditation

He looked so tiny lying there,
    so vulnerable –
    like a little china doll,
    like thistledown swaying in the breeze –
    and I wanted simply to hold him in my arms
    and protect him from the world outside.
Could this be God's Son, I asked,
    the one destined to be great,
    the Prince of Peace,
    a ruler over Israel?
Surely not!
It had been hard enough to believe at the start,
    when the angel first broke the news –
    to think that I, Mary, had been chosen above all others,
    singled out to bear in my womb the Messiah –
    but now, as I gazed down into the manger,
    and saw those little arms waving,
    that sweet innocent face wrinkled up in sleep,
    and those eyes so tightly shut,

it seemed doubly impossible,
out of the question,
a foolish fancy of my fevered imagination.
Be sensible, I told myself,
there's no way God could take such a gamble,
no possibility, if the fate of the world truly hung in the balance,
that he would stake it all on a helpless child,
least of all one born where we found ourselves –
a stable of all places!
And, as if to prove the point, that very moment Jesus awoke,
tears filling his eyes,
a scream of protest on his lips,
and I realised he was hungry,
well past his usual feed.
It dawned on me then, the staggering implications –
he needed me, this child,
not just for food, or warmth, or protection,
but for everything,
his very future in my hands.
Would God allow that?
Could he ever need *us* as much as *we* need him?
No, there had to be some mistake –
it just couldn't be, could it?
Could it?

Prayer

Gracious God,
you came to our world in fulfilment of your promises of old,
your word embodied in a child lying in a manger.
You loved us so much
that you staked everything
to break down the barriers that keep us from you.
You shared our humanity from birth to death,
so that with you we might share your eternity,
life in all its fullness.
You became God with us,
so that we might become one with *you*.
Teach us that, as you needed Mary's response then,
you need *our* response now;

our willingness to accept your mercy
and experience the blessings you so long to give us.
Come again now and be born in our hearts,
 so that we may truly love you
 and joyfully serve you, this and every day;
 through Jesus Christ our Lord.
Amen.

11
DON'T TALK TO STRANGE MEN

Shepherd

Reading: Luke 2:8-14

In that region there were shepherds living in the fields, keeping watch over their flock by night. Then an angel of the Lord stood before them, and the glory of the Lord shone around them, and they were terrified. But the angel said to them, 'Do not be afraid; for see – I am bringing you good news of great joy for all the people: to you is born this day in the city of David a Saviour, who is the Messiah, the Lord. This will be a sign for you: you will find a child wrapped in bands of cloth and lying in a manger.' And suddenly there was with the angel a multitude of the heavenly host, praising God and saying, 'Glory to God in the highest heaven, and on earth peace among those whom he favours!'

Meditation

Don't talk to strange men.
Have you ever heard that expression?
I have,
    dozens of times,
    far more than I care to remember.
Why do I say that?
Because all too often it's me they mean by it,
    me the one people look at
    as, arm wrapped protectively round their child's shoulder,
    they usher them away –
    the look on their faces saying it all:
    'Keep away, he spells trouble!'
Yes, that's how they see us –
    not as shepherds,
    but as vermin,
    the lowest of the low.
And the worst thing is
    after a while it's hard not to believe it,
    all one's feelings of dignity and self-respect

eaten away by the continual suspicion,
   the poisonous asides,
   the sly innuendoes.
I think that's what made the other night so special –
   the night we saw the angels,
   heard the good news,
   went to Bethlehem to see for ourselves.
It wasn't simply that the Messiah was born,
   amazing though that was,
   but the fact *we* were chosen to hear the news,
   given pride of place before all others!
Don't misunderstand me, we'd have rejoiced whoever was the first,
   for, despite what folk may say,
   we're as God-fearing as the next person,
   and we'd been looking forward to the day of the Messiah
   just like them,
   hoping and praying it might be in our lifetime.
But to hear the news firsthand,
   to be given a personal invitation
   to see the newborn Saviour for ourselves,
   that was beyond all our dreams,
   and it meant more to us than I can ever tell you.
Suddenly we were worth something again,
   recognised and valued as individuals.
Suddenly we could hold our heads up high
   and look the world full in the face,
   confident we had as much right to walk this earth as anyone.
Suddenly it didn't bother us any more what others thought,
   whether they loved us or loathed us,
   for we were important to God,
   and what else could matter?
I've no doubt some will judge even now,
   just as they always have,
   still pass us by with the same dismissive gesture,
   the same self-righteous glance of disdain.
But I don't care any more,
   for there's another saying you may have heard
   which to me says it all:
   'Beauty is only skin-deep'.
I know what that means now,
   for God has demonstrated to me
   that he looks beneath the surface,

behind the outer show,
and sees the person hidden there,
deep within –
a person more precious to him
than you would ever dare imagine.

Prayer

Gracious God,
  though we know it is wrong to judge by appearances
  we still do it, day after day.
Our hidden prejudices lurk so deep
  that we are unable to overcome them
  despite our best intentions.
Instead of seeing people as they really are,
  we see only a caricature,
  blinded by our own assumptions
  and our blinkered view of the world.
Forgive us all the times we have dealt unfairly as a result –
  the hurt and misunderstanding we have caused,
  the relationships which have been broken
  or never even started,
  and the opportunities which have been denied.
Teach us to see with your eyes
  and to look for the worth in everyone,
  remembering always that you came among us in Christ,
  sharing our life and death,
  not for the elite few but for all.
In his name we pray.
Amen.

12

I HAD MIXED FEELINGS, TO TELL THE TRUTH

Mary

Reading: Luke 2:15-20

When the angels had left them and gone into heaven, the shepherds said to one another, 'Let us go now to Bethlehem and see this thing that has taken place, which the Lord has made known to us.' So they went with haste and found Mary and Joseph, and the child lying in the manger. When they saw this, they made known what had been told them about this child; and all who heard it were amazed at what the shepherds told them. But Mary treasured all these words and pondered them in her heart. The shepherds returned, glorifying and praising God for all they had heard and seen, as it had been told them.

Meditation

I had mixed feelings, to tell the truth,
    not just before the birth but afterwards too.
Does that surprise you?
It did me.
I thought I'd be ecstatic once the child was born,
    over the moon –
    isn't that how we mums are meant to feel?
He was my firstborn after all,
    a beautiful bouncing boy,
    so why wasn't I bursting with happiness?
Well, I was, of course,
    part of me anyway,
    yet there was so much I didn't understand,
    and so many things to take the edge off the moment.
There was Joseph for a start.
Oh, he was supportive – don't think I'm complaining –
    once he got over the shock of the pregnancy anyway,
    and you can hardly blame him if that took a while, can you?
But, imagined or not, I always felt there was a shadow in his eyes
    when he looked at Jesus,

as if to say, 'What *really* happened?'
And then there were those visits after the birth –
    first the shepherds,
    then those strangers from the East with their lavish gifts.
It was gratifying, obviously,
    not every child gets that sort of attention, after all.
But what made them come? – that's what I keep asking.
What did their homage signify?
Don't think I'm ungrateful,
    but I really wish sometimes Jesus could have been an ordinary child,
    and the three of us left to enjoy our happiness –
    no fuss,
    no angels,
    no promises,
    simply the joy of being together.
But any last chance of that disappeared after those words of Simeon,
    that curious warning of his about the future.
I've tried not to let it get to me,
    but it's preyed on my mind ever since,
    always that fear within me of tragedy round the corner.
So, you see, I had mixed feelings,
    very mixed,
    and I still do have, as much now as ever.
I want to rejoice,
    to enjoy my boy while I still have him.
I want to count my blessings and thank God for all he's given.
But there's been a price to pay already,
    and deep within I've a horrible feeling
    that this business of being God's servant,
    of accepting his will and serving his kingdom,
    involves a far greater cost than I'd ever begun to imagine,
    and a price I'd rather not pay.

Prayer

Gracious God,
    alongside the blessings of discipleship
    there is always also the cost –
    sacrifices which will inevitably be asked of us,
    demands which we inevitably must face,
    responsibilities which we must inevitably accept.
Hard though it is to accept, let alone understand,
    there can be no joy without sorrow,
    no pleasure without pain,
    no life without death.
Yet however great the price may be,
    the rewards of service far outweigh it,
    for you promise all who serve you
    lasting blessings which will never fail;
    treasure in heaven which nothing shall ever destroy.
Help us, then, to offer all that is asked of us,
    until finally we rejoice in everything you hold in store
    for us and all your people;
    through Jesus Christ our Lord.
Amen.

13

THERE WAS SOMETHING ABOUT THAT COUPLE

Priest

Reading: Luke 2:21-24, 39-40

After eight days had passed, it was time to circumcise the child; and he was called Jesus, the name given by the angel before he was conceived in the womb. When the time came for the purification according to the law of Moses, they brought him up to Jerusalem to present him to the Lord (as it is written in the law of the Lord, 'Every firstborn male shall be designated as holy to the Lord'), and they offered a sacrifice according to what is stated in the law of the Lord, 'a pair of turtledoves or two young pigeons'.

When they had finished everything required by the law of the Lord, they returned to Galilee, to their own town of Nazareth. The child grew and became strong, filled with wisdom; and the favour of God was upon him.

Meditation

There was something about that couple,
 something that caught my attention the moment I saw them.
Happiness, I suppose it was,
 the joy of sharing a newborn baby.
Only it was more than that,
 for I've seen a multitude of parents over the years,
 each coming bubbling with excitement,
 skipping with delight,
 and yet none had that look of wide-eyed wonder which these had.
It was as though they thought their child different from any other,
 a unique gift from God to be handled with infinite care,
 treasured beyond all price.
Oh, I know every parent feels their baby's special –
 in their eyes the most beautiful thing ever born –
 yet with these two it was more than that.
It was almost as if they were in awe of the child,
 elated yet terrified at the responsibility of parenthood.
You think I'm exaggerating,
 reading too much into an innocent moment?

Well, possibly.
She was very young after all,
   and this was their first child –
   everything new,
   unknown,
   unexplored.
Yet I still say I've never seen a look quite like they had.
Probably it will always remain a mystery,
   for though no doubt they'll come back
   for the occasional festival or ceremony,
   I'm not sure I'll recognise them when they do.
Yet perhaps I may find the answer despite that,
   for when his mother handed me the child,
   and announced his name – Jesus –
   she did so as if it should mean something to me,
   as if I would understand straightaway
   why the child was so important,
   as if he was a gift not just to *them*,
   but to *me*,
   to *you*,
   and to *everyone*.

Prayer

Gracious God,
   we remember today the joy you brought through Jesus
   to those whose lives were touched by his birth –
   Mary, Joseph, shepherds, magi, Simeon and Anna –
   their lives overflowing with praise and thanksgiving.
Forgive us that the joy we have felt in turn
   can sometimes be lost as the years go by,
   dulled by familiarity
   or swamped by the cares of daily life.
Speak the good news to us again
   and enter our hearts afresh.
So may we know once more the gladness
   which only Christ can bring,
   and may it shine from us as a living testimony to others
   of the wonder of your love made known through him.
In his name we ask it.
Amen.

14

IT WAS AS THOUGH A WAVE OF PEACE ENGULFED ME

Simeon

Reading: Luke 2:25-35

Now there was a man in Jerusalem whose name was Simeon; this man was righteous and devout, looking forward to the consolation of Israel, and the Holy Spirit rested on him. It had been revealed to him by the Holy Spirit that he would not see death before he had seen the Lord's Messiah. Guided by the Spirit, Simeon came into the temple; and when the parents brought in the child Jesus, to do for him what was customary under the law, Simeon took him in his arms and praised God, saying, 'Master, now you are dismissing your servant in peace, according to your word; for my eyes have seen your salvation, which you have prepared in the presence of all peoples, a light for revelation to the Gentiles and for glory to your people Israel.'

And the child's father and mother were amazed at what was being said about him. Then Simeon blessed them and said to his mother Mary, 'This child is destined for the falling and the rising of many in Israel, and to be a sign that will be opposed so that the inner thoughts of many will be revealed – and a sword will pierce your own soul too.'

Meditation

It was as though a wave of peace engulfed me,
    a great surge of tranquillity flooding my soul
    with a quietness beyond expression –
    for I held him in my arms,
    God's promised Messiah –
    there, in that little wrinkled face,
    that tiny, vulnerable child staring up at me,
    the fulfilment of God's eternal purpose.
I just can't tell you what that meant to me,
    not only the joy but the relief I felt,
    for there had been times when my faith had begun to waver.
No, I don't just mean my conviction
    that I'd see the Messiah's coming,

though I did question that sometimes, it's true.
It went deeper than that,
    to the very heart of my faith,
    to those words of the prophet
    about us being a light to the Gentiles,
    bringing glory to God through our life and witness.
I'd always believed that implicitly,
    the vision stirring my imagination and firing my faith,
    but over the years the flame had begun to splutter,
    doused by the harsh realities which surrounded me.
The fact is we'd turned inwards rather than outwards,
    our concern more for ourselves than the world beyond,
    and, if anything, our horizons were growing narrower by the day.
It was understandable, of course,
    the oppression we'd suffered across the centuries
    enough to dampen anyone's fervour,
    but that didn't make it any easier to stomach,
    still less offer any grounds for hope.
Could things change, I wondered?
Was there really any chance we might recapture that old spark,
    that sense of sharing in the divine purpose,
    testifying to his glory,
    or was that dream destined to die for ever?
It was impossible not to ask it.
But that day, there in the temple, suddenly it all changed –
    faith vindicated,
    hope realised –
    for I knew then beyond all doubt
    that God had been faithful to his purpose,
    his chosen servant there in my arms,
    the one who would bring light to the world,
    salvation to all.
I saw him with my own eyes,
    touched him with my own hands,
    and after that I could die happy,
    my joy complete,
    my faith rekindled,
    my soul at peace.

Prayer

Gracious God,
  you have promised that in the fullness of time
  your kingdom shall come;
  a kingdom in which there shall be no more war or violence,
  no more hatred or injustice,
  no more sickness, suffering or sorrow,
  but in which all will dwell in peace.
It is a vision which gives us hope and inspiration,
  and we long for that day
  when, together with all your people,
  we shall see it realised.
But we would not be honest
  if we pretended never to have any doubts.
When we look at the sin and suffering in our world,
  the corruption, oppression and violence which seems so rife,
  there are times when we wonder
  if that hope is simply a vain delusion,
  a chasing after the wind.
Teach us to go on believing,
  even when everything seems to count against such belief.
Help us to trust that your will shall be done
  and, in faith, to do whatever we can,
  however small it may seem,
  to bring your kingdom nearer.
In the name of Christ we ask it.
Amen.

15

WELL, WE MADE IT AT LAST

Magi

Reading: Matthew 2:1-12

In the time of King Herod, after Jesus was born in Bethlehem of Judea, wise men from the East came to Jerusalem, asking, 'Where is the child who has been born king of the Jews? For we observed his star at its rising, and have come to pay him homage.' When King Herod heard this, he was frightened, and all Jerusalem with him; and calling together all the chief priests and scribes of the people, he inquired of them where the Messiah was to be born. They told him, 'In Bethlehem of Judea; for so it has been written by the prophet: "And you, Bethlehem, in the land of Judah, are by no means least among the rulers of Judah; for from you shall come a ruler who is to shepherd my people Israel."' Then Herod secretly called for the wise men and learned from them the exact time when the star had appeared. Then he sent them to Bethlehem, saying, 'Go and search diligently for the child; and when you have found him, bring me word so that I may also go and pay him homage.' When they had heard the king, they set out; and there, ahead of them, went the star that they had seen at its rising, until it stopped over the place where the child was. When they saw that the star had stopped, they were overwhelmed with joy. On entering the house, they saw the child with Mary his mother; and they knelt down and paid him homage. Then, opening their treasure chests, they offered him gifts of gold, frankincense, and myrrh. And having been warned in a dream not to return to Herod, they left for their own country by another road.

Meditation

Well, we made it at last.
After all the setbacks,
   all the frustration,
   we finally found the one we were looking for –
   our journey over,
   the quest completed.

And I can't tell you how relieved we were.
You see, we'd begun to fear we'd be too late,
   the time for celebration long since past
   by the time we eventually arrived.
It was that business in Jerusalem which caused the delay,
   all the waiting
   while Herod and his entourage rummaged around
   trying to discover what we were on about.
They were unsettled for some reason,
   taken aback, it seemed, by the news we brought,
   apparently unaware a king had been born among them.
A rival claimant, they must have thought,
   and who could tell what trouble that might stir up?
Anyway, they pointed us in the right direction if nothing else,
   but we'd wasted time there we could ill-afford,
   and although the star reappeared to lead us again
   we were almost falling over ourselves with haste
   by the time we reached Bethlehem.
It was all quiet,
   just as we feared –
   no crowds,
   no family bustling around offering their congratulations,
   no throng of excited visitors,
   just an ordinary house –
   so ordinary we thought we'd gone to the wrong place.
But we went in anyway,
   and the moment we saw the child, we knew he was the one –
   not just the King of the Jews,
   but a prince among princes,
   a ruler among rulers,
   a King of kings!
We were late,
   much later than intended,
   the journey far more difficult than we ever expected,
   but it was worth the effort,
   worth struggling on,
   for, like they say, 'Better late than never!'

Prayer

Gracious God,
    such is your love for us that you go on calling
    however long it takes for us to respond,
    and you go on leading
    however tortuous our journey of faith may be.
We may put off a decision,
    keep you at arm's length –
    still you are there to guide,
    striving to draw us to yourself.
We may encounter obstacles which impede our progress,
    which cause us to take wrong directions,
    which obscure the truth,
    yet always you are there to set us back on the way.
Teach us that your love will never let us go,
    and so help us to make our response
    and bring our lives to you in joyful homage,
    knowing that you will continue to lead us
    until our journey's end;
    through Jesus Christ our Lord.
Amen.

16

Do you know what we gave him?

Magi

Reading: Matthew 2:10-11

When they saw that the star had stopped, they were overwhelmed with joy. On entering the house, they saw the child with Mary his mother; and they knelt down and paid him homage. Then, opening their treasure chests, they offered him gifts of gold, frankincense, and myrrh.

Meditation

Do you know what we gave him –
    that little boy in Bethlehem?
Go on, have a guess!
A rattle?
A toy?
A teddy bear?
No, nothing like that!
In fact, nothing you'd associate with a child at all,
    even if he *was* destined to be a king.
Gold, that's what I brought!
And my companions?
Wait for it!
Frankincense and myrrh!
Yes, I thought you'd be surprised,
    for, to tell the truth
    we're pretty amazed ourselves looking back,
    unable to imagine what on earth possessed us
    to choose such exotic and unusual gifts.
It wasn't so much that they were costly,
    though they were, of course –
    to a family like his they were riches beyond their dreams.
But we could more than afford it –
    little more than small change to men of our means.
No, it wasn't the price that troubled us afterwards,
    but the associations,

the possible meaning his parents might have read into our presents
    when we'd gone.
Not the gold, there was no problem there –
    a gift fit for a king and designed to say as much, of course.
But frankincense?
Well, the main use his people have for that, as we learned later,
    is to sweeten their sacrifices,
    to pour out on to their burnt offerings
    so that the fragrance might be pleasing to their God.
Hardly the most appropriate gift for a baby.
But compared with myrrh!
Don't tell me you don't know?
It was a drug used to soothe pain,
    either for that or as a spice for embalming –
    more fitting for a funeral than a birth,
    having more to do with suffering and death than celebration!
So what were we thinking of?
What possible significance could gifts like those have for a little child?
Frankly, I have no idea.
Yet at the time the choice seemed as obvious to us
    as following the star,
    as though each were all part of some greater purpose
    which would one day become clear to all.
Were we right?
Well, after all I've said, I rather hope not,
    for if this king was born to die,
    to be offered in sacrifice rather than enthroned in splendour,
    then his must be an unusual kingdom,
    very different from most we come across –
    in fact, you might almost say, not a kingdom of this world at all!

Prayer

Lord Jesus Christ,
    you were born so that you might die.
You took on our humanity
    so that you might experience also our mortality.
Only through identifying yourself so totally with us
    could you bridge the gap that separates us from God.
You showed us the way of love, and you followed it to the end.

You proclaimed forgiveness,
    and you paid the price to make it possible.
In life and in death, you testified to the grace of the Father
    and his purpose for all the world.
Help us, as we celebrate again your birth,
    never to forget that this was just the beginning of the story.
As we greet you now as the child of Bethlehem,
    so let us greet you also as the crucified Saviour
    and the risen Lord,
    and may we offer you; this and every day;
    our joyful worship in grateful praise.
Amen.

17

IT WAS AS THOUGH ALL HELL WAS LET LOOSE

Mother in Bethlehem

Reading: Matthew 2:13-18

Now after they had left, an angel of the Lord appeared to Joseph in a dream and said, 'Get up, take the child and his mother, and flee to Egypt, and remain there until I tell you; for Herod is about to search for the child, to destroy him.' Then Joseph got up, took the child and his mother by night, and went to Egypt, and remained there until the death of Herod. This was to fulfil what had been spoken by the Lord through the prophet, 'Out of Egypt I have called my son.'

When Herod saw that he had been tricked by the wise men, he was infuriated, and he sent and killed all the children in and around Bethlehem who were two years old or under, according to the time that he had learned from the wise men. Then was fulfilled what had been spoken through the prophet Jeremiah: 'A voice was heard in Ramah, wailing and loud lamentation, Rachel weeping for her children; she refused to be consoled, because they are no more.'

Meditation

It was as though all hell was let loose,
    the most terrible day in my life,
    as suddenly the soldiers burst in upon us –
    cold,
    cruel,
    clinical –
    wresting our little ones from us,
    ignoring *our* screams for mercy,
    their screams of terror,
    and hacking them down in cold blood before our very eyes.
There are simply no words to describe how we felt –
    the fear,
    the horror,
    the emptiness,
    the rage,

and above all, the helplessness –
　　unable to do anything but watch grief-stricken
　　as our world fell to pieces.
One moment life was full of promise,
　　the next, utterly bereft.
One moment we were laughing with our children,
　　and the next sobbing our hearts out as we laid them to rest.
Why did it have to happen?
What could have possessed even Herod to do such a thing?
And, most of all, how could God ever have allowed it?
I'll never understand that, as long as I live – never!
It's thrown a cloud over everything, even faith itself,
　　for I can't help thinking of an event not so very different,
　　that moment of our nation's deliverance,
　　centuries back, from Egypt,
　　when, after the death of their firstborn,
　　Pharaoh at last let our people go.
A glorious chapter in our history, so they tell us,
　　and maybe it was,
　　but I can't help thinking of all *those* mums
　　and the agony *they* must have gone through,
　　while we skipped away to freedom.
We were spared *then* of course –
　　the blood of a lamb setting us apart –
　　but not *this* time –
　　this time we were left to face the full force of unbridled evil,
　　hatred incarnate,
　　humanity at its most vile –
　　and all, apparently, because Herod heard some rumour
　　that the Messiah had been born
　　somewhere here in Bethlehem.
How much longer must it go on?
How much more suffering must there be,
　　before God decides to do something about it?
I'm sorry, but it seems to me
　　if he really loves this world as he says he does,
　　then it's about time he provided another lamb,
　　another sacrifice,
　　just like he provided before,
　　only this time one to save not just a few of us,
　　those specially chosen, set apart,
　　but everyone.

Prayer

Lord,
    it is not easy sometimes to keep on believing
    faced by the cold realities of this world.
Life brings us joy and beauty,
    but it brings also pain and sorrow,
    times occasionally so testing
    that they stretch faith to the limit.
Tragedy and disaster strike us all, irrespective of virtue,
    untold suffering afflicting the most innocent.
We cannot make sense of it, try though we might,
    and we cannot help wondering sometimes why you allow it.
Yet you have shown us
    through your suffering and death in Jesus
    that you are not remote from our need,
    but, in a way we don't understand, a victim of it,
    sharing in our grief,
    enduring our sorrow,
    feeling our pain.
And through your willingness to bear that for our sakes,
    you give us the promise
    that one day such things will be over.
It doesn't answer all the questions,
    but it gives us a glimpse into your heart
    which bleeds for us,
    and longs to tend our wounds.
Teach us to hold on to that truth,
    until that day when your kingdom comes;
    through Jesus Christ our Lord.
Amen.

LENT

LENT

18

IT TOOK ME BY SURPRISE

John the Baptist

Reading: Mark 1:9-13

In those days Jesus came from Nazareth of Galilee and was baptised by
John in the Jordan. And just as he was coming up out of the water, he
saw the heavens torn apart and the Spirit descending like a dove on him.
And a voice came from heaven, 'You are my Son, the Beloved; with you I
am well pleased.' And the Spirit immediately drove him out into the
wilderness. He was in the wilderness forty days, tempted by Satan; and
he was with the wild beasts; and the angels waited on him.

Meditation

It took me by surprise, I don't mind admitting it,
    his going off into the desert like that
    the moment after his baptism.
You see, I thought that was my role,
    to fulfil the words of the prophet –
    'A voice crying in the wilderness:
    "Prepare the way of the Lord."'
And I'd done it well,
    patiently,
    faithfully,
    determined to play my part, come what may.
They'd come in their thousands,
    flocking out to me like there was no tomorrow –
    to be baptised,
    to confess their sins,
    to await the Messiah.
They were ready and waiting,
    eager to receive him,
    hungry for his coming.
And at last we saw him,
    striding down into the water,
    his identity unmistakable –

not simply Jesus of Nazareth,
but the Deliverer,
the Son of God,
the Saviour of the world!
I was ecstatic, you can imagine.
It was like a dream come true,
    the answer to all my prayers.
And as he came up out of the water
    I was waiting for the next move,
    wondering what would follow.
I'm not quite sure what I expected,
    but something dramatic at the very least –
    a bolt from heaven perhaps,
    a fanfare of trumpets,
    a raising of the standard,
    I don't know –
    but some sign,
    some symbol to let us know beyond all doubt
    that the moment had come,
    the waiting was over,
    and the kingdom was here.
Only what did he do?
Well, like I say, he disappeared.
No pep talk,
    no message for the crowd,
    just off and away without so much as a backward glance,
    and no hide nor hair of him seen for weeks afterwards.
To be frank, I was annoyed at first,
    for it all seemed such an anticlimax,
    but on reflection I can't blame him,
    for I think it took *him* by surprise as much as it did *me*.
When I recall now how he looked
    coming up out of the water after his baptism,
    so joyful,
    so radiant,
    almost as though he'd heard God rather than me talking to him,
    I just can't believe he had any idea
    that minutes later he'd be making off into the wilderness.
It was like he had no say in the matter,
    as though an unseen hand was guiding him,
    so that the one event progressed naturally from the other –
    a moment of joy –

a time of trial;
a wonderful high –
a desperate low,
a certainty of faith –
a wrestling with doubt.
Yet by all accounts it's been the making of him,
almost as if faith needed to be forged on the anvil of temptation,
tested to the limit
before the weight of the world could be hung upon it.
I think I'm beginning to see it now,
to understand that it wasn't just the wilderness of Judea
he faced out there,
but the desert of the soul,
and he needed to experience both if God was to use him,
for, strange though it may seem,
God is often more at work when we don't see it
than when we do.

Prayer

Lord God,
there are times when you seem very distant;
when, for all our prayers,
it seems to us that even you have abandoned us.
There is so much in life we cannot make sense of,
and we can feel bewildered
by the uncertainty and mystery of it all.
Yet, whether we see it or whether we don't,
you are always there at work,
bringing good out of evil,
joy out of sorrow,
hope out of despair,
light out of darkness.
Teach us then to put our trust in you,
knowing that though all else fail us, you never will.
Amen.

19

I THOUGHT I HAD HIM

The Devil

Reading: Luke 4:1-13

Jesus, full of the Holy Spirit, returned from the Jordan and was led by the Spirit in the wilderness, where for forty days he was tempted by the devil. He ate nothing at all during those days, and when they were over, he was famished. The devil said to him, 'If you are the Son of God, command this stone to become a loaf of bread.' Jesus answered him, 'It is written, "One does not live by bread alone."'

Then the devil led him up and showed him in an instant all the kingdoms of the world. And the devil said to him, 'To you I will give their glory and all this authority; for it has been given over to me, and I give it to anyone I please. If you, then, will worship me, it will all be yours.' Jesus answered him, 'It is written, "Worship the Lord your God, and serve only him."'

Then the devil took him to Jerusalem, and placed him on the pinnacle of the temple, saying to him, 'If you are the Son of God, throw yourself down from here, for it is written, "He will command his angels concerning you, to protect you," and "On their hands they will bear you up, so that you will not dash your foot against a stone."' Jesus answered him, 'It is said, "Do not put the Lord your God to the test."' When the devil had finished every test, he departed from him until an opportune time.

Meditation

I thought I had him.
Not just once but three times
   I thought I'd caught him out,
   stopped him in his tracks before he'd barely had time to get started!
And I was close,
   even *he*, I expect, would give me that.
Oh, he started off well enough –
   sure of his destiny,
   confident of his ability to grasp it.
But then he would have, wouldn't he,

coming out into the wilderness like that straight after his baptism,
    heart still skipping within him,
    the memory fresh,
    the voice of God ringing in his ears.
But forty days on –
    forty days of gnawing hunger, desert heat and night-time chill –
    and then it was a different story,
    hard then to think of anything but the pain in his belly
    and the simple comforts of home.
So I saw my chance,
    and made my move.
Nothing crude or clumsy –
    no point scaring him off unnecessarily –
    just a subtle whisper,
    a sly suggestion:
    'Turn this stone into bread.'
And he was tempted, don't be fooled.
I could see by the gleam in his eyes and the way he licked his lips
    that, if you'll pardon the expression, he was chewing it over.
It wouldn't have taken much to make him crack, I'm certain of it;
    one whiff of a fresh-baked loaf
    and I'm sure he'd have given in –
    why didn't I think of it!
Only then he remembered those cursed scriptures of his,
    and all my hard work was undone in a moment:
    'One does not live by bread alone.'
It was a setback,
    but I pressed on, confident I was making ground.
And soon after he was up on the mountains,
    the world stretching out before him as far as the eye could see.
'All this is yours!' I whispered.
    'Just forget this Messiah business and grab it while you can.'
Oh, you may sneer with hindsight at my methods,
    but it's worked before,
    many a lofty ideal sacrificed on the altar of ambition.
But not Jesus –
    in fact, this time not even a suggestion of compromise:
    'It is written, "Worship the Lord your God, and serve only him."'
So I took him in his imagination up on to the temple
    and played my trump card:
    'Go on,' I urged him, 'Throw yourself off.
    If you are who you think you are, God will save you,

for *it is written*:
"He will command his angels concerning you, to protect you.
On their hands they will bear you up,
   so that you will not dash your foot against a stone."'
A master-stroke, so I thought,
   quoting his own scriptures at him like that,
   and, let's face it, we all like a little reassurance, don't we,
   however strong our faith;
   the knowledge, should the worst come to the worst,
   that there'll be someone to bail us out when we need them?
'Why should he be any different?' I reasoned –
   he was as human as the next man,
   as vulnerable as the rest of your miserable kind.
But, somehow, even then he held firm:
   'It is said,' he answered,
   '"Do not put the Lord your God to the test."'
Well, that was it,
   I knew I was beaten.
There was nothing left to throw at him,
   so I slithered away to lick my wounds.
But I'll be back, you mark my words,
   and next time, when it's his whole life in the balance,
   a question of do or die,
   then we'll see what he's really made of, won't we?
Then we'll see which of us is finally the stronger.

Prayer

Lord of all,
   we are reminded today
   that even Jesus faced temptation during his lifetime –
   the temptation to compromise his convictions,
   to abandon his calling,
   to serve himself rather than others.
Teach us to recognise
   the many similar temptations *we* face in our turn;
   some easy to spot
   but others so subtle and insidious
   that we give in to them without even realising it.
Give to us a clear sense of what you would have us do

and all you would have us be,
and grant us the courage and commitment we need
to stand firm whenever temptation strikes.
So may we stay true to you,
and offer our faithful service,
in the name of Christ.
Amen.

20
HE WAS BACK AT LAST!

John the Baptist

Reading: Luke 4:14-15

Then Jesus, filled with the power of the Spirit, returned to Galilee, and a report about him spread through all the surrounding country. He began to preach and teach in their synagogues and was praised by everyone.

Meditation

He was back at last!
After countless days of silence,
   no sight nor sound of him,
   suddenly he was back where he belonged
   and taking the world by storm.
It was a relief, believe me,
   for I'd begun to wonder what I'd done,
   whether I'd somehow put my foot in it,
   even got the wrong man.
You see, he'd come to me there in the Jordan,
   and I'd thought immediately, 'This is the one,
   the Saviour God has promised,
   the lamb that takes away the sin of the world!'
And what an honour,
   what a joy for me, John, to baptise him,
   to be there at the beginning of the Messiah's ministry,
   the inauguration of God's kingdom!
Only then he disappeared,
   without trace,
   the last I saw of him making off into the wilderness,
   alone.
What's going on, I wondered?
Where's he off to?
I wanted him back here at the sharp end where he was needed –
   wasn't that what he'd come for –
   to bring light into darkness,

joy out of sorrow,
   hope in despair?
But he was gone,
   and as the days passed with no word,
   no sign,
   no news,
   so the doubts began to grow.
Had I misunderstood,
   presumed too much?
Had I caused offence,
   given the wrong signals?
I wondered,
   and I worried,
   day after day my confusion growing,
   and I'd all but given up hope,
   ready to write the whole business off as some sad mistake,
   when suddenly he was back,
   the word spreading like fire,
   his name on every tongue –
   Jesus of Nazareth,
   preacher and teacher,
   the talk of the town.
I still don't know what he got up to out there,
   why he needed to spend so long out in the desert,
   but it doesn't matter any more,
   for he's here now where we need him,
   and he's come back stronger and surer,
   almost as though the wilderness
   meant as much to him as his baptism,
   if not more!'
Does that make sense to you?
It does to me.

Prayer

Loving God,
   we thank you for all those times
   when you have come to our aid,
   just when we have begun to lose hope.
We face problems and difficulties
   to which we see no solution,

only for you to give us guidance when we need it most.
We feel hopelessly alone,
    only to discover you by our side.
We wrestle with sorrow and despair,
    only for your light to break through the darkness,
    bringing joy and hope through the knowledge of your love.
Teach us, through such experiences,
    to remember that, however bleak a moment may seem,
    you will never abandon us or forsake us,
    and in that confidence may we live each day;
    through Jesus Christ our Lord.
Amen.

21

SHALL I TELL YOU SOMETHING STRANGE?

John the Baptist

Reading: Luke 7:18b-19, 21-23

John summoned two of his disciples, and sent them to the Lord to ask, 'Are you the one who is to come, or are we to wait for another?' Jesus had just then cured many people of diseases, plagues, and evil spirits, and had given sight to many who were blind. And he answered them, 'Go and tell John what you have seen and heard: the blind receive their sight, the lame walk, the lepers are cleansed, the deaf hear, the dead are raised, the poor have good news brought to them. And blessed is anyone who takes no offence at me.'

Meditation

Shall I tell you something strange?
Almost funny you might call it, were it not so sad.
It's about me,
    the voice in the wilderness,
    the baptiser in the Jordan,
    the one sent to prepare the way of the Lord.
Well, I managed that, didn't I?
Or at least so they'll tell you –
    I made straight a path in the wilderness,
    I paved the way for his coming,
    and, yes, I have to say I made a good job of it,
    too good in a sense,
    for, much to my embarrassment, many were so impressed
    they followed me instead of him.
But it wasn't just them who got it wrong,
    it was me,
    for when Jesus finally came I was as unprepared as any.
Oh, I didn't realise it at the time,
    far from it –
    in fact, I thought I was an example to them all,
    the one who, more than any other,

understood who he was and what he came to do.
'Behold the lamb of God!' I told them,
    'the one who comes to take away the sin of the world.'
A good speech, wouldn't you say?
But it was just words,
    sounding impressive,
    but belying the truth beneath.
And it wasn't long after –
    when his ministry had begun and mine ended,
    when he was travelling the byways of Judah
    and I was rotting in prison –
    that I found myself questioning everything.
'Could he be the Messiah?' I asked,
    'the one we'd so long waited for?'
If he was, then why was so little happening –
    why so little evidence of his kingdom getting closer?
I should have known different, of course I should,
    and, yes, you may well say a hint of jealousy
    coloured my judgement.
But, honestly, how would you have felt in my position,
    knowing that, having given your all,
    more would be asked,
    even life itself?
It won't be long now before they come for me,
    I'm under no illusions.
There's no escape,
    no possibility of a last-minute reprieve;
    that wife of Herod's won't rest
    until she sees me dead and buried,
    the voice in the wilderness silenced for ever.
I wasn't prepared for that when I started,
    and I still wouldn't have been, just a day ago.
But thank God he's given me time to think,
    to hear what Jesus is doing,
    to understand what it's all leading up to,
    and I'm ready now,
    at last I'm ready,
    prepared for anything
    prepared for everything!

Prayer

Gracious God,
    there are times when, like John the Baptist,
    we find ourselves in the wilderness of doubt and despair.
We look at our lives, at the world, even at you,
    and we are overwhelmed by a sense of hopelessness,
    by questions as to why you do not act to establish your kingdom
    or respond to us in our time of need.
Help us at such moments when all seems dark
    to put our faith in you,
    trusting that your light will finally shine again.
Inspire us with the knowledge that time and again
    it has been in the wilderness experiences of people's lives
    that you have been supremely at work –
    challenging, deepening and strengthening their faith,
    equipping them for new avenues of service,
    and opening the way to a richer experience of your love.
In that assurance, lead us forward;
    through Jesus Christ our Lord.
Amen.

22

CAN YOU BELIEVE WHAT HE TOLD US?

Listener to the Sermon on the Mount

Reading: Matthew 5:38-45

You have heard that it was said, 'An eye for an eye and a tooth for a tooth.' But I say to you, Do not resist an evildoer. But if anyone strikes you on the right cheek, turn the other also; and if anyone wants to sue you and take your coat, give your cloak as well; and if anyone forces you to go one mile, go also the second mile. Give to everyone who begs from you, and do not refuse anyone who wants to borrow from you.

You have heard that it was said, 'You shall love your neighbour and hate your enemy.' But I say to you, Love your enemies and pray for those who persecute you, so that you may be children of your Father in heaven; for he makes his sun to rise on the evil and on the good, and sends rain on the righteous and on the unrighteous.

Meditation

Can you believe what he told us?
'Love your enemies', that's what he said!
Pray for those who abuse you,
    and if someone slaps you in the face, turn the other cheek!
Well, I ask you, what sort of talk is that?
He's on another planet, this fellow –
    cloud-cuckoo land!
Oh, it sounds wonderful, granted,
    but can you see it working?
I can't.
No, we have to be sensible about these things,
    realistic.
We'd all like the world to be different,
    but it's no use pretending, is it?
'Love your enemies' –
    where will that get us?
They'll see us coming a mile off!
And as for 'turn the other cheek' –
    well, *you* can if you want to, but not me;

I'll give them one back with interest –
    either that or run for it!
I'll tell you what, though,
    we listened to him,
    all of us,
    just about the biggest crowd I've ever seen,
    hanging on to his every word,
    listening like I've rarely known people listen before.
Why?
Well, you could see he meant what he was saying for one thing –
    the way he dealt with the hecklers and cynics:
    never losing his cool,
    never lashing out in frustration,
    ready to suffer for his convictions if that's what it took.
He practised what he preached,
    and there aren't many you can say that about, are there?
But it was more than that.
Like it or not it was his message itself;
    that crazy message,
    so different from any we'd ever heard before –
    impractical,
    unworkable,
    yet irresistible.
It gave us a glimpse of the way life could be,
    the way it should be –
    and he actually made us feel that one day it might be!
No, I'm not convinced, sad to say –
    life's just not like that –
    but I wish it was.
I wish I had the courage to try his way,
    the faith to give it a go,
    for we've been trying the way of the world
    for as long as I can remember,
    and look where that's got us!

Prayer

Lord,
    we are told that the strongest survive,
    that we need to look after number one,
    that in this world it's a question of never mind the rest

so long as we're all right.
But you call us to another way –
    the way of humility, sacrifice and self-denial,
    of putting the interests of others before our own.
You stand accepted wisdom on its head,
    claiming that the meek shall inherit the earth,
    and telling us that it is those who are willing to lose their lives
    who will truly find them.
Lord, it is hard to believe in this way of yours,
    and harder still to live by it,
    for it runs contrary to everything we know about human nature,
    yet we have seen for ourselves that the world's way
    leads so often to hurt, sorrow and division.
Give us, then, faith and courage
    to live out the foolishness of the gospel,
    and so to bring closer the kingdom of Christ,
    here on earth.
In his name we ask it.
Amen.

23

'ASK,' HE SAID, 'AND YOU WILL RECEIVE'

Another listener to the Sermon on the Mount

Reading: Matthew 6:31-33; 7:7-11

Do not worry, saying, 'What will we eat?' or 'What will we drink?' or 'What will we wear?' For it is the Gentiles who strive for all these things; and indeed your heavenly Father knows that you need all these things. But strive first for the kingdom of God and his righteousness, and all these things will be given to you as well.

Ask, and it will be given you; search, and you will find; knock, and the door will be opened for you. For everyone who asks receives, and everyone who searches finds, and for everyone who knocks, the door will be opened. Is there anyone among you who, if your child asks for bread, will give a stone? Or if the child asks for a fish, will give a snake? If you then, who are evil, know how to give good gifts to your children, how much more will your Father in heaven give good things to those who ask him!

Meditation

'Ask,' he said, 'and you will receive.'
Just like that,
    or so at least it sounded.
As though all we have to do is put in our request,
    place our order,
    and at the drop of a hat it will be there before us,
    served up on a plate,
    exactly to our requirements.
Do you believe that?
I'm not sure I do.
And I'm not sure I want to either,
    for if he really meant that,
    then where would it all end,
    when could we ever stop asking?
We couldn't, could we?
Not while there's still suffering in the world,

still need,
sorrow,
hunger,
disease,
despair.
It wouldn't be right –
a dereliction of duty, you might call it.
And anyway, even if we could wipe those out,
rid the world of its many ills,
that wouldn't be the end of it, not by a long way,
for there would always be something else to ask for –
a gift we know we lack,
a dream still unfulfilled,
a person we long to reach –
always just one more favour
before we could be completely satisfied.
It would end up with God at our beck and call,
bowing to our every whim,
dancing to our tune, instead of us responding to his.
So no, he couldn't have meant that, could he?
But what then?
What was Jesus getting at
with that weird but wonderful promise?
I've wrestled with that day after day,
and I've begun to wonder
if maybe we're looking at it the wrong way round,
too much at self and too little at Jesus.
'Do not worry about your life,' he told us,
'what you will eat or what you will drink,
or about your body, what you will wear.
Strive first for the kingdom of God and his righteousness,
and all these things will be given to you as well.'
Ask for what matters, isn't that what he was saying –
for those things in life which can bring you lasting happiness –
treasures in heaven rather than pleasure on earth?
It's not that this life was unimportant to him.
He cared about the world's suffering
more than anyone I've ever known.
But he came to tackle not simply the symptoms but the cause,
not just the way things look but the way they are –
the way we think,
the way we speak,

the way we act,
each transformed deep inside.
I may be wrong, of course,
but I think that's what he meant;
something like it anyway.
Ask God for guidance, strength, faith, renewal.
Ask him to teach, use, shape, forgive you.
Ask for these things,
earnestly,
honestly –
the gifts of his kingdom –
and you *will* receive
until your cup runs over!

Prayer

Loving God,
you long to shower us with blessings,
to fill our lives with good things,
yet there are times when, through our weakness of faith,
we frustrate your gracious purpose
and deprive ourselves of the inexpressible riches
you so freely offer.
We do not seek, so we do not find.
We do not ask, so we do not receive.
We concern ourselves with the fleeting pleasures of the moment
and so fail to grasp treasures which endure for eternity.
Forgive us the shallowness of our values
and the limitations of our understanding.
Teach us to set our hearts
on those things which truly have the power to satisfy,
which you so yearn to share with us.
In Christ's name.
Amen.

24

IT WAS DARK WHEN I WENT TO HIM

Nicodemus

Reading: John 3:1-6; 19:38-42

Now there was a Pharisee named Nicodemus, a leader of the Jews. He came to Jesus by night and said to him, 'Rabbi, we know that you are a teacher who has come from God; for no one can do these signs that you do apart from the presence of God.' Jesus answered him, 'Very truly, I tell you, no one can see the kingdom of God without being born from above.' Nicodemus said to him, 'How can anyone be born after having grown old. Can one enter a second time into the mother's womb and be born?' Jesus answered, 'Very truly, I tell you, no one can enter the kingdom of God without being born of water and Spirit. What is born of the flesh is flesh, and what is born of the Spirit is spirit.'
(later, following the death of Jesus, we read)
Joseph of Arimathea, who was a disciple of Jesus, though a secret one because of his fear of the Jews, asked Pilate to let him take away the body of Jesus. Pilate gave him permission; so he came and removed his body. Nicodemus, who had at first come to Jesus by night, also came, bringing a mixture of myrrh and aloes, weighing about a hundred pounds. They took the body of Jesus and wrapped it with the spices in linen cloths, according to the burial custom of the Jews. Now there was a garden in the place where he was crucified, and in the garden there was a new tomb in which no one had ever been laid. And so, because it was the Jewish day of Preparation, and the tomb was nearby, they laid Jesus there.

Meditation

It was dark when I went to him that first time,
　　the middle of the night when all was quiet –
　　and can you blame me?
It just wouldn't have done, would it,
　　a man in my position to be seen associating with Jesus?
Even a hint of involvement
　　and my fellow Pharisees would have lynched me on the spot!

He was the enemy,
  the blasphemer,
  the one who threatened everything we stood for –
  not just misguided,
  but dangerous,
  evil –
  a threat to our society,
  a challenge to the very heart of our religion.
I knew all that,
  or at least I knew the theory,
  and, yes, I'd been as shocked as any
  by some of the things he'd said,
  not to mention the things he'd done.
Yet I couldn't get him out of my mind, try as I might.
I can't say why exactly,
  for it wasn't any one word or deed that hooked me –
  it was all of them together,
  the way each reinforced the other,
  combining to make him the person he was.
He spoke of love,
  and he showed what love was all about.
He talked of forgiveness,
  and I simply haven't met a more forgiving man.
He talked of life,
  and there was a quality to his own life that I couldn't help but envy.
He talked of God,
  and I could see God was more real,
  more personal,
  more special to him,
  than I'd ever have dreamed possible for anyone.
So I went
  and I talked.
I listened
  and I learned.
Nervous, true,
  hesitant,
  strictly incognito,
  and so very, very slow to understand.
Yet, little by little, the truth broke through my confusion,
  a ray of light in the darkness,
  new birth for my parched and barren soul.
It was dark when I went again,

a night far blacker than that first night,
 for they'd taken their revenge by then, as I knew they would,
 done him to death on the cross.
And as he hung there in agony,
 his gasps piercing the air,
 suddenly the sun vanished and darkness fell.
That had them worried, you can well imagine,
 more than a few scuttling off in panic.
But not me,
 for I had seen the truth he spoke of
 and found the life he promised.
So, while others stumbled blindly in the darkness,
 for me it was lighter than the lightest day,
 and brighter than the brightest sunshine.

Prayer

Lord Jesus Christ,
 you tell us to walk in the light,
 and to be witnesses to it through the things we do
 and the people we are.
You call us to let your light shine through us
 so that others might see the good works we do
 and give glory to God.
Forgive us that all too often we do the opposite,
 hiding our light under a bushel,
 even sometimes to the point of secret discipleship.
Afraid of what others might think
 and concerned that admitting faith in you
 may prejudice our standing in this world,
 we keep our beliefs private,
 imagining they can be kept between us and you.
Forgive us the feebleness of our commitment
 and the weakness of our love.
Help us to recognise everything you have done for us
 while we still walked in darkness,
 and so teach us to acknowledge you proudly
 as the light of our lives,
 whatever the cost might be.
In your name we pray.
Amen.

25
WE WERE LOST FOR WORDS

Pharisee

Reading: Mark 2:23-3:6

One sabbath, he was going through the grainfields; and as they made their way his disciples began to pluck heads of grain. The Pharisees said to him, 'Look, why are they doing what is not lawful on the sabbath?' And he said to them, 'Have you never read what David did when he and his companions were hungry and in need of food? He entered the house of God, when Abiathar was high priest, and ate the bread of the Presence, which it is not lawful for any but the priests to eat, and he gave some to his companions.' Then he said to them, 'The sabbath was made for humankind, and not humankind for the sabbath; so the Son of Man is lord even of the sabbath.'

Again he entered the synagogue, and a man was there who had a withered hand. They watched him to see whether he would cure him on the sabbath, so that they might accuse him. And he said to the man who had the withered hand, 'Come forward.' Then he said to them, 'Is it lawful to do good or to do harm on the sabbath, to save life or to kill?' But they were silent. He looked around at them with anger; he was grieved at their hardness of heart and said to the man, 'Stretch out your hand.' He stretched it out, and his hand was restored. The Pharisees went out and immediately conspired with the Herodians against him, how to destroy him.

Meditation

We were lost for words,
    stunned into silence by the sheer cheek of the man.
It was as though he was hell-bent on getting our backs up,
    determined to flout the Law in whatever way he could.
All right, so maybe it can be an ass sometimes,
    taken to the letter,
    but if he had his doubts,
    did he have to be quite so public about them?
Better surely to have talked them through with the experts,
    those with a lifetime's experience in such matters.

But, oh no, not Jesus.
He knew we were watching him,
    so what did he do?
Plucked corn on the sabbath, that's what.
A minor transgression, I grant you,
    but it was a matter of principle;
    if we turned a blind eye to it,
    who could say what might follow?
Yet, when we courteously pointed out his mistake,
    he had the gall to quote scripture at us,
    some obscure passage completely out of context –
    not just impudent, you see, but a blasphemer to boot!
And then what?
Just a short while later, and there he was in the synagogue,
    catching sight of some chap with a gammy hand.
Minding his own business, the fellow was,
    and quite rightly,
    mind fixed on the worship where it should be.
Only, you've guessed it – 'Come here,' says Jesus.
And before you can say Moses, the hand's fixed, right as rain.
Oh, he had all the answers to any challenge we put to him:
    'Is it lawful to do good or to do harm on the sabbath,
    to save life or to kill?'
Very clever!
But why couldn't he have waited? –
    that's what I'd like to know.
What was the hurry
    when the poor fellow had been like that since the day he was born?
It was outright provocation, nothing less,
    determined to make his point, never mind the consequences.
We didn't answer him, of course –
    well, it was a trick question, wasn't it?
But if he thought he'd won the day he was mistaken,
    for we were determined to have the last laugh.
The Law's the Law,
    and even though you might feel we were straining at a gnat,
    you must see it was the thin end of the wedge.
We saw it all too clearly,
    and much though it grieved us to do it,
    we went out and began plotting his downfall.
Sabbath or no sabbath, the man had to be stopped,
    whatever it might take to do it!

Prayer

Sovereign God,
  like the Pharisees of old
  we too are often guilty of finding fault with others
  when in reality the problem lies in ourselves.
We are so busy looking for specks in the eyes of others
  that we fail to see the log in our own.
Day by day we are guilty of hypocrisy
  without even beginning to realise it.
Forgive us for the way we preach one rule for others
  while we reserve one quite different for ourselves.
Forgive us for dwelling on the letter of the law
  whilst completely overlooking the spirit.
Teach us to recognise
  that your will is summed up in the simple commandment:
  to love,
  and so may that love which flows from you
  come to characterise our every thought and action.
In the name of Christ we ask it.
Amen.

26

I CAN'T TELL YOU HOW AWFUL IT WAS

Jairus

Reading: Mark 5:21-24, 35-43

When Jesus had crossed again in the boat to the other side, a great crowd gathered around him; and he was by the sea. Then one of the leaders of the synagogue named Jairus came and, when he saw him, fell at his feet and begged him repeatedly, 'My little daughter is at the point of death. Come and lay your hands on her, so that she may be made well, and live.' So he went with him.

While he was still speaking, some people came from the leader's house to say, 'Your daughter is dead. Why trouble the teacher any further?' But overhearing what they said, Jesus said to the leader of the synagogue, 'Do not fear, only believe.' He allowed no one to follow him except Peter, James, and John, the brother of James. When they came to the house of the leader of the synagogue, he saw a commotion, people weeping and wailing loudly. When he had entered, he said to them, 'Why do you make a commotion and weep? The child is not dead but sleeping.' And they laughed at him. Then he put them all outside, and took the child's father and mother and those who were with him, and went in where the child was. He took her by the hand and said to her, 'Talitha cum,' which means, 'Little girl, get up!' And immediately the girl got up and began to walk about (she was twelve years of age). At this they were overcome with amazement. He strictly ordered them that no one should know this, and told them to give her something to eat.

Meditation

I can't tell you how awful it was,
    how devastated I felt
    when my servants burst through the crowd to break the news.
There was no need for them to speak;
    one look at their faces said it all –
    she was dead,
    my beautiful, precious daughter lost to me for ever –
and it was as though my whole world fell apart in that moment.

I'd dared to hope, you see;
    I'd actually believed that this man Jesus
    might yet save her where all others had failed,
    and when he agreed to come, my heart had missed a beat,
    skipping in anticipation
    at the promise of that awful cloud lifting at last.
But I knew now it was all over –
    and, quite simply, I was overcome,
    nothing and no one seeming to matter any more;
    not even Jesus.
To be honest I'd forgotten he was still there,
    his presence past significance beside the intensity of my grief –
    until suddenly I heard his voice,
    felt his hand upon my shoulder,
    and I realised *he'd* not forgotten *me*,
    his concern anything but at an end.
'Do not fear,' he told me, 'only believe.'
As simple as that –
    no embellishment,
    no explanation,
    just that quiet, unruffled instruction.
Well, I didn't know what to think!
Hadn't the man been listening?
My daughter was dead,
    all hope extinguished,
    nothing now anyone could do, not even him.
Yet there was something about his presence
    which made it impossible to argue,
    so we walked on together,
    and, to be truthful, I was glad of his company –
    the calmness,
    the peace,
    and the sense of purpose which radiated from him,
    somehow giving solace in my hour of despair.
He'd discover what had happened soon enough,
    and, who could tell, maybe even then
    he might have some crumb of comfort to offer.
But when we got back home –
    the family sobbing their hearts out,
    my wife just about inconsolable –
    then, as if I didn't have enough on my plate,
    his attitude really began to trouble me,

for he carried on as if nothing had happened,
   as if it were all fussing over a storm in a teacup.
'Why all the commotion?' he asked, 'She's only sleeping.'
Sleeping!
I could hardly believe my ears!
What was wrong with the fellow?
Could he really not see it, even now?
Little wonder the neighbours laughed at him.
Yet somehow I didn't have the heart to argue –
   it just didn't seem worth the hassle –
   so I let him usher everyone out of the house,
   everyone but myself and the family,
   and then we went in to where she was lying,
   just where I'd left her a short time before,
   but so white now,
   so still,
   so cold.
I watched in a daze as he reached out,
   scarcely able to see with the tears running down my face,
   and then I heard a voice,
   his voice,
   gentle but firm,
   'Little girl, get up!'
And, believe it or not, she did!
She opened her eyes and walked towards us,
   for all the world as though she'd simply been sleeping after all!
I can't make sense of it, no –
   what he did or how he did it is beyond my ability to fathom –
   but I tell you this,
   my daughter was dead,
   and he brought her back to life,
   my heart was broken,
   and he filled it again with joy,
   and if he can do that, then, quite honestly, what can't he do?
It seems to me nothing is beyond him!

Prayer

Lord Jesus Christ,
    you promise new life to those who follow you –
    not just a different quality of life here and now,
    though that is a part of it,
    but life beyond the grave; life eternal.
We thank you for the way you foreshadowed that promise
    during your earthly ministry,
    demonstrating your sovereign, life-giving power.
You raised Lazarus,
    you raised the daughter of Jairus,
    you raised the son of a widow,
    and finally, after three days in the tomb,
    you rose yourself!
Through word and deed you have given us the assurance
    that nothing in life or in death
    can ever separate us from your love.
Lord Jesus Christ, the resurrection and the life,
    we praise you.
Amen.

27

I WAS SICK

The woman who touched Jesus' cloak

Reading: Mark 5:25-34

Now there was a woman who had been suffering from haemorrhages for twelve years. She had endured much under many physicians, and had spent all that she had; and she was no better, but rather grew worse. She had heard about Jesus, and came up behind him in the crowd and touched his cloak, for she said, 'If I but touch his clothes, I will be made well.' Immediately her haemorrhage stopped; and she felt in her body that she was healed of her disease. Immediately aware that power had gone forth from him, Jesus turned about in the crowd and said, 'Who touched my clothes?' And his disciples said to him, 'You see the crowd pressing in on you; how can you say, "Who touched me?"' He looked all around to see who had done it. But the woman, knowing what had happened to her, came in fear and trembling, fell down before him, and told him the whole truth. He said to her, 'Daughter, your faith has made you well; go in peace, and be healed of your disease.'

Meditation

I was sick –
   sick of body,
   sick of mind,
   sick of spirit –
   fed up with having my hopes raised only to be dashed again,
   fed up with everything.
I'd suffered for so long,
   my strength failing,
   my fears multiplying,
   and I was ready to give up,
   to say goodbye to it all,
   to curl up in some dark corner and let life slip away.
But then suddenly I saw him, just a few yards in front of me,
   the man they were all talking about –
   Jesus of Nazareth,

prophet,
teacher,
worker of miracles –
and it took only one glance to convince me
he was the answer to my prayers.
Yes, I was desperate, admittedly,
ready to believe anything, clutch at any straw,
but there was more to it than that,
for I could see immediately that this man was unique,
everything about him proclaiming his love for others.
So I pushed my way through the crowds
and I reached out and touched him,
just the faintest of contacts, that's all,
yet immediately I felt whole again,
a knowledge deep within that I was well.
But before I had time to celebrate I froze in horror,
for he stopped,
and turned,
and looked around curiously,
eyes sweeping over the crowd.
Goodness knows how he'd felt my touch amongst so many,
but he had,
and I realised then the awfulness of what I'd done,
breaking every commandment in the book
by touching him in my condition.
I waited for the rebuke,
the explosion of anger which would shatter my illusions,
yet it never came;
just that one simple question:
'Who touched me?'
There was no escape.
Much as I longed to melt away into the crowd,
I knew there could be no deceiving this man,
so I shambled forward and blurted out the whole story,
pleading for forgiveness,
begging him to make allowances.
I still feared the worst,
but finally I dared to meet his eyes,
and there he was,
gently returning my gaze,
a look of love and understanding which I shall never forget.
'Daughter,' he said, 'your faith has made you well.

Go in peace, and be healed of your disease.'
It was true, the disease had gone,
　　but there was more than that,
　　much, much more.
I'd found new meaning, new hope, new purpose,
　　strength which I'd never known before,
　　peace such as I'd never imagined possible.
He sensed my need that day before I even expressed it,
　　responding instinctively to my silent plea;
　　and I'm whole now –
　　whole in body,
　　whole in mind,
　　whole in spirit –
　　ready for whatever life might bring,
　　ready for anything!

Prayer

Lord Jesus Christ,
　　you touched the sick and made them well;
　　you touched the lepers and made them clean;
　　you touched the blind and made them see;
　　you touched the lame and made them walk.
In these and so many other ways you brought healing
　　but, more wonderful still, you brought wholeness,
　　a health of body, mind and spirit.
Reach out to all who suffer today,
　　and work through all those
　　to whom you have entrusted the ministry of healing
　　in all its many forms.
Grant your renewing, restoring touch through them,
　　and grant also the blessing which you alone can bring,
　　your strength and inner peace
　　which nothing we may face can finally destroy.
In your name we ask it.
Amen.

28

WAS HE JUST TESTING ME?

The Syrophoenician woman

Reading: Mark 7:24-30

From there he set out and went away to the region of Tyre. He entered a house and did not want anyone to know he was there. Yet he could not escape notice, but a woman whose little daughter had an unclean spirit immediately heard about him, and she came and bowed down at his feet. Now the woman was a Gentile, of Syrophoenician origin. She begged him to cast the demon out of her daughter. He said to her, 'Let the children be fed first, for it is not fair to take the children's food and throw it to the dogs.' But she answered him, 'Sir, even the dogs under the table eat the children's crumbs.' Then he said to her, 'For saying that, you may go – the demon has left your daughter.' So she went home, found the child lying on the bed, and the demon gone.

Meditation

Was he just testing me?
I'm still not sure even now,
   but I think he must have been.
How else can you explain his reaction when first I approached him,
   the very last thing I expected,
     out of character with everything I'd been told of the man.
Aloof, some have put it, trying to put things kindly –
   detached,
   curt,
   matter of fact.
But that wasn't how I saw it, not at the time anyway –
   rude more like,
   heartless,
   dismissive.
To be frank, I could have burst into tears on the spot.
But I didn't –
   I couldn't afford to, could I? –
   my hurt counting as nothing beside my daughter's health,

and she needed help from this man
whether he liked it or not.
So I stuck at it,
    protesting my case,
    and persistence paid off,
    the change in his attitude immediate and remarkable.
Your request is granted, he told me,
    just like that –
    no messing,
    no strings attached –
    just that simple response, and it was done!
She was healed,
    my little daughter well again,
    her spirit tranquil,
    her mind at rest,
    body and soul made whole, just as he'd promised me.
But why then that initial response,
    so cold, so cruel, so callous?
Why put me down only to lift me up?
Was he just testing me?
In part he was, I'm sure,
    his way of ensuring that my faith was real
    and my commitment total,
    yet I've come to believe it was more than that,
    for I've considered since the message he shared
    and the wonders he performed,
    the life he lived and the love he showed,
    and I see there a man whose concern was to break down the barriers
    that keep us apart,
    to heal our divisions and make us one.
He saw the faith I had,
    the resolve,
    the dedication,
    and he used that to test not just me
    but the crowds which thronged about him,
    to show them that his love wasn't simply for the few,
    as they seemed to imagine,
    but for everyone,
    even an undeserving Gentile like me!

Prayer

Lord Jesus Christ,
    it is hard sometimes when our prayers do not seem to be answered;
    even harder when you seem remote and disinterested,
    seemingly unmoved by our faith.
Yet sometimes you are speaking precisely through
    that apparent lack of response,
    challenging us or those around us
    to look more deeply into a given situation
    and to broaden our horizons.
Help us, then, never to lose heart,
    but rather to persevere in prayer,
    knowing that you do hear us
    and will respond in your own way and time.
Amen.

29

LORD, I DO BELIEVE

Father of the epileptic boy

Reading: Mark 9:14-24

When they came to the disciples, they saw a great crowd around them, and some scribes arguing with them. When the whole crowd saw him, they were immediately overcome with awe, and they ran forward to greet him. He asked them, 'What are you arguing about with them?' Someone from the crowd answered him, 'Teacher, I brought you my son; he has a spirit that makes him unable to speak; and whenever it seizes him, it dashes him down; and he foams and grinds his teeth and becomes rigid; and I asked your disciples to cast it out, but they could not do so.' He answered them, 'You faithless generation, how much longer must I be among you? How much longer must I put up with you? Bring him to me.' And they brought the boy to him. When the spirit saw him, immediately it convulsed the boy, and he fell on the ground and rolled about, foaming at the mouth. Jesus asked the father, 'How long has this been happening to him?' And he said, 'From childhood. It has often cast him into the fire and into the water, to destroy him; but if you are able to do anything, have pity on us and help us.' Jesus said to him, 'If you are able! – All things can be done for the one who believes.' And immediately the father of the child cried out, 'I believe; help my unbelief!'

Meditation

Lord, I do believe,
   truly.
Despite my doubts,
   despite my questions,
   I do believe.
Not that my faith is perfect, I'm not saying that –
   there's still much that puzzles me,
   much I'd like to ask you about further, given the chance.
But I believe you're different,
   that you can change lives in a way others can't,
   that you can bring hope where there's despair,

joy where there's sorrow,
    peace where there's turmoil,
    love where there's hate.
And I need those things now as never before,
    not for myself, but for my son.
He's suffering, you see,
    troubled in body and mind,
    day after day thrown into terrible convulsions.
And, Lord, I'm afraid of what might happen,
    what he might do to himself when the fits come upon him.
It's breaking my heart seeing him like this,
    having to stand by helpless as he writhes and groans.
Yet I've tried everything –
    every doctor,
    every healer,
    even your own disciples,
    all to no avail.
Not one has been able to help,
    none able to provide the answer I long to find.
So I've come finally to you,
    my last throw of the dice,
    and I'm begging you, Lord:
    help!
Oh, I know I don't deserve it –
    I'm not pretending otherwise.
I have my doubts, all too many –
    barely understanding half of what you teach,
    and even what does make sense is hard to accept.
I don't have the makings of a disciple, I realise that,
    all kinds of things wrong in my life –
    ask anyone.
And though I want to change,
    to become the person you would have me be,
    I'm not sure I can come anywhere near it.
In fact, though I say I believe,
    I'm not even certain of that,
    for I'm torn in two,
    half of me sure, half of me not,
    my faith and doubt warring together,
    each battling for the upper hand,
    each ebbing and flowing as the mood takes me.
Yet I've seen what you've been able to do for others,

I've heard about the wonders you perform,
  and I'm sure that if anyone can help me, then it's you.
So you see, I do believe a little,
    not as much as I'd like,
    not as much as I should,
    but I do believe,
    and I'm trying so hard to believe more.
In the meantime, I'm begging you, Lord,
    on bended knee, I'm begging you:
    help my unbelief.

Prayer

Lord,
  you know our faith isn't perfect.
There is much that we don't understand,
    much that we question,
    and much that is not all it ought to be.
Despite our love for you,
    we find it difficult to trust as we know we should,
    the things we don't believe
    triumphing over the things we do.
Yet, for all its weakness,
    you know that our faith is real,
    and you know that we long to serve you better.
Take, then, what we are and what we offer,
    and, through your grace, provide what we lack
    until the faith we profess with our lips
    may be echoed in our lives,
    and our faith be made complete.
Amen.

30

THEY THOUGHT I WAS MAD

The Roman centurion

Reading: Luke 7:1-10

After Jesus had finished all his sayings in the hearing of the people, he entered Capernaum. A centurion there had a slave whom he valued highly, and who was ill and close to death. When he heard about Jesus, he sent some Jewish elders to him, asking him to come and heal his slave. When they came to Jesus, they appealed to him earnestly, saying, 'He is worthy of having you do this for him, for he loves our people, and it is he who built our synagogue for us.' And Jesus went with them, but when he was not far from the house, the centurion sent friends to say to him, 'Lord, do not trouble yourself, for I am not worthy to have you come under my roof; therefore I did not presume to come to you. But only speak the word, and let my servant be healed. For I also am a man set under authority, with soldiers under me; and I say to one, "Go", and he goes, and to another, "Come", and he comes, and to my slave, "Do this", and the slave does it.' When Jesus heard this he was amazed at him, and turning to the crowd that followed him, he said, 'I tell you, not even in Israel have I found such faith.' When those who had been sent returned to the house, they found the slave in good health.

Meditation

They thought I was mad when I sent for him like that,
    a small deputation meekly appealing for help.
Why ask, they said, when you can command?
Why waste time with polite requests
    when you have only to say the word and it is done?
And, of course, they had a point,
    for I had the power, had I wished to use it,
    to compel Jesus to come,
    whether he wanted to or not.
I was a Roman soldier, remember,
    and a centurion to boot,
    one of the ruling elite,

a man of authority,
   used to having my own way.
Yet it wasn't that simple, not this time.
I knew it even before I met the man
   from all the accounts I heard of him.
I could command my men,
   win their trust, their respect, their allegiance,
   but I couldn't win their souls,
   not as Jesus had won the heart and soul of the multitude.
I could fight with the best of them,
   no battle too fierce for me,
   no enemy too strong,
   but I couldn't take on the forces of evil,
   the powers of darkness,
   still less hope to rout them as he was doing.
I could build up or tear down, keep peace or make war,
   but I couldn't restore the broken-hearted,
   heal the sick or raise the dead as he had done.
He spoke with an authority I could never hope to equal,
   acted with a power no person alive could ever begin to match,
   and, to be honest, I was in awe of him –
   there's no other word for it –
   conscious that he was no ordinary man
   but one sent by God,
   before whom and beside whom I was as nothing.
I had no claim on his mercy,
   no reason to expect his help.
It was all down to him –
   his goodness,
   his grace –
   and he didn't disappoint me,
   my servant restored to health even as we spoke.
Was my faith so very special?
It didn't feel like it at the time, despite what he said.
But if you think it was, let me tell you its source,
   for there's no secret.
I saw what *I* could do,
   I saw what *he* had done,
   I saw what needed doing,
   and I put them together, as simple as that.
The rest was down to him.

Prayer

Sovereign God,
 there are things we can do ourselves
 and things only you can do;
 there are times when we have the resources in ourselves
 to cope with a situation
 and times when we depend utterly on you for help.
Teach us to know the difference,
 and help us to remember
 that, though our own reserves may run dry,
 yours never will.
Give us an appreciation of our own abilities
 and of yours,
 and help us to get the balance right;
 through Jesus Christ our Lord.
Amen.

31

YOU JUST CAN'T IMAGINE WHAT IT WAS LIKE

Legion

Reading: Luke 8:26-39

Then they arrived at the country of the Gerasenes, which is opposite Galilee. As he stepped out on land, a man of the city who had demons met him. For a long time he had worn no clothes, and he did not live in a house but in the tombs. When he saw Jesus, he fell down before him and shouted at the top of his voice, 'What have you to do with me, Jesus, Son of the Most High God? I beg you, do not torment me' – for Jesus had commanded the unclean spirit to come out of the man. (For many times it had seized him; he was kept under guard and bound with chains and shackles, but he would break the bonds and be driven by the demon into the wilds.) Jesus then asked him, 'What is your name?' He said, 'Legion'; for many demons had entered him. They begged him not to order them to go back into the abyss.

Now there on the hillside a large herd of swine was feeding; and the demons begged Jesus to let them enter these. So he gave them permission. Then the demons came out of the man and entered the swine, and the herd rushed down the steep bank into the lake and was drowned.

When the swineherds saw what had happened, they ran off and told it in the city and in the country. Then people came out to see what had happened, and when they came to Jesus, they found the man from whom the demons had gone sitting at the feet of Jesus, clothed and in his right mind. And they were afraid. Those who had seen it told them how the one who had been possessed by demons had been healed. Then all the people of the surrounding country of the Gerasenes asked Jesus to leave them; for they were seized with great fear. So he got into the boat and returned. The man from whom the demons had gone begged that he might be with him; but Jesus sent him away, saying, 'Return to your home, and declare how much God has done for you.' So he went away, proclaiming throughout the city how much Jesus had done for him.

Meditation

You just can't imagine what it was like –
   the turmoil, the agony, the confusion I went through,

day after day,
year after year,
my tortured mind hell-bent, so it seemed,
on self-destruction.
It would have been less painful, perhaps,
had my reason gone completely;
at least then the nightmare world I lived in
would have been the only one I knew.
But it wasn't like that –
I was still cursed with those occasional lucid moments,
those awful interludes when sanity briefly returned
and I witnessed the man I'd become –
like a wild beast, scavenging in the wilds,
an outcast from Hades, skulking there among the tombs.
I could have wept with the shame of it,
the torment I felt so dreadful that words can't describe it,
and, yes, there were times
when I'd have gladly hurled myself from the cliff-top,
dashed my head against the rocks,
anything to escape that degradation to which I'd sunk.
Believe me, I came close on many occasions,
but then the madness would take hold again,
its horrors almost welcome after that awful glimpse of reality.
To cap it all, there were crowds sometimes
who came to watch me, do you realise that? –
gawping, giggling groups of sightseers
queuing to see this freak everyone was talking about.
Can you imagine how it felt,
listening to their gasps of incredulity,
watching as their eyes widened in disbelief,
sensing their revulsion, their pity, their disgust?
I expected more of the same that day Jesus came by –
yet another dose of humiliation to endure,
but when he kept on coming
instead of keeping his distance,
when he looked me eye to eye
with no trace of fear or repugnance,
suddenly I knew this man was different from the usual visitors –
and it threw me completely.
I didn't know if I was afraid or excited,
and perhaps that explains what happened next,
for suddenly it was as though all the demons in my head

were let loose at once,
a thousand voices clamouring for attention,
yelling,
shrieking,
cursing,
screaming,
my mind torn now this way, now that,
sensing both threat and hope,
the prospect of rebuke and the promise of redemption.
I begged him to go – can you believe that? –
    even though I longed for him to stay.
I actually implored him to leave me in 'peace',
    though he alone could bring that greatest of gifts
    which I craved so desperately.
Had it been anyone else they'd have been off like a shot,
    no further reason needed for leaving me to my fate.
But not Jesus.
There was still no sign of rejection from him,
    just a calm, unshakable authority,
    and an inner quietness which I longed to share.
Don't ask me what happened next –
    I still can't make sense of it and I don't think I ever will –
    but the next moment it was as though all hell broke lose,
    noise, chaos, confusion everywhere,
    and then . . .
    suddenly . . .
    all was still . . .
    not just the world outside,
    but the world within,
    body, mind and spirit,
    a tranquillity such as I'd never even dared to imagine!
It was over,
    the whole ghastly business put behind me,
    and I've learned to forget over the years,
    to let go and start again.
But one thing I won't forget, as long as I live,
    is what Jesus did for me that day –
    the way he reached out to me in my need and set me free,
    the way he touched me with his peace
    and brought rest to my soul!

Prayer

Lord,
  we talk of peace but all too rarely find it,
  for our minds are full of a multitude of concerns
  which pull us this way and that
  until we feel bewildered and confused.
We hear your still, small voice bidding us to let go and rest,
  but always there is another call,
  another demand on our attention pressing in upon us,
  and, before we know it, your word is drowned
  in the noisy bustle of life.
Lord, we cannot ignore the world
  or our responsibilities within it,
  and we would not want to,
  for there is so much you have given us there which is good,
  but help us always to make time for you within it,
  so that, even when chaos seems to reign,
  your quietness may fill our souls,
  bringing an inner calm which cannot be shaken.
Amen.

32

I EXPECTED HIM TO CONDEMN ME LIKE ALL THE REST

The woman caught in adultery

Reading: John 8:2-11

Early in the morning he came again to the temple. All the people came to him and he sat down and began to teach them. The scribes and the Pharisees brought a woman who had been caught in adultery; and making her stand before all of them, they said to him, 'Teacher, this woman was caught in the very act of committing adultery. Now in the law Moses commanded us to stone such women. Now what do you say?' They said this to test him, so that they might have some charge to bring against him. Jesus bent down and wrote with his finger on the ground. When they kept on questioning him, he straightened up and said to them, 'Let anyone among you who is without sin be the first to throw a stone at her.' And once again he bent down and wrote on the ground. When they heard it, they went away, one by one, beginning with the elders; and Jesus was left alone with the woman standing before him. Jesus straightened up and said to her, 'Woman, where are they? Has no one condemned you?' She said, 'No one, sir.' And Jesus said, 'Neither do I condemn you. Go your way, and from now on do not sin again.'

Meditation

I expected him to condemn me like all the rest,
  to shake his head in disgust and send me to my death.
Just another self-righteous busybody, that's what I thought –
  you know the sort,
  the kind always up on their soap box,
  sounding off about something or other,
  telling folk how they ought to live their lives.
Not that it mattered much this time who he was,
  for there was no getting away from it, I'd broken the law,
  caught, as they say, well and truly in the act –
  no way anyone could get me out of that one,
  even if they'd wished to.

And you could see from the smug look of the Pharisees
    that they felt the same –
    lips twisted with contempt,
    eyes glittering with hatred,
    their hands positively itching to pick up the first stone
    and strike me down.
It was just a matter of time,
    a question of completing the necessary formalities
    before the verdict was given.
So I cowered there trembling,
    waiting for the fateful signal for them to begin,
    expecting each moment to be my last.
I waited . . .
    and I waited . . .
    sweat trickling down my brow,
    limbs shaking in terror . . .
But it didn't happen,
    no word,
    no sign,
    nothing.
What could it mean?
A reprieve?
Surely not.
But what then?
Some heartless trick to prolong my agony,
    an unforeseen last-minute technicality,
    or simply a pause while they gathered the rocks to stone me?
There was only one way to find out,
    so I looked up,
    tense,
    fearful . . .
    then stopped,
    transfixed,
    catching my breath in astonishment,
    for we were alone,
    just the two of us,
    me and Jesus,
    not another soul to be seen.
I thought I was dreaming for a moment,
    either that or the stoning had despatched me
    unbeknown to another life.
But then he spoke,

his eyes gentle yet piercing as he voiced my unspoken question:
    'Woman, where are your accusers?'
They were gone, each one of them,
    none able, apparently, to throw the first stone;
    and even as I struggled to take it in, he spoke again,
    those marvellous, memorable words:
    'Neither do I condemn you.'
I should have danced for joy, shouldn't I? –
    whooped with delight,
    laughed in exultation –
    for I was free,
    not simply reprieved but forgiven,
    invited to go back and start again.
But I didn't laugh.
I broke down in tears,
    the sobs convulsing my body,
    tears streaming down my face,
    for suddenly, faced by this astonishing man,
    I saw myself as I really was . . .
    and became my own accuser.
I'd expected death, and been given life,
    feared judgement, and been shown mercy;
    what had seemed the end was suddenly a new beginning –
    and it was all too much to take in!
Not any more, though.
I understand now what he's done for me,
    and I look back still to that day with wonder,
    my whole being throbbing with praise,
    for he met me in my need and made me whole,
    he saw me at my worst,
    and dared to believe the best!

Prayer

Lord Jesus Christ,
    you did not come to judge or condemn the world,
    but in order to save it.
Where others saw the bad in people,
    you saw the good.
You recognised the value in everyone,
    and instilled in all a sense of worth.

Such was your willingness to show acceptance to the unacceptable
    that many were scandalised by your behaviour.
Forgive us that we too can be equally self-righteous,
    more concerned with judgement than mercy.
Forgive us for failing to see in ourselves
    the evil which we are so ready to see in others.
Teach us to look at the world with your eyes,
    and to deal graciously in all our relationships,
    just as you have dealt graciously with us.
Amen.

33

I WAS SCARED AT FIRST

One of the little children

Reading: Mark 10:13-16

People were bringing little children to him in order that he might touch them; and the disciples spoke sternly to them. But when Jesus saw this, he was indignant and said to them, 'Let the little children come to me; do not stop them; for it is to such as these that the kingdom of God belongs. Truly I tell you, whoever does not receive the kingdom of God as a little child will never enter it.' And he took them up in his arms, laid his hands on them, and blessed them.

Meditation

I was scared at first,
    scared of the noise, the crowds, the confusion –
    a sea of faces unlike anything I'd seen before.
It seemed that everyone wanted to see Jesus –
    everyone, that is, except us;
    we just wanted to get back to our friends
    and enjoy ourselves as we'd been doing before.
Who was he anyway, that's what we wanted to know?
What made him so special, so important?
Yet it was no use arguing,
    one look at my mother's face told me that –
    she was determined I was going to see him, like it or not.
So there we were, pushing through the crowd,
    her hand clasping mine
    in case I should have any ideas about escaping –
    and slowly fear turned to rebellion.
OK, I'd go if I had to,
    but if she imagined I was going to play the sweet innocent child
    she could think again.
I resolved instead to give Jesus an audience he wouldn't forget in a hurry,
    to scowl, sulk, scream the place down if I had to,
    anything to make clear whose idea this daft business was.

Yet that's not the way it worked out.
I had the scowl ready all right,
    a sullen snarl to be proud of,
    but the moment I saw him it just melted away,
    all hostility and resentment forgotten.
I can't tell you why exactly,
    but there was something quite extraordinary about him,
    an interest, warmth and concern which seemed to flow over you,
    impossible to resist.
Instead of treating us like kids he made us feel important,
    as though we were real people,
    worth something to him,
    special –
    and suddenly, instead of sulking,
    we were beaming with sheer delight,
    even, would you believe, when he picked us up
    and started to pray for us.
There's not many I'd have let do that, I can tell you!
He was so different from the rest of those with him –
    you could tell they were itching to get rid of us,
    their annoyance at our intrusion all too clear.
Yet do you know what Jesus said to them?
That the kingdom of God belongs to children like us!
I can't think why, for we were no angels, not by a long way,
    and I can't imagine he was under any illusions –
    presumably he saw something in us we didn't.
I tell you what, though –
    we'd have followed him anywhere after that,
    walked to the ends of the earth and back had he asked us.
No, we didn't understand quite who he was
    or what he'd come to do –
    but that didn't matter –
    we knew instinctively that he was someone special,
    a man we could trust completely,
    with our very lives if necessary,
    and that was enough.
What more could we have wanted?
What more could anyone ask?

Prayer

Gracious God,
    we thank you for the great adventure of life
    in all its endless diversity and richness.
We thank you that, whoever we are,
    there is always more to learn,
    more to explore and more to experience.
Keep our minds open to that special truth
    for, as the years pass,
    we can lose our sense of childlike wonder and fascination,
    becoming worldly-wise or blasé about life,
    taking for granted those things
    which once had the power to stir our imagination,
    and sinking into an ever-deeper rut of cynicism
    and over-familiarity.
Help us to recapture something of the innocence and spontaneity
    of our childhood years;
    the ability to look at the world with open eyes,
    to trust in the future and to celebrate the present.
Gracious God, give us faith in life and faith in you;
    through Jesus Christ our Lord.
Amen.

34
IT WAS A LOT TO ASK, WASN'T IT?

The rich ruler

Reading: Luke 18:18-25

A certain ruler asked him, 'Good Teacher, what must I do to inherit eternal life?' Jesus said to him, 'Why do you call me good? No one is good but God alone. You know the commandments: "You shall not commit adultery; You shall not murder; You shall not steal; You shall not bear false witness; Honour your father and mother."' He replied, 'I have kept all these since my youth.' When Jesus heard this, he said to him, 'There is still one thing lacking. Sell all that you own and distribute the money to the poor, and you will have treasure in heaven; then come, follow me.' But when he heard this, he became sad; for he was very rich. Jesus looked at him and said, 'How hard it is for those who have wealth to enter the kingdom of God! Indeed, it is easier for a camel to go through the eye of a needle than for someone who is rich to enter the kingdom of God.'

Meditation

It was a lot to ask, wasn't it,
    too much to expect of anyone?
I was ready to do my bit, after all,
    happy to be more than generous if that's what he wanted;
    but to give up everything,
    to leave it all behind so that I could follow him,
    well, quite simply, it wasn't on.
So I left,
    disappointed,
    disillusioned,
    preferring the riches I could handle now
    to the promise of treasure in heaven.
It was a shame though –
    had he asked for a quarter,
    a half,
    even the bulk of my wealth,
    I'd have said yes, happily enough,

for he had something I didn't,
a tranquillity, an assurance, a sense of purpose beyond price,
more precious than anything money can buy,
and I wanted to share it,
to be part of something which really mattered,
to grasp hold of a prize which would never fade,
never perish.
Did I have my regrets?
Of course I did,
and I prayed many times for help to accept his challenge,
yet somehow, though I longed to respond,
the resolve was never quite there.
Until today, that is,
for I arrived here in Jerusalem for the Passover,
and I saw a crowd gathering in the streets,
and, there among them, a man struggling under a cross,
collapsing in exhaustion,
writhing in agony as they nailed him up to die,
and do you know what? – it was Jesus.
Don't ask how it could happen, for I'll never know –
how anyone could kill a man like that just makes no sense –
yet I understood one thing.
He'd given his all,
everything,
precisely what he'd asked of me,
and more besides!
And suddenly,
as I watched him suffer,
as I heard his groans,
as I saw him take his final breath,
his words came flooding back,
cutting deep into my soul:
'Sell all that you own and distribute the money to the poor,
and you will have treasure in heaven;
then come, follow me.'
It wasn't much to ask, was it?

Prayer

Gracious God,
   no one can ever give us more than you have given,
   for you have blessed us with life itself –
   life overflowing with good things, life eternal –
   and to make that gift possible you gave of yourself,
   not just a little but all.
You bore the limitations of our flesh;
   you endured rejection, humiliation
   and finally death on a cross;
   and, most awesome of all,
   through Christ you took on yourself
   the dreadful burden of human sinfulness,
   experiencing the despair and isolation that brings.
Forgive us that, despite all this,
   we give so grudgingly in return.
Forgive us that though our words say one thing,
   our lives say another.
Forgive us that so often our thoughts are little for you,
   none for others
   and all for ourselves.
Help us to catch again a glimpse into the wonder of your love
   which you have freely given,
   and so may we spontaneously give something back
   in joyful and heartfelt thanksgiving;
   through Jesus Christ our Lord.
Amen.

35

WE WERE ON OUR OWN SUDDENLY

Thaddaeus

Reading: Matthew 10:1-23

Then Jesus summoned his twelve disciples and gave them authority over unclean spirits, to cast them out, and to cure every disease and every sickness. These are the names of the twelve apostles: first, Simon, also known as Peter, and his brother Andrew; James son of Zebedee, and his brother John; Philip and Bartholomew; Thomas and Matthew the tax-collector; James son of Alphaeus, and Thaddaeus; Simon the Cananaean, and Judas Iscariot, the one who betrayed him.

These twelve Jesus sent out with the following instructions: 'Go nowhere among the Gentiles, and enter no town of the Samaritans, but go rather to the lost sheep of the house of Israel. As you go, proclaim the good news, "The kingdom of heaven has come near." Cure the sick, raise the dead, cleanse the lepers, cast out demons. You received without payment; give without payment. Take no gold, or silver, or copper in your belts, no bag for your journey, or two tunics, or sandals, or a staff; for labourers deserve their food. Whatever town or village you enter, find out who in it is worthy, and stay there until you leave. As you enter the house, greet it. If the house is worthy, let your peace come upon it; but if it is not worthy, let your peace return to you. If anyone will not welcome you or listen to your words, shake off the dust from your feet as you leave that house or town. Truly I tell you, it will be more tolerable for the land of Sodom and Gomorrah on the day of judgement than for that town.

'See, I am sending you out like sheep into the midst of wolves; so be wise as serpents and innocent as doves. Beware of them, for they will hand you over to councils and flog you in their synagogues; and you will be dragged before governors and kings because of me, as a testimony to them and the Gentiles. When they hand you over, do not worry about how you are to speak or what you are to say; for what you are to say will be given to you at that time; for it is not you who speak, but the Spirit of your Father speaking through you. Brother will betray brother to death, and a father his child, and children will rise against parents and have them put to death; and you will be hated by all because of my name. But the one who endures to the end will be saved. When they persecute you in one town, flee to the next; for truly I tell you, you will not have gone through all the towns of Israel before the Son of Man comes.

Meditation

We were on our own suddenly,
 sent out in the Master's name to proclaim the good news,
 to announce the dawn of his kingdom –
 and it came as a rude awakening!
We'd been happy until then,
 perfectly content to sit at his feet as he talked,
 just the twelve of us and him, comfortably ensconced together.
I think we'd all have stayed and listened to him for ever,
 given the choice,
 his words a constant source of inspiration,
 his company a pleasure to share.
It was a piece of cake, following Jesus, so we thought,
 each of us only too delighted he'd called us
 to be part of his intimate circle,
 one of his chosen disciples.
Only that was then, and this was now.
Suddenly the easy life was over
 and it was time for us to play our part.
He wanted us to go out with the message he brought,
 to share in his mission,
 even one day carry it on ourselves;
 and the picture he painted of what we could expect
 seemed very bleak,
 not a prospect we welcomed at all.
Like sheep among wolves, he called it,
 and out there, in the thick of things,
 we soon realised what he meant –
 the demands, the pressures,
 the corruption, the hostility utterly bewildering,
 pressing in upon us until we didn't know where to turn next,
 shattering our illusions,
 sapping our strength,
 battering our convictions –
 honestly, I don't know how he coped.
We were glad to get back to him, I can tell you,
 glad to lick our wounds and take shelter under his wings.
Yet we knew it couldn't last –
 the time would come,
 sooner rather than later,
 when we had to go back and face the world again.

'No good hiding your lamp under a bushel,' he told us,
   'it's there to be seen,
   to bring light to others,
   or else what use is it to anyone?'
He was right, of course, we knew that,
   but we still hoped it could wait a while,
   just a little longer until we were ready.
You feel the same, do you?
I'm not surprised,
   for it's easy to believe when you're among friends, isn't it? –
   so much harder when the world seems against you;
   easy to trust when there's nothing asked of you –
   so very different when it actually starts to cost.
Yet that's why he called us;
   that's what it means to follow Jesus –
   not simply to come *to* him but to go *for* him,
   to show the reality of our faith through serving others,
   to find our life through losing it.
It's a costly business, there's no denying it,
   the demands sometimes overwhelming –
   just as he said they would be –
   but he's not asking from us any more than he gave himself,
   for he offered everything,
   even life itself,
   convinced that though the price may be high,
   the rewards are higher,
   and if that was enough for Jesus,
   then, scared though I may be,
   it's enough for me.

Prayer

Lord Jesus Christ,
   you do not simply call us to *believe* the good news;
   you call us to *share* it.
Forgive us for all too often failing to do that.
We have been happy to *come* to you
   but reluctant to *go out* in your name,
   afraid of what might be asked of us
   and unsure of our ability to respond to the challenge.
Help us to understand that discipleship without service

is no discipleship at all,
and that faith without witness
is a denial of the gospel which we claim to believe.
Teach us, then, not only to rejoice in the love you have shown us
but, through word and deed, to share it with those around us,
for your kingdom's sake.
Amen.

36

DO YOU KNOW WHAT THEY'RE SAYING ABOUT HIM?

Resident of Nazareth

Reading: Matthew 13:54-58

He came to his home town and began to teach the people in their synagogue, so that they were astounded and said, 'Where did this man get this wisdom and these deeds of power? Is not this the carpenter's son? Is not his mother called Mary? And are not his brothers James and Joseph and Simon and Judas? And are not all his sisters with us? Where then did this man get all this? And they took offence at him. But Jesus said to them, 'Prophets are not without honour except in their own country and in their own house.' And he did not do many deeds of power there, because of their unbelief.

Meditation

Do you know what they're saying about him?
You're not going to believe it!
There are all kinds of rumours flying about –
    that he's Moses, Elijah or another of the prophets –
    but some are now actually claiming he's the Messiah,
    the one we've waited for all this time,
    God's promised deliverer!
I said you wouldn't believe it, didn't I?
Yet plenty do, apparently,
    a great multitude always around him,
    hanging on to his every word,
    applauding his every action,
    following his every move with open adulation.
And the worst of it is he's done nothing to discourage them,
    no attempt whatsoever to cool their ardour a little
    or prompt a moment's reasoned reflection.
I'd swear he's coming to believe what they're saying about him,
    allowing the hype and hysteria to go to his head –
    at least that's how it seemed the other day
    when he strolled back here into Nazareth,

entourage in tow.
Barely back five minutes,
    and there he was in the synagogue
    interpreting the scriptures,
    telling us how we should live our lives,
    as though he was an expert or something,
    privy to some special relationship with God denied the rest of us.
Well, he may have fooled others,
    but he didn't fool us –
    no chance of pulling the wool over *our* eyes.
We've watched him grow up, you see,
    followed his progress
    from when he was a bundle in his mother's arms,
    and we knew exactly who we were dealing with.
Oh, he'd always been a nice enough lad, I'm not denying that,
    never any trouble like some I might mention,
    but he was just an ordinary young man,
    Jesus the carpenter's son,
    from the back streets of Nazareth,
    a local boy with, let's face it, dubious origins to put it kindly.
No, I won't go into that,
    hardly fair to stir up old dirt,
    but you get my drift, don't you?
We knew all about this man the crowds were flocking to,
    and, frankly, the idea of him being sent by God was laughable.
The proof was in the pudding,
    for what did he actually do here when it came down to it? –
    precious few of those signs and wonders
    everyone was raving about –
    and, quite frankly, after all the hullabaloo
    we felt he was a bit of a let-down.
It's strange, though, for no one else has said that,
    not to my knowledge, anyway.
I hear fresh reports about him day after day,
    and always it's the same story –
    healing the sick,
    cleansing lepers,
    even raising the dead.
Funny he couldn't do it here.
There must be an answer somewhere, mustn't there?
Probably right under my nose if only I could see it.
But it's no good – we know the truth, don't we?

We've seen it with our own eyes,
    so, whatever else, the fault can't lie with us.
It can't, can it?

Prayer

Loving God,
    you tell us not to judge others,
    but we find it so hard not to.
You tell us that, on those occasions when we do need to judge,
    we should do so rightly,
    but again we find that so difficult,
    for although we strive to be open-minded and objective
    in the decisions we make,
    the fact is we rarely succeed.
We are shaped by a multitude of influences
    which have gone together to create the people we are,
    and the way we look at the world is so coloured by each one
    that we find it impossible sometimes
    to see beyond our preconceived ideas.
Even when the truth is staring us in the face
    we can fail to spot it,
    so ingrained have these ideas become.
Break through the barriers which shut our minds fast,
    and help us to see things both as they really are
    and as you can help them become.
Loving God, fill us with the mind of Christ,
    to his glory.
Amen.

37

I WAS ASHAMED, IF I'M TRUTHFUL

The widow at the treasury

Reading: Luke 21:1-4

He looked up and saw rich people putting their gifts into the treasury; he also saw a poor widow put in two small copper coins. He said, 'Truly I tell you, this poor widow has put in more than all of them; for all of them have contributed out of their abundance, but she out of her poverty has put in all she had to live on.'

Meditation

I was ashamed, if I'm truthful,
    desperately praying that no one would notice me,
    for what would they think
    when they saw those two miserable coins of mine;
    what sort of person would they take me for?
They seemed little short of an insult,
    worse, in some ways, than bringing nothing at all,
    and believe me, I'd toyed seriously
    with staying away altogether to spare my blushes.
It had been different once,
    when my husband was alive –
    then I could hold my head up in any company,
    my gifts, if not extravagant, were more than generous.
But times were hard,
    a matter of getting through from one day to the next
    as best I could;
    life's little luxuries a thing of the past,
    and many of its necessities too.
Yet there was one thing I was resolved to do, come what may,
    even if it meant going short,
    and that was to continue offering something to God.
So there I was, that day in the temple,
    surreptitiously bringing my feeble gift.
It wasn't much, I know,

not in the eyes of the world, anyway,
but to me it was a small fortune,
the last thing I had in the world.
Well, you can imagine my horror when I arrived there
to find this crowd with Jesus watching.
It was my worst nightmare come true,
my pathetic offering exposed to the full glare of public scrutiny,
and I felt certain I would die of shame,
waiting with weary resignation
for the inevitable howl of laughter or snort of disgust.
And when Jesus nodded towards me
I could feel the colour rising to my cheeks,
skin crawling with embarrassment.
Yet then, he spoke,
his words, would you believe, not of condemnation but praise,
singling me out as an example to follow
rather than an object of ridicule.
It's the thought which counts, we sometimes say,
and Jesus understood that.
Somehow he knew how much that gift had cost me,
and to him those small pieces of copper
were like nuggets of gold!
I went out that morning with my heart singing,
head held high after all,
and I brought my offering from then on
without any hesitation or any sense of unworthiness,
for I understood that God sees things differently from us,
that he measures the gift not by how much it's worth,
but by how much it means!

Prayer

Gracious God,
you give to us out of love,
more and more blessings poured out upon us day after day.
Forgive us for so often giving to you out of habit or duty.
We make our offering in worship
because it is expected of us.
We make time for personal devotion
because we feel we ought to.
We make time for others

because our conscience pricks us.
The end result may seem worthy,
    but the true value is small.
Teach us instead to give joyfully,
    not because we must but because we may.
Teach us to offer our money, our worship and our service
    as a gesture of love and an expression of our appreciation.
Help us to understand that it is not the gift that matters so much
    as the spirit in which it is given,
    and may that awareness inspire all we offer to you;
    through Jesus Christ our Lord.
Amen.

38

I'VE NEVER BEEN SO EMBARRASSED

James the son of Zebedee

Reading: Matthew 20:20-27

Then the mother of the sons of Zebedee came to him with her sons, and kneeling before him, she asked a favour of him. And he said to her, 'What do you want?' She said to him, 'Declare that these two sons of mine will sit, one at your right hand and one at your left, in your kingdom.' But Jesus answered, 'You do not know what you are asking. Are you able to drink the cup that I am about to drink?' They said to him, 'We are able.' He said to them, 'You will indeed drink my cup, but to sit at my right hand and at my left, this is not mine to grant, but it is for those for whom it has been prepared by my Father.'

When the ten heard it, they were angry with the two brothers. But Jesus called them to him and said, 'You know that the rulers of the Gentiles lord it over them, and their great ones are tyrants over them. It will not be so among you; but whoever wishes to be great among you must be your servant, and whoever wishes to be first among you must be your slave.'

Meditation

I've never been so embarrassed;
    the way his face fell as we stood before him
    will be etched on my memory for ever.
Oh, he tried to let us down gently,
    concerned for our feelings as always,
    but I could tell he was disappointed in us,
    dismayed that we should even have thought of asking.
To be fair, it was our mother's idea,
    though we played along quite happily,
    glad, in fact, she'd taken the initiative.
'Think of the future,' she told us.
    'What's going to happen then?'
And she was genuinely troubled,
    understandably so,

for we'd packed in our jobs,
    left home, family, livelihood, everything
    to follow Jesus,
    and she wanted to know, quite simply, what was in it for us.
Yes, it may sound shabby now,
    a sordid quest for gain,
    but at the time it seemed perfectly reasonable,
    a quite natural thing to ask.
After all, we'd no idea what the future might bring,
    what demands would be made of us,
    what sacrifices expected,
    so it seemed only fair to seek some assurances,
    some guarantee of long-term security.
Remember as well that we'd been the first to respond,
    so why not be the first to benefit? –
    it wasn't like we were jumping the queue.
Only that's not how the others saw it!
They were incensed,
    more angry than I've ever seen them,
    and as to the accusations they hurled at us,
    well, they're best left unsaid.
But with Jesus it was different.
There was no anger from him,
    no disgust at our request;
    rather, if anything, anxiety, concern.
It was as though we were spoilt children
    with no idea what we were asking –
    and I'm afraid that just about sums it up.
We'd followed him,
    listened to his words,
    witnessed his deeds,
    but we'd taken in precious little of what he'd tried to show.
We knew he was special,
    the promised Messiah,
    the Son of God,
    but we hadn't begun to understand what that meant.
We thought we were serving *him*,
    but we were still serving *self*,
    our welfare, *our* interests, *our* future all that really mattered to us.
No wonder he shook his head.
It was a moment I prefer to forget, except for one thing:
    it taught us something we needed to learn,

something we should have seen sooner
if we'd only had eyes to see it –
the truth that those who wish for greatness will never find it,
that those who strive to be first will be last,
and the last will be first.

Prayer

Lord Jesus Christ,
    we want to serve you, and we like to believe we do,
    but unwittingly we can turn even our faith
    into a way of serving ourselves.
We gain strength through fellowship and worship
    but neglect your call to mission.
We focus on our own concerns in prayer
    and forget about the world beyond.
We expect *you* to reward *our* trust
    and respond to the requests we bring to you,
    when, in fact, *we* should be seeking *your* will.
Even our deeds of kindness
    can finally be more about our own sense of righteousness
    than the needs of those we think we are serving.
Lord Jesus, overcome the stranglehold of self
    and help us to understand
    that true discipleship brings its own reward,
    for the more we give the more we shall receive.
In your mercy, hear our prayer.
Amen.

39

HE MADE IT ALL SOUND SO EASY

The Scribe

Reading: Mark 12:28-31

One of the scribes came near and heard them disputing with one another, and seeing that Jesus answered them well, he asked him, 'Which commandment is the first of all?' Jesus answered, 'The first is, "Hear, O Israel: the Lord our God, the Lord is one; you shall love the Lord your God with all your heart, and with all your soul, and with all your mind, and with all your strength." The second is this, "You shall love your neighbour as yourself." There is no other commandment greater than these.'

Meditation

He made it all sound so easy,
   so simple.
The whole Law,
   everything we'd been struggling to understand
   for so many years,
   summed up in two little commandments:
   you shall love the Lord your God
   with all your heart and mind and soul;
   you shall love your neighbour as yourself.
It sounds perfect, doesn't it?
What our faith is all about – in a nutshell.
And for the most part I agreed with him –
   spot on!
Love God,
   love your neighbour;
   I've no problem with that –
   it's what I've tried to do all my life.
But love your neighbour as yourself –
   that's where I come unstuck;
   for though you may not believe it,
   and though it may rarely seem like it,

I don't love myself at all.
Oh, I give a good impression, I know –
    I'm as selfish as the next person,
    invariably putting *my* interests before others,
    more often than not wrapped up in my own affairs –
    I can't deny that.
But beneath the facade,
    whenever I have the courage to look deep inside,
    I'm ashamed of what I see,
    ashamed of what I am.
Love myself?
With all my weakness,
    all my greed,
    all my pride?
You must be joking!
Only he wasn't, that's the mystery;
    there was no irony from Jesus when he said those words,
    no sarcasm,
    no hidden agenda.
Love your neighbour as yourself, he told us,
    and he meant it;
    he actually believed that I was lovable.
I just can't tell you what that means,
    what hope it gives me –
    him to say such a thing of all people!
For he was under no illusions,
    no false sense of my worthiness.
He knew me as I was,
    better than anyone,
    with all my faults,
    all my ugliness,
    yet he still believed I was worth something.
Am I convinced?
Well, not as much as I'd like to be,
    for there are still times when I look at myself
    and turn away in shame.
I'm not pretty,
    not special,
    not a nice person at all when you get down to it.
But I've begun to understand that inside this stranger I call me,
    beneath the mask I put on for the world,
    there's a person who God truly values,

an individual unique and precious to him,
and if *he* believes that, despite everything,
who am *I* to argue?

Prayer

Gracious God,
  we marvel that you can love us,
    for there is so little about us that deserves it.
We look into the mirror of our souls
  and we are repelled by what we see there,
    for the image is marred by greed, pride, selfishness, envy
    and so much else that destroys not just others
    but ourselves too.
Yet, incredibly, you value us
  to the point that we are precious in your sight,
    special enough even to die for.
If you can accept us despite everything,
  teach us to do the same,
    and, in learning to love ourselves as you do,
    help us also to love others and love you;
    through Jesus Christ our Lord.
  Amen.

40

WAS IT GUILT THAT MADE THEM TURN ON ME?

The woman who anointed Jesus' head

Reading: Mark 14:3-9

While he was at Bethany in the house of Simon the leper, as he sat at the table, a woman came with an alabaster jar of very costly ointment of nard, and she broke open the jar and poured the ointment on his head. But some were there who said to one another in anger, 'Why was the ointment wasted in this way? For this ointment could have been sold for more than three hundred denarii, and the money given to the poor.' And they scolded her. But Jesus said, 'Let her alone; why do you trouble her? She has performed a good service for me. For you always have the poor with you, and you can show kindness to them whenever you wish; but you will not always have me. She has done what she could; she has anointed my body beforehand for its burial. Truly I tell you, wherever the good news is proclaimed in the whole world, what she has done will be told in remembrance of her.'

Meditation

Was it guilt that made them turn on me?
I couldn't help but wonder,
    for there were some there who'd welcomed me very differently
    the last time I saw them,
    eager not only to share my company but my bed as well.
Oh yes, there were a few skeletons in the cupboard that day,
    enough to wreck many a career and destroy many a family.
Is that what they thought –
    that I'd come to tell all,
    expose them for the hypocrites they were?
It would have served them right if I had.
But no, they had nothing to fear,
    such revelations were the last thing on my mind.
I wanted to see Jesus, that's all,
    for I'd come to recognise that here was a man
    different from any I'd known before,

concerned not for himself but for others,
　　his only desire, it seemed, to bring a little light
　　into the darkness of this world.
I'd taken some convincing, mind you –
　　the kind of man I was used to made cynicism come easy –
　　but I'd watched him talking with the multitude,
　　healing the sick, comforting the distressed;
　　I'd seen him welcoming the poor, embracing the little children,
　　accepting the unacceptable;
　　and I knew then, beyond all doubt,
　　that he was genuine through and through,
　　offering a glimpse of the way life could and should be.
Quite simply I was entranced,
　　captivated,
　　longing to discover that life for myself.
I had no right to be there, I knew that,
　　but I wanted to respond,
　　to show him that he'd touched me
　　in a way no one else had ever done –
　　not my body but my soul –
　　so I burst in with my perfume,
　　ignoring the gasps, the protests, the cries of outrage,
　　and in a wild impulsive gesture I poured it over his head,
　　anointing him with love.
You should have seen their faces!
I actually think some thought I was making a pass at him.
But not Jesus –
　　he understood –
　　the compassion in his eyes as he looked up at me,
　　the concern, the welcome,
　　sending a tingle down my spine,
　　for these told me in a way words never could
　　that he had time for me,
　　time for the person I was
　　as much as the person I could become.
It cost me something that day,
　　not just the perfume but my career,
　　for there was no way I could carry on selling my body
　　after that encounter,
　　but I've this horrible feeling that Jesus is going to pay far more
　　for the love he has for us,
　　for as he leapt to my defence that day he said the strangest of things,

words which have troubled me ever since –
something about anointing his body for burial.
Could he really have meant it?
He's too good for this world, I've always said that,
  but surely no one could want to remove him from it,
  not even his enemies.
No one would want to do that –
  would they?

Prayer

Lord,
  there are many ready to sneer at faith.
'Who do they think they are?'
'What makes *them* so special?'
We've all heard the kind of thing people throw at us.
Yet we know that you love us
  not because we deserve it
  but solely through your grace.
We recognise our faults, we acknowledge our sinfulness,
  and we realise full well that we will never be perfect,
  but we ask you to help us live more authentically as your disciples
  and to offer our lives as best we can
  as a joyful outpouring of thanksgiving
  and a spontaneous expression of praise.
Amen.

41

I THOUGHT HE MIGHT BE THE ONE WE WERE WAITING FOR

Judas Iscariot

Reading: Matthew 10:16-23, 34-39

'See, I am sending you out like sheep into the midst of wolves; so be wise as serpents and innocent as doves. Beware of them, for they will hand you over to councils and flog you in their synagogues; and you will be dragged before governors and kings because of me, as a testimony to them and the Gentiles. When they hand you over, do not worry about how you are to speak or what you are to say; for what you are to say will be given to you at that time; for it is not you who speak, but the Spirit of your Father speaking through you. Brother will betray brother to death, and a father his child, and children will rise against parents and have them put to death; and you will be hated by all because of my name. But the one who endures to the end will be saved. When they persecute you in one town, flee to the next; for truly I tell you, you will not have gone through all the towns of Israel before the Son of Man comes.

'Do not think that I have come to bring peace to the earth; I have not come to bring peace, but a sword. For I have come to set a man against his father, and a daughter against her mother, and a daughter-in-law against her mother-in-law; and one's foes will be members of one's own household. Whoever loves father or mother more than me is not worthy of me; and whoever loves son or daughter more than me is not worthy of me; and whoever does not take up the cross and follow me is not worthy of me. Those who find their life will lose it, and those who lose their life for my sake will find it.'

Meditation

I thought he might be the one we were waiting for,
    the Messiah promised of old,
    coming at last to deliver his people.
The Prince of Peace, isn't that what the prophet called him?
And my heart had thrilled at the prospect –
    to think that after years of oppression, hatred and cruelty

there might finally be harmony between the nations,
an end to violence and bloodshed,
divisions put aside once and for all.
Idealistic, I know,
even naïve some might call it,
but I dared to hope,
to actually believe that we might see a world at one with itself.
Yet has it happened?
Well, not as far as I can see.
In fact, quite the opposite, that's what troubles me.
I hate to say it,
but I'm starting to think I got it wrong about Jesus,
that he's not at all the man I thought he was.
Just look around and ask yourself one question:
what he's actually done? –
for it seems to me it's not peace he's brought but division.
I see people day after day arguing about who he is,
what he's come for,
what he's doing.
I've seen families divided,
marriages broken,
friendships destroyed,
all because people can't agree.
And today, do you know what he told us to expect?
More of the same, that's what!
I couldn't believe it –
just when I hoped he might have some strategy to counter it
he tells us it has to be.
And as if that's not enough, the problem is getting worse.
There are some now openly hostile,
and making no secret of their feelings,
to the point that I fear deeply for his safety.
It's his own fault.
He's got people's backs up once too often,
spoken out of turn when he should have kept quiet,
and there's really no telling where it might end.
He came to unite us, so I thought –
to usher in a new era of harmony and peace,
but it hasn't worked out that way,
his coming, if anything, adding to the problem.
For while some would do anything for him,
worshipping the ground he walks on,

others would stop at nothing to see him silenced,
    once and for all.
Me? I really don't know what to believe any more,
    but if Jesus genuinely believes he can bring us peace,
    then he must be living in another world,
    that's all I can say,
    for I can't see it coming in this one,
    can you?

Prayer

Lord of all,
    we long to see peace in our world,
    but the disturbing truth is that faith itself
    seems to contribute towards division.
We look at history,
    and across the centuries we see a sorry catalogue of atrocities
    in the name of religion.
We look at the Church,
    and even today, despite all the efforts to build unity,
    there is still suspicion between various factions,
    sometimes to the point of outright hostility.
We know this shouldn't be,
    and yet we know also that peace doesn't come easily,
    for it can never be achieved
    simply through covering over the causes of our division.
Help us, then, to work for peace in whatever ways we can,
    but give us the faith and the courage we need
    to accept the consequences which may result from our efforts,
    until one day your will is done,
    your kingdom comes
    and all things are made new;
    through Jesus Christ our Lord.
Amen.

42

IT WAS A CHILLING PICTURE HE GAVE US

Andrew

Reading: Mark 13:3-13

When he was sitting on the Mount of Olives opposite the temple, Peter, James, John and Andrew asked him privately, 'Tell us, when will this be, and what will be the sign that all these things are about to be accomplished?' Then Jesus began to say to them, 'Beware that no one leads you astray. Many will come in my name and say, "I am he!" and they will lead many astray. When you hear of wars and rumours of wars, do not be alarmed; this must take place, but the end is still to come. For nation will rise against nation, and kingdom against kingdom; there will be earthquakes in various places; there will be famines. This is but the beginning of the birth pangs.

'As for yourselves, beware; for they will hand you over to councils; and you will be beaten in synagogues; and you will stand before governors and kings because of me, as a testimony to them. And the good news must first be proclaimed to all nations. When they bring you to trial and hand you over, do not worry beforehand about what you are to say; but say whatever is given you at that time, for it is not you who speak, but the Holy Spirit. Brother will betray brother to death, and a father his child, and children will rise against parents and have them put to death; and you will be hated by all because of my name. But the one who endures to the end will be saved.'

Meditation

It was a chilling picture he gave us,
    so unlike those he usually painted,
    so different from those we'd come to expect –
    one which shattered all our illusions,
    throwing everything we thought we'd understood into the balance.
No homely parables this time to bring the message home,
    no comforting promises,
    but a scenario which made us draw our breath in amazement –
    stark,

shocking,
scary –
warnings of doom and disaster,
of trials and temptation,
of beatings and betrayal.
I don't know why,
    but we'd never thought of the future in that way before,
    never expected anything other than joy and blessings.
Not that we had a clear picture, mind you –
    we were more interested in this world than the next –
    but when the kingdom did come
    and the sheep were separated from the goats,
    well, we were pretty confident which side we'd be on.
Only, listening to Jesus, suddenly we weren't so sure after all.
His words wiped the smiles off our faces,
    sent shivers down our spines,
    for they brought home as never before the cost of discipleship,
    the faith, commitment and perseverance needed
    to see our journey through to the end.
We'd imagined, until then, it would be plain sailing,
    a matter simply of plodding along until the race was run,
    the sacrifices we might make now
    more than compensated when the prizes were handed out.
But here was a different prospect altogether,
    the possibility that our love might grow cold,
    our faith be undermined,
    our courage fail,
    our horizons be clouded –
    and the awful thing was we knew it could too easily come true.
We'd grown smug,
    complacent,
    too certain of our righteousness,
    too blasé about our destiny;
    but we realised then there could be no shortcuts,
    no easy options –
    the way is hard and the gate narrow,
    and only a few will find it.
Yes, it was a chilling picture all right –
    one that left us stunned and shaken –
    yet I'm glad he painted it
    for we needed to look again at the faith we professed,
    to consider again the response we'd made,

and then to match our stride to his,
whatever it might take,
wherever it might lead.

Prayer

Lord,
it is easy to grow careless in discipleship –
to imagine that through confessing you as Lord
we have done all that ever needs to be done.
But you call us not simply to acknowledge you
but to follow you,
sharing in the work of your kingdom
and striving to live as your people.
Teach us, then, to walk by your side day by day,
so that we do not find ourselves excluded from that kingdom
when it finally comes.
Amen.

HOLY WEEK

43

HELLO, I THOUGHT, WHAT'S GOING ON HERE?

One of the owners of the colt

Reading: Luke 19:29-40

When he had come near Bethphage and Bethany, at the place called the Mount of Olives, he sent two of the disciples, saying, 'Go into the village ahead of you, and as you enter it you will find tied there a colt that has never been ridden. Untie it and bring it here. If anyone asks you, "Why are you untying it?" just say this, "The Lord needs it."' So those who were sent departed and found it as he had told them. As they were untying the colt, its owners asked them, 'Why are you untying the colt?' They said, 'The Lord needs it.' Then they brought it to Jesus; and after throwing their cloaks on the colt, they set Jesus on it. As he rode along, people kept spreading their cloaks on the road. As he was now approaching the path down from the Mount of Olives, the whole multitude of the disciples began to praise God joyfully with a loud voice for all the deeds of power that they had seen, saying, 'Blessed is the king who comes in the name of the Lord! Peace in heaven, and glory in the highest heaven!' Some of the Pharisees in the crowd said to him, 'Teacher, order your disciples to stop.' He answered, 'I tell you, if these were silent, the stones would shout out.'

Meditation

Hello, I thought, what's going on here?
And you can hardly blame me,
    for there I was, minding my own business,
    when suddenly these fellows I've never clapped eyes on
    appeared from nowhere
    and, cool as you like, started to make off with our donkey!
In broad daylight, too, that's what I couldn't get over –
    bold as brass,
    without so much as a by-your-leave!
Well, you can imagine my surprise, can't you?
Hardly the kind of goings-on you expect in a quiet village like ours.
So I asked them straight, 'What's your game?'
And that's when they spoke those special words:

'The Lord needs it.'
Not the fullest of explanations, admittedly,
    but it was all I needed,
    for straightaway it all came flooding back –
    that day when Jesus came by
    and for a wonderful few moments I met him face to face.
No, you won't have heard about it,
    for it wasn't the sort of encounter to hit the headlines –
    no stunning healing or unforgettable miracle needed in my case,
    but he touched my life as surely and wonderfully as any,
    offering a new direction,
    a fresh start from which I've never looked back.
Quite simply, he changed my life,
    and though I'm not the sort to shout it from the rooftops
    I wanted to respond nonetheless,
    to show Jesus how much he meant to me,
    how much I valued what he'd done.
This was it,
    the chance I'd been waiting for,
    my opportunity to give something back at last.
Hardly earth-shattering stuff, I grant you –
    the loan of a donkey –
    but that didn't matter;
    the fact was that Jesus had need of me –
    it was all I needed to know.
He arrived soon after, and I followed him to Jerusalem,
    where the crowds were waiting to greet him,
    wild with excitement,
    shouting their praises,
    throwing down their cloaks in welcome –
    and, small though it had been, I knew I'd done my bit
    to make that great day possible.
Never forget that, whoever you are,
    however little you think you have to offer,
    for some day, some time, your moment will come –
    a day when your contribution to his kingdom
    will be requested in those lovely words:
    'The Lord needs it.'

Prayer

Lord,
    we are not all called
    to positions of eye-catching responsibility in your service,
    but we all have a part to play nonetheless.
Whoever we are, whatever our gifts,
    we each have a contribution to make which you can use
    in fulfilling something of your eternal purpose.
Teach us, then, to listen for your voice
    and, when you call, to respond gladly,
    offering whatever you ask whenever you need it,
    to the glory of your name.
Amen.

44

YOU SHOULD HAVE HEARD THEM!

Simon the Zealot

Reading: Matthew 21:1-11

When they had come near Jerusalem and had reached Bethphage, at the Mount of Olives, Jesus sent two disciples, saying to them, 'Go into the village ahead of you, and immediately you will find a donkey tied, and a colt with her; untie them and bring them to me. If anyone says anything to you, just say this, "The Lord needs them." And he will send them immediately.' This took place to fulfil what had been spoken through the prophet, saying, 'Tell the daughter of Zion, Look, your king is coming to you, humble, and mounted on a donkey, and on a colt, the foal of a donkey.' The disciples went and did as Jesus had directed them; they brought the donkey and the colt, and put their cloaks on them, and he sat on them. A very large crowd spread their cloaks on the road, and others cut branches from the trees and spread them on the road. The crowds that went ahead of him and that followed were shouting, 'Hosanna to the Son of David! Blessed is the one who comes in the name of the Lord! Hosanna in the highest heaven!' When he entered Jerusalem, the whole city was in turmoil, asking, 'Who is this?' The crowds were saying, 'This is the prophet Jesus from Nazareth in Galilee.'

Meditation

You should have heard them!
What a noise!
What a sight!
What a welcome!
I'm telling you, I've never seen the like,
   not in all my born days,
   and there's been a few of those.
We've had kings here,
   governors,
   would-be messiahs,
   and they've all had their moments,
   their fans out in force to greet them,

but nothing like this,
    nowhere near it!
They came in their thousands,
    waiting to meet him,
    the news of his coming having raced before him.
And it wasn't just his followers,
    it was everyone,
    men, women and children plucking branches from the trees,
    tearing off their cloaks,
    carpeting the road before him,
    their voices hoarse with shouting.
'Hosanna!' they cried.
'Blessed is he who comes in the name of the Lord!'
It was treason, of course,
    and probably heresy too,
    but no one cared –
    devil take the consequences, this was a time for rejoicing,
    and rejoice we did.
Yet if that was unusual –
    the abandonment,
    the jubilation –
    there were stranger things to follow,
    for just a few days later,
    less than a week in fact,
    the scene was so very different.
The same people by and large,
    once more part of a crowd,
    but this time not love but hatred in their faces,
    not welcome but rejection,
    their waving hands suddenly shaking fists,
    their 'Hosanna to the Son of David'
    all at once 'We have no king but Caesar'.
I wouldn't have believed it possible if I hadn't seen it for myself,
    but the sad fact is I not only saw it,
    in my own way I was part of the whole sorry business,
    for when the crisis came I was found wanting,
    concerned only to save my skin
    with no thought as to his.
It was a chilling lesson,
    and one that I, like so many others, learned the hard way –
    the lesson that it's easy to call someone king,
    much harder to actually serve them.

Prayer

Lord Jesus Christ,
    we are good at singing your praises
    when life is going according to plan.
It is another matter when our expectations are overturned,
    our preconceptions challenged
    and our faith tested to the limit.
Yet if we are serious about calling you king,
    then it means accepting your authority
    and allowing you freedom to rule in our lives.
Teach us to be faithful in the good times and the bad,
    giving you honour in whatever we may face
    and confessing you, through word and deed,
    as King of kings and Lord of lords,
    to the glory of your name.
Amen.

45

HE WAS ANGRY

James

Reading: Mark 11:15-19

Then they came to Jerusalem. And he entered the temple and began to drive out those who were selling and those who were buying in the temple, and he overturned the tables of the money-changers and the seats of those who sold doves; and he would not allow anyone to carry anything through the temple. He was teaching and saying, 'Is it not written, "My house shall be called a house of prayer for all the nations"? But you have made it a den of robbers.' And when the chief priests and the scribes heard it, they kept looking for a way to kill him; for they were afraid of him, because the whole crowd was spellbound by his teaching. And when evening came, Jesus and his disciples went out of the city.

Meditation

He was angry,
    more angry than I've ever seen him,
    more angry than I dreamt he could be.
It was so unlike him, that's what surprised me,
    so different from everything we'd come to expect.
The model of gentleness he'd been up till then,
    always willing to see the best,
    ready to make allowances
    where others rushed in to condemn.
Goodness knows, there'd been provocation enough,
    the way the Pharisees goaded him,
    the scribes heckled,
    the Sadducees found fault,
    but despite everything they threw at him –
    the insults,
    the lies,
    the accusations –
    he never let it get to him,
    somehow keeping his cool

when all around him were losing theirs.
But not this time.
I could sense it the moment he set foot in the temple –
     not just anger,
     but outrage,
     seething within him before finally boiling over
     in an explosion of fury.
We were stunned by the way he acted,
     not quite sure what to do with ourselves.
I mean, words are one thing,
     but to create a scene like that –
     it just wasn't done.
But here was a face of Jesus we hadn't seen before,
     disturbing yet challenging.
He saw God's house turned into a market-place,
     a centre of extortion, injustice and corruption,
     and suddenly the frustration he'd bottled up for so long
     came pouring out –
     his sorrow and disappointment
     at a world hell-bent on destroying itself
     when salvation was so nearly in its grasp.
It sealed his fate, that day,
     the writing on the wall after such a blatant act of defiance,
     and the funny thing is I think he knew it,
     almost, you might say, timed it to happen that way.
Did he want to die?
I'm not sure of that, for he loved life as much as any of us.
But what he saw there in the temple
     seemed to convince him there was no other way,
     no other course open to him than to tackle evil head on,
     however awful the consequences,
     however great the price.
No wonder he was angry!

Prayer

Lord,
  we are not good at showing anger;
  at least, not as it is meant to be shown.
We are ready enough to show our temper,
  easily riled by the most innocuous of things
  and capable, at our worst, of destructive fits of rage,
  but such anger is rarely justified,
  almost always serving merely to give vent to our own feelings
  at the cost of someone else's.
Your anger is so very different,
  for it is not about your hurt but ours.
You see injustice and exploitation,
  and your blood boils for the oppressed.
You see the peddling of drugs and the sale of pornography,
  and your heart burns within you at the innocent led astray.
You see hatred, violence, cruelty,
  and your spirit seethes for those caught up in its wake.
Whatever destroys hope, denies love or despoils life
  arouses wrath within you.
Teach us to share that anger
  and to channel it in your service,
  committing ourselves to do all in our power
  to fight against evil and to strive for your kingdom;
  through Jesus Christ our Lord.
Amen.

46

IT WAS READY FOR US,
JUST AS HE'D SAID IT WOULD BE

Peter

Reading: Luke 22:7-13

Then came the day of Unleavened Bread, on which the Passover lamb
had to be sacrificed. So Jesus sent Peter and John, saying, 'Go and prepare
the Passover meal for us that we may eat it.' They asked him, 'Where do
you want us to make preparations for it?' 'Listen,' he said to them,
'when you have entered the city, a man carrying a jar of water will meet
you; follow him into the house he enters and say to the owner of the
house, "The teacher asks you, 'Where is the guest room, where I may eat
the Passover with my disciples?'" He will show you a large room upstairs,
already furnished. Make preparations for us there.' So they went and found
everything as he had told them; and they prepared the Passover meal.

Meditation

It was ready for us, just as he'd said it would be,
    everything arranged,
    everything in its place,
    down to the very last detail,
    as if our arrival there had been planned long before;
    yet – can you believe it? – still the penny didn't drop!
It was only later –
    after we'd shared supper together,
    after his enemies had come for him in the garden,
    after they'd beaten him, broken him,
    nailed him to the cross –
    it was only then that the awesome truth suddenly hit us:
    he *had* planned it! –
    every move, every step, meticulously prepared,
    weeks, months, even years beforehand –
    and our minds reeled at the enormity of it all.
When we'd walked by his side,
    blissfully unaware of anything untoward,
    he'd known that death was waiting for him,

lurking greedily around the corner.
When we watched as he healed the sick and comforted the distressed,
    his thoughts all for others rather than himself,
    he was aware, nonetheless, of the awful fate in store for him,
    the horror, the hurt, the humiliation.
When we'd accompanied him proudly as he entered Jerusalem,
    basking in his reflected glory,
    revelling in the adulation,
    he'd had one eye already fixed on the days ahead –
    on this last meal we would share together,
    on the darkness to come in Gethsemane,
    on the torture of crucifixion.
Suddenly it all made sense –
    how that stranger had been waiting to meet us inside the city,
    how we'd only to say 'The teacher asks . . .'
    and it was done,
    how we were shown upstairs to that little room
    without any need for explanation.
He'd realised, all along,
    probably from the very beginning,
    that this moment would come,
    that the path he had chosen would lead to suffering and death,
    yet still he carried on,
    undeterred,
    undaunted.
And as that truth dawned on me, a lump came to my throat,
    for he'd done it, willingly, for people like me.
He'd known I would deny him,
    that we'd all fail him in our own way,
    yet it didn't matter,
    still he cared enough to die for us.
He saw us at our worst,
    recognising our deepest weaknesses,
    yet still he walked the way of the cross,
    faithful to the last.
I can't believe it, even now –
    that anyone could love us that much –
    but it's true,
    I saw the proof for myself.
We deserved nothing, as he well knew,
    yet he went to the cross
    and gave everything.

Prayer

Lord Jesus Christ,
  you didn't just accept death for our sakes;
  you chose it.
You didn't simply let things happen;
  you planned them in advance,
  knowing the way you would take,
  down to that final agony on the cross.
The only thing you couldn't guarantee was resurrection –
  that had to be taken on trust.
You staked all, you gave all,
  and you did it willingly for our sakes.
Such love is too wonderful to comprehend,
  but we thank you for it from the bottom of our hearts.
Lord Jesus Christ, receive our praise.
Amen.

47

HE COULDN'T MEAN ME, SURELY?

Philip

Reading: Mark 14:17-25

When it was evening, he came with the twelve. And when they had taken their places and were eating, Jesus said, 'Truly I tell you, one of you will betray me, one who is eating with me.' They began to be distressed and to say to him one after another, 'Surely, not I?' He said to them, 'It is one of the twelve, one who is dipping bread into the bowl with me. For the Son of Man goes as it is written of him, but woe to that one by whom the Son of Man is betrayed! It would have been better for that one not to have been born.'

While they were eating, he took a loaf of bread, and after blessing it he broke it, gave it to them, and said, 'Take; this is my body.' Then he took a cup, and after giving thanks he gave it to them, and all of them drank from it. He said to them, 'This is my blood of the covenant, which is poured out for many. Truly I tell you, I will never again drink of the fruit of the vine until that day when I drink it new in the kingdom of God.'

Meditation

He couldn't mean me, surely? –
   that's what I kept telling myself –
   one of the others perhaps, but not me.
I would stay true, if nobody else did,
   dependable to the last,
   someone he could stake his life on if he needed to.
Yet could he?
Deep down, despite my protestations, I wondered,
   for, to tell the truth, I was scared out of my wits,
   dreading what the future might hold for us.
It was suddenly all too real,
   the prospect of suffering and death,
   those warnings Jesus had given
   no longer simply words we could push aside,
   but fact staring us in the face.

His enemies were gathering for the kill,
   greedily waiting their moment,
   and it was only a matter of time
   before they came for the rest of us.
We'd kept on smiling until then,
   putting a brave face on things as best we could,
   if not for his sake then our own.
But suddenly there could be no more running away,
   for in that stark sentence he spelt out the awful truth:
   'One of you will betray me.'
We protested, of course, vehement in our denials,
   yet one by one we looked away, unable to meet his gaze.
It *wasn't* me, I'm glad to say,
   but, of course, you'll know that by now, won't you?
It was Judas who finally couldn't take it,
   Judas whose name will go down in history
   as the one who betrayed Jesus.
Yet somehow that doesn't help,
   for the truth is this:
   when the moment came we were all found wanting,
   all more concerned for our own safety than his.
Maybe we didn't betray him,
   but don't think we're feeling smug about it,
   still less like twisting the knife in Judas,
   for that moment – there in the upper room –
   made us all take a long hard look at ourselves,
   and we didn't much like what we saw.

Prayer

Merciful God,
   it's not easy being honest with ourselves,
   for sometimes we prefer to keep things hidden
   rather than face the disturbing truth.
Occasionally we may glimpse our darker side,
   but we push it away,
   attempting to deny its existence even to ourselves,
   but the knowledge of our weakness is always there,
   lurking in the shadows.
Help us, then, to open our hearts before you
   and acknowledge our faults,

in the knowledge that you gave your Son for us
while we were yet sinners.
Cleanse, redeem, renew, restore,
and by your grace help us
to come to terms with the people we are,
so that one day we might become
the people you would have us be;
through Jesus Christ our Lord.
Amen.

48

'DO WHAT YOU HAVE TO DO,' HE TOLD ME

Judas

Reading: John 13:21-30

Jesus was troubled in spirit, and declared, 'Very truly, I tell you, one of you will betray me.' The disciples looked at one another, uncertain of whom he was speaking. One of his disciples – the one whom Jesus loved – was reclining next to him; Simon Peter therefore motioned to him to ask Jesus of whom he was speaking. So while reclining next to Jesus, he asked him, 'Lord, who is it?' Jesus answered, 'It is the one to whom I give this piece of bread when I have dipped it in the dish.' So when he had dipped the piece of bread, he gave it to Judas son of Simon Iscariot. After he received the piece of bread, Satan entered into him. Jesus said to him, 'Do quickly what you are going to do.' Now no one at the table knew why he said this to him. Some thought that, because Judas had the common purse, Jesus was telling him, 'Buy what we need for the festival'; or, that he should give something to the poor. So, after receiving the piece of bread, he immediately went out. And it was night.

Meditation

'Do what you have to do,' he told me.
And I realised then, as he looked at me,
    from the expression in his eyes,
    that he knew full well what I'd been up to,
    and understood precisely what I had planned for later that evening.
Call me a fool, but I thought until then I'd covered my tracks,
    played the part of doting disciple to a tee.
And I was right to a point,
    for my fellow apostles fell for it hook, line and sinker.
You should have seen their faces
    when Jesus suddenly turned during supper
    and solemnly announced that one of us would betray him.
'Who is it, Lord?' they gasped. 'Surely not I?'
But they actually believed it might be –
    as much one of them as me.

Not Jesus though –
    I realised the moment he looked at me
    that there was no pulling the wool over *his* eyes.
He saw through the charade,
    behind the lamb to the wolf,
    beneath the dove to the serpent,
    and suddenly I was ashamed,
    sickened by what I was doing,
    disgusted at what I'd become.
I should have stopped it there and then,
    confessed everything before them all and begged for mercy.
But I didn't.
I was too proud,
    afraid of losing face,
    terrified of what Caiaphas might do to me
    if I failed to deliver the goods.
So I slithered out of the room,
    leaving the rest of them wide-eyed in disbelief.
It still wasn't too late, even then –
    I could have called a halt to the whole business,
    and I only wish I had.
But I didn't –
    I led the soldiers into the garden,
    and greeted Jesus with a kiss –
    the last revolting act of a repulsive evening.
It was bad enough betraying a friend,
    but what made it worse
    was that we'd eaten together such a short time before.
He'd washed my feet,
    shared bread and wine,
    kept faith with me to the very last, despite everything.
If he'd cursed me,
    accused me,
    rebuked me,
    it would have made it easier.
If he'd only shown some sign of resentment,
    maybe then I could have lived with myself,
    knowing he wasn't so perfect after all.
But there was none of that.
A hint of sorrow, perhaps,
    but apart from that, only love,
    compassion, forgiveness.

He knew what was happening, yet it made no difference.
He knew I was leading him to his death,
   and he carried on regardless.
Why?
You tell me!
I only hope he had more idea what he was doing than I had.

Prayer

Lord Jesus Christ,
   you knew one of your disciples would betray you,
   another deny you,
   and the rest forsake you,
   yet still you went to your death.
You know that we are no better
   and that, with far less reason,
   we continue to betray, deny and forsake you today,
   yet still you love *us*.
Despite the weakness of our faith
   and the poverty of our discipleship,
   you go on caring,
   faithful to us no matter how faithless we may be to you.
Accept our thanksgiving,
   and give us strength to show our gratitude
   through staying true to our calling,
   wherever the path may lead,
   for your name's sake.
Amen.

49

WHY DIDN'T HE ESCAPE WHILE HE HAD THE CHANCE?

The Temple policeman

Reading: John 18:1-14

After Jesus had spoken these words, he went out with his disciples across the Kidron valley to a place where there was a garden, which he and his disciples entered. Now Judas, who betrayed him, also knew the place, because Jesus often met there with his disciples. So Judas brought a detachment of soldiers together with police from the chief priests and the Pharisees, and they came there with lanterns and torches and weapons. Then Jesus, knowing all that was to happen to him, came forward and asked them, 'For whom are you looking?' They answered, 'Jesus of Nazareth.' Jesus replied, 'I am he.' Judas, who betrayed him, was standing with them. When Jesus said to them, 'I am he', they stepped back and fell to the ground. Again he asked them, 'For whom are you looking?' And they said, 'Jesus of Nazareth.' Jesus answered, 'I told you that I am he. So if you are looking for me, let these men go.' This was to fulfil the word that he had spoken, 'I did not lose a single one of those whom you gave me.' Then Simon Peter, who had a sword, drew it, struck the high priest's slave, and cut off his right ear. The slave's name was Malchus. Jesus said to Peter, 'Put your sword back into its sheath. Am I not to drink the cup that the Father has given me?'

So the soldiers, their officer, and the Jewish police arrested Jesus and bound him. First they took him to Annas, who was the father-in-law of Caiaphas, the high priest that year. Caiaphas was the one who had advised the Jews that it was better to have one person die for the people.

Meditation

Why didn't he escape while he had the chance? –
    that's what I can't work out.
He had only to melt away into the shadows,
    slip quietly off into the darkness,
    and we'd have missed him for sure,
    our quarry once again slipping through our fingers.

Right fools we'd have looked then!
But, luckily for us, it didn't work out that way.
Don't ask me why, for I still can't make sense of it,
    but for some reason he actually came looking for us,
    determined, apparently, to give himself up.
Was he fed up, perhaps, with the constant harrying,
    the knowledge that we were always there,
    plotting behind his back,
    waiting for the chance to bring him down.
Some have said so,
    yet he'd never appeared troubled before,
    our attentions, seemingly, of no importance to him.
Whatever it was, though, the fact is *he* took the initiative,
    and we were taken aback,
    such assurance the last thing we'd expected.
You should have seen us,
    enough men and weapons to bring down an army,
    and there he was surrendering without a murmur,
    even rebuking that hot-headed disciple of his
    for taking a swipe at Malchus.
It was astonishing,
    yet that's how it continued –
    no argument,
    no resistance,
    no attempt to defend himself –
    not even when he stood before Pilate,
    his life on the line.
He submitted willingly,
    almost eagerly,
    like a lamb led to the slaughter.
Well, we achieved what we were sent to do.
We got our man where we wanted him,
    nailed for all to see on a cross.
Yet somehow it doesn't feel right,
    the whole business leaving a strange taste in the mouth,
    for the truth of the matter is this:
    we didn't take his life from him as we'd planned –
    he gave it to us!

Prayer

Lord Jesus Christ,
  before we ever loved you, you loved us;
  before we ever looked for you, you were seeking us out;
  before we ever made a response, you were guiding our footsteps.
Always you have been there taking the initiative,
  just as you did throughout your ministry
  and even at the time of your death.
In love you offered your life,
  and in love you continue to reach out,
  never resting until our journey is over and the race is won.
To you be praise and glory, honour and thanksgiving,
  now and for evermore.
Amen.

50

HE WAS UNSURE OF HIMSELF

Peter

Reading: Luke 22:39-46

He came out and went, as was his custom, to the Mount of Olives; and the disciples followed him. When he reached the place, he said to them, 'Pray that you may not come into the time of trial.' Then he withdrew from them about a stone's throw, knelt down, and prayed, 'Father, if you are willing, remove this cup from me; yet, not my will but yours be done.' Then an angel from heaven appeared to him and gave him strength. In his anguish he prayed more earnestly, and his sweat became like great drops of blood falling down on the ground. When he got up from prayer, he came to the disciples and found them sleeping because of grief, and he said to them, 'Why are you sleeping? Get up and pray that you may not come into the time of trial.'

Meditation

He was unsure of himself,
    for the first time in his life
    unsure of his ability to face the future,
    and it hurt him more than the pain he was finally to suffer.
You see, there'd never been any doubt until then,
    never even the slightest suggestion of hesitation.
Despite the hostility, the resentment, the abuse from so many,
    he'd set his face resolutely towards Jerusalem,
    knowing from the very beginning where it would all end.
He understood it all,
    the pain and humiliation he must suffer,
    conscious of it even way back
    in those heady days of his baptism,
    yet he'd carried on willingly,
    the prospect seeming to hold no fear for him,
    and we'd marvelled at the faith, the love,
    the courage of the man,
    the sheer commitment

which gave him such awesome strength and inner purpose.
But suddenly, that evening, it was all so very different,
   a shadow blotting out the light which had shone so brightly.
I saw despair in his eyes rather than hope,
   fear rather than laughter,
   sorrow rather than joy,
   and, most terrible of all, that desperate look of uncertainty,
   so alien,
   so devastating,
   so crushing a burden.
It was all suddenly too real,
   no longer theory but fact –
   the agony and the isolation he was about to face –
   and, like any of us would in his place, he wanted to back away,
   find an easier course,
   a less dreadful option.
It struck me then, as never before,
   that he didn't know what lay beyond death
   any more than I did.
He'd always believed,
   always trusted,
   but he had no more certainty than you and me –
   only the assurance of faith,
   the conviction borne of trust,
   and there in the darkness,
   as the chill of night took hold,
   it all hung on a thread
   as he wrestled with the torment of doubt.
I know what I'd have done had I been him –
   quite simply, I wouldn't have stopped running
   until Jerusalem was just a memory!
But not Jesus.
He stayed quietly in the garden, as I knew he would,
   and he offered not just his *faith* but his *doubt* to God –
   'not *my* will but *yours* be done'.
Well, he was sure of one thing after that –
   there was no way back,
   death now a cast-iron certainty;
   but it wasn't dying itself that was the problem for him,
   it was not knowing whether it would all be worth it,
   whether it could actually make a difference
   to this world we live in,

and there was no way of answering that for certain
this side of eternity.
He was unsure –
of himself,
of his faith,
of his ability to face the future –
but despite it all he risked everything,
offering life itself,
so that we might know the truth,
and be free from death –
free for all eternity!

Prayer

Loving God,
you call us to live by faith, not by sight,
to put our faith in things unseen rather than seen,
and most of the time we are able to do that.
But occasionally we are faced by circumstances
which cause us to doubt,
throwing a shadow over everything we believe.
We question our ability to keep going,
we wonder what is happening to us,
and though we look to you for assurance, we do not find it.
Help us when such moments come
to know that you have been there before us in Christ
and that you understand what we are facing.
Inspire us through the faith and courage he showed,
and so help us to trust in your purpose
even when we cannot see the way ahead.
In his name we pray.
Amen.

51

ANGRY? YOU BET I WAS!

Annas

Reading: John 18:19-24

Then the high priest questioned Jesus about his disciples and about his teaching. Jesus answered, 'I have spoken openly to the world; I have always taught in synagogues and in the temple, where all the Jews come together. I have said nothing in secret. Why do you ask me? Ask those who heard what I said to them; they know what I said.' When he had said this, one of the police standing nearby struck Jesus on the face, saying, 'Is that how you answer the high priest?' Jesus answered, 'If I have spoken wrongly, testify to the wrong. But if I have spoken rightly, why do you strike me?' Then Annas sent him bound to Caiaphas the high priest.

Meditation

Angry? You bet I was!
Wouldn't you have been?
It beggared belief the things this man had said and done –
    violating the sabbath,
    flouting the scripture,
    contradicting our teaching,
    presuming even to forgive sins –
    who did he think he was, the Son of God or something?
I was seething,
    barely able to restrain myself as he stood before me,
    so when one of my men lashed out
    and struck him across the face,
    let's put it this way, I made no attempt to intervene.
It wouldn't have been so bad had he been a priest or a rabbi –
    at least then he'd have had some claim to authority,
    some grounds perhaps to speak out.
But he wasn't any of those, was he? –
    just some self-styled teacher from Galilee
    without even the first idea about the finer points of the law.

Yet was he sorry when they dragged him in?
Was there any sign of remorse,
    even a hint of regret?
Not a bit of it!
Blatant defiance, more like,
    a total disregard for his spiritual betters.
I'll give him one thing, though –
    he made no attempt to duck the issue as some might have done,
    no cowering behind half-truths or lame excuses.
We'd been prepared for that,
    even hauled in some false witnesses just in case,
    but it was clear they wouldn't be needed,
    this man happy, apparently, to condemn himself
    out of his own mouth.
That's the one thing I can't understand –
    he made it easy for us,
    almost too easy,
    as though he wanted it all to happen,
    as though he welcomed the prospect of death.
It wasn't just the trial that set me thinking, but before that:
    why, for example, he came to Jerusalem in the first place –
    he must have known the knives were out for him;
    and why he waited there in the garden
    after Judas slipped away into the darkness –
    did he really have no idea we'd set him up?
Perhaps he was just teasing us,
    believing God would deliver him at the last?
Or did he expect the mob to rise up in rebellion,
    to take us by storm and set him free?
Well, if he did, he showed no sign of it.
It's a mystery to me, I have to confess,
    and there are times when I catch myself thinking
    we were the ones set up that night,
    not *him* –
    that for all *our* scheming *he* was the one
    who finally called the tune.
I'm wrong of course,
    I must be,
    for where did it get him? –
    off to Caiaphas,
    off to Herod,
    off to Pilate,

off finally to the cross and that ghastly, grisly end.
Not even Jesus could have wanted that, could he?
Surely not!

Prayer

Lord Jesus Christ,
    you refused to compromise
    even though you knew what it would cost you to stay true.
You continued to proclaim the good news, heal the sick,
    comfort the broken-hearted and forgive the contrite;
    so long as you had breath within your body
    you were determined to go on loving come what may –
    and you did so to the very end,
    even as you hung in agony on the cross.
Give us a similar resolve to stay true to you,
    honouring the call we have received in turn.
By your grace, help us to walk the way of love,
    faithful to the last, for your name's sake.
Amen.

52
'Truth!' I said. 'What is truth?'
Pilate

Reading: John 18:33-38

Then Pilate entered the headquarters again, summoned Jesus, and asked him, 'Are you the King of the Jews?' Jesus answered, 'Do you ask this on your own, or did others tell you about me?' Pilate replied, 'I am not a Jew, am I? Your own nation and the chief priests have handed you over to me. What have you done?' Jesus answered, 'My kingdom is not from this world. If my kingdom were from this world, my followers would be fighting to keep me from being handed over to the Jews. But as it is, my kingdom is not from here.' Pilate asked him, 'So you are a king?' Jesus answered, 'You say that I am a king. For this I was born, and for this I came into the world, to testify to the truth. Everyone who belongs to the truth listens to my voice.' Pilate asked him, 'What is truth?'

Meditation

'Truth!' I said. 'What is truth?'
No, I wasn't trying to be clever,
    despite what some people may tell you.
I really meant it,
    for I'd encountered so many over the years
    convinced they had the answer,
    each swearing blind that they knew best,
    party to some special knowledge denied to others.
Well, they couldn't all be right, could they? –
    and, the way I see it, none of them were.
Some were downright crazy,
    others well-intentioned but misguided,
    a few with genuine insights to offer,
    but not one of them had the truth,
    the whole truth and nothing but the truth.
Life just isn't like that – black and white –
    and anyone who thinks otherwise is potentially dangerous,
    all the makings of a dictator or fanatic –

believe me, I've trodden that road myself.
So when this Jesus fellow trotted out the same old refrain
    you can understand my being sceptical.
Quite simply, I'd seen it all before.
Or at least, that's what I thought;
    only it soon became apparent that there was more to this man
    than met the eye,
    something quite out of the ordinary.
I'd expected him to launch straightaway into some diatribe,
    to tell me, as they always do, why *he* was right and *I* was wrong.
But he didn't.
He just looked at me with an expression that left me mystified,
    unlike anything I'd seen before.
None of the usual cocktail of fear and bravado,
    laced with a liberal dash of resentment,
    not even the remotest suggestion of it.
Instead there was what seemed like pity, concern,
    even compassion –
    as though he was genuinely disappointed I didn't understand,
    as though he longed for my eyes to be opened,
    as though he actually cared about the way I responded.
It threw me completely, I don't mind admitting it;
    after all, I was the one conducting the trial, not him.
At least, that's how it should have been,
    yet it didn't feel that way.
It was as though my life was being weighed there in the balance,
    and found sadly wanting.
Ridiculous, a man in my position . . .
    to feel I had to answer to some Judean nobody,
    but, try as I might, I just couldn't shake the feeling off,
    and the more I tried to wriggle off the hook,
    the more hopelessly impaled I became.
Do you *still* ask 'What is truth?'
I don't, for I know the answer now –
    I saw it there that day in the eyes of that man,
    and I wish to God I hadn't, for it's haunted me ever since –
    the knowledge that for the first time in my life
    I had the chance to make a stand,
    to commit myself to something which really mattered,
    and I let it slip through my fingers
    for fear of the consequences.
I held the difference between life and death in my hands that day,

his fate in my hands,
and I decided finally on death.
The trouble is I'm not sure whose fate we're talking about –
his, or mine?

Prayer

Gracious God,
  we look for truth but we are often disappointed.
What seems certain is suddenly shaken;
  what seems trustworthy turns out to be false;
  what seems clear becomes a puzzle;
  what seems good unexpectedly proves bad.
Few things in life are quite what they appear
  and, as a result, we can feel like a ship without an anchor,
  tossed about in a sea of confusion.
Help us to put our trust in the one thing that doesn't change:
  your love revealed in Jesus Christ,
  the same today, yesterday and for ever,
  and in him may we find the truth that sets us free.
Amen.

53

HE WAS A FOOL, THAT'S WHAT I THOUGHT

Herod

Reading: Luke 23:1-12

Then the assembly rose as a body and brought Jesus before Pilate. They
began to accuse him, saying, 'We found this man perverting our nation,
forbidding us to pay taxes to the emperor, and saying that he himself is
the Messiah, a king.' Then Pilate asked him, 'Are you the king of the
Jews?' He answered, 'You say so.' Then Pilate said to the chief priests
and the crowds, 'I find no basis for an accusation against this man.' But
they were insistent and said, 'He stirs up the people by teaching
throughout all Judea, from Galilee where he began even to this place.'

When Pilate heard this, he asked whether the man was a Galilean.
And when he learned that he was under Herod's jurisdiction, he sent
him off to Herod, who was himself in Jerusalem at that time. When
Herod saw Jesus, he was very glad, for he had been wanting to see him
for a long time, because he had heard about him and was hoping to see
him perform some sign. He questioned him at some length, but Jesus gave
him no answer. The chief priests and the scribes stood by, vehemently
accusing him. Even Herod with his soldiers treated him with contempt
and mocked him; then he put an elegant robe on him, and sent him back
to Pilate. That same day Herod and Pilate became friends with each
other; before this they had been enemies.

Meditation

He was a fool, that's what I thought.
Why else walk into that trap the Pharisees had set for him?
Why else be taken in by a betrayer's kiss?
Why else keep silent,
   when a simple denial might have saved him?
Only a fool would make mistakes like those,
   so I decided to treat him like one,
   show him up for the clown he was.
We dressed him like a king,
   bowed in mock obeisance,

declared our undying love and loyalty.
'Come on,' we shouted,
  'show us a sign,
  perform a wonder,
  work a miracle!'
And we fell about laughing until our sides ached
  and the tears rolled down our faces.
It sounds quite a party, doesn't it?
Only it wasn't, not if you really want to know,
  for beneath the facade it wasn't laughter we felt,
  but amazement,
  awe,
  dread,
  disbelief.
How come? – I hear you ask.
What did he say? What did he do?
Yet that's just it –
  he did nothing,
  said nothing,
  just stood there calmly,
  meeting everything we threw at him
  with a quiet unshakeable dignity.
And as he stood there,
  unbowed,
  unbroken,
  suddenly I knew he hadn't walked into any trap,
  fallen for any kiss,
  wasted any last chance for freedom.
He'd seen it all coming, every last detail –
  suffering, rejection, death –
  and he'd been waiting for it to happen,
  waiting for the last piece of the jigsaw to fit into place.
It was no accident, this trial and interrogation,
  no unfortunate mistake or cruel twist of fate –
  it was planned long before,
  part of some greater purpose I couldn't even begin to fathom,
  and it exposed at a stroke the pathetic emptiness of my life.
I tried to brush it aside,
  to pretend I had no need of him,
  but it was no good – there was no escaping the truth.
Maybe I couldn't have saved him from his fate that day –
  not given the mood the crowds were in –

but he could have saved *me* from *mine*,
    and I tossed away my opportunity for fear of the consequences,
    terrified of what it all might cost.
I sent him away finally, unable to take it any longer,
    and they nailed him to a cross,
    an unimaginably awful death.
Yet I tell you what,
    however ridiculous it may sound,
    it wasn't him who was the fool that day –
    it was me!

Prayer

Gracious God,
    your way can sometimes seem like foolishness –
    the way of sacrifice and self-denial,
    of love in the face of hatred,
    faithfulness in the face of rejection.
In the eyes of the world the message of Christ crucified
    continues to look like folly,
    but to us it is a revelation of your power and wisdom,
    a demonstration of your mercy,
    and the most marvellous expression of your saving grace.
Teach us to show our gratitude not just through words
    but through following his way,
    ready in turn to be fools for Christ.
Amen.

54

'REMEMBER ME,' HE CRIED

Mother of one of the thieves

Reading: Luke 23:39-43

One of the criminals who were hanged there kept deriding him and saying, 'Are you not the Messiah? Save yourself and us!' But the other rebuked him, saying, 'Do you not fear God, since you are under the same sentence of condemnation? And we indeed have been condemned justly, for we are getting what we deserve for our deeds, but this man has done nothing wrong.' Then he said, 'Jesus, remember me when you come into your kingdom.' He replied, 'Truly I tell you, today you will be with me in Paradise.'

Meditation

'Remember me,' he cried.
'When you come into your kingdom,
   remember the poor wretch who suffered and died beside you.'
What made him ask it?
I really don't know,
   but there was something about that man Jesus
   which clearly touched him,
   enough apparently, despite the agony he endured,
   to inspire that last desperate plea.
It came as a complete surprise, that's for sure,
   for he wasn't a religious man;
   his faith – not just in God but in everything –
   long broken by then.
You see, he knew he'd done wrong,
   and he wanted to change,
   to put the past behind him and start again,
   but what hope did he have,
   for how many were there ready to give him a second chance,
   willing to believe he could mend his ways?
None.

One mistake,
    one moment's madness,
    and he was an outcast,
    a reject,
    condemned to spend the rest of his life in the gutter,
    devoid of hope,
    devoid of meaning.
No wonder he couldn't take it.
Eventually he just snapped,
    throwing not just scruples but caution to the wind,
    and after that there could only be one result.
It broke my heart when they caught him,
    for he was still my son, whatever he'd done,
    yet he seemed resigned by then,
    as if he accepted he deserved punishment for his crimes.
But as they lifted up his cross
    he caught sight of Jesus nailed there beside him,
    and his expression changed in a moment,
    from dull despair to anger, disbelief, dismay.
I knew what he was thinking,
    for I felt it too:
    why this man? –
    a man who was so clearly innocent,
    not an ounce of evil in him,
    not even the faintest suggestion of hatred or malice.
He took everything the crowds threw at him,
    the insults,
    the ridicule,
    the rejection,
    and even when the other fellow hanging there beside him
    joined in the abuse,
    hurling down curses –
    his reaction never changed;
    no anger,
    no resentment,
    no curses in return.
It was the first time I'd seen anything like it –
    the *only* time –
    and clearly it touched my son as much as it touched me,
    for next thing I knew I heard his voice,
    calling out, loud and clear:
    'Jesus, remember me when you come into your kingdom.'

I caught my breath then,
    afraid what might happen next,
    for why should Jesus listen, there of all places –
    no one else ever did –
    what reason to think he'd have time for anything
    but his own agony.
Yet he turned with a look I shall never forget –
    such love,
    such joy,
    such acceptance in his face –
    and he spoke those wonderful words:
    'Today you will be with me in Paradise.'
Was it true?
Well, I can't tell you, can I,
    not in this life anyway –
    if you want proof, you must wait and see.
But I *can* tell you this,
    when they cut my boy down I held him in my arms,
    and you should have seen the smile on his face –
    the peace and joy which radiated from him,
    happiness which I'd given up hoping ever to see again.
It was enough for me.
I knew then,
    beyond doubt,
    beyond question,
    that Jesus had heard his prayer,
    and answered him!

Prayer

Lord Jesus Christ,
    whoever we are, whatever we have done,
    it is never too late to respond to your love.
You are always ready to forgive and forget,
    always waiting to pick up the pieces of our lives
    and help us start again.
That is why you came –
    to offer a clean break to everyone who recognises their need;
    a new beginning in this life and the life to come.
And that is why we come to you now

seeking your help and mercy,
for we know our weakness and our sin is ever before us.
Lord Jesus Christ, we join in the words
of that simple and unforgettable prayer:
'When you come into your kingdom, remember me.'
Amen.

55

I STILL CAN'T BELIEVE MY LUCK

Barabbas

Reading: Mark 15:6-15

Now at the festival he used to release a prisoner for them, anyone for whom they asked. Now a man called Barabbas was in prison with the rebels who had committed murder during the insurrection. So the crowd came and began to ask Pilate to do for them according to his custom. Then he answered them, 'Do you want me to release for you the King of the Jews?' For he realised that it was out of jealousy that the chief priests had handed him over. But the chief priests stirred up the crowd to have him release Barabbas for them instead. Pilate spoke to them again, 'Then what do you wish me to do with the man you call the King of the Jews?' They shouted back, 'Crucify him!' Pilate asked them, 'Why, what evil has he done?' But they shouted all the more, 'Crucify him!' So Pilate, wishing to satisfy the crowd, released Barabbas for them; and after flogging Jesus, he handed him over to be crucified.

Meditation

I still can't believe my luck,
    still, after all this time, can't believe
    that I got off that day scot-free.
What on earth possessed the mob to let *me* off the hook
    and send *Jesus* to the cross? –
    I'll never make sense of it.
All right, so I wasn't a follower of his –
    my way more one of force than persuasion –
    but even I couldn't help being impressed by the man.
He was so clearly innocent, any fool could see that –
    a good man, through and through,
    sincere,
    gentle,
    honest,
    refusing to compromise his convictions
    despite the torment they put him through –

the very idea of him inciting a revolt frankly laughable.
Yes, maybe he had stirred up the crowd's expectations
    through his signs and wonders,
    allowed them to believe he was the promised Messiah,
    but what of it? –
    he was hardly a revolutionary, was he? –
    not in the sense I wish he'd been, anyway,
    rebellion the last thing in his mind.
I knew it.
They knew it.
So why turn against him?
Why hand him over to the enemy
    to be butchered like a common criminal,
    and let me, a known trouble-maker, wriggle off the hook? –
    it just didn't add up.
Yet that's what they did,
    and the strange thing is
    he made no attempt to defend himself,
    no attempt to expose the ludicrousness of the charges
    or explain the true nature of his claims.
You might almost have thought he wanted to die, the way he acted.
Not that I'm complaining –
    I wouldn't be here now had things worked out differently –
    only I can't help wondering sometimes
    what actually went on that day,
    whether there was more going on than anyone realised,
    some hidden force at work.
It should have been me instead of him,
    anyone rather than a man like that,
    but it wasn't –
    he suffered the punishment I deserved,
    by some strange twist of fate his death buying me freedom.
It's a mystery, isn't it?

Prayer

Gracious God,
    we have no claim on your love,
    for we know that there is no good in us,
    nothing deserving your mercy.
Yet through Christ you have endured the punishment

which should have been ours,
you have paid the penalty for our sins
and carried the burden
which should have been on our shoulders.
By his wounds we are healed,
   by his love made whole,
   by his death given life.
There are no words to express our debt to you,
   yet you ask nothing more
   than that we receive the gift you have given.
Gracious God, we come again
   and we give you thanks for the wonder of your grace;
   through Jesus Christ our Lord.
Amen.

56

WHAT GOT INTO US THAT DAY?

One of the mob

Reading: John 19:1-16

Then Pilate took Jesus and had him flogged. And the soldiers wove a crown of thorns and put it on his head, and they dressed him in a purple robe. They kept coming up to him, saying, 'Hail, King of the Jews!' and striking him on the face. Pilate went out again and said to them, 'Look, I am bringing him out to you to let you know that I find no case against him.' So Jesus came out, wearing the crown of thorns and the purple robe. Pilate said to them, 'Here is the man!' When the chief priests and the police saw him, they shouted, 'Crucify him! Crucify him!' Pilate said to them, 'Take him yourselves and crucify him; I find no case against him.' The Jews answered him, 'We have a law, and according to that law he ought to die, because he has claimed to be the Son of God.'

Now when Pilate heard this, he was more afraid than ever. He entered his headquarters again and asked Jesus, 'Where are you from?' But Jesus gave him no answer. Pilate therefore said to him, 'Do you refuse to speak to me? Do you not know that I have power to release you, and power to crucify you?' Jesus answered him, 'You would have no power over me unless it had been given you from above; therefore the one who handed me over to you is guilty of a greater sin.' From then on Pilate tried to release him, but the Jews cried out, 'If you release this man, you are no friend of the emperor. Everyone who claims to be a king sets himself against the emperor.'

When Pilate heard these words, he brought Jesus outside and sat on the judge's bench at a place called The Stone Pavement, or in Hebrew Gabbatha. Now it was the day of Preparation for the Passover; and it was about noon. He said to the Jews, 'Here is your King!' They cried out, 'Away with him! Away with him! Crucify him!' Pilate asked them, 'Shall I crucify your King?' The chief priests answered, 'We have no king but the emperor.' Then he handed him over to them to be crucified.

Meditation

What got into us that day?
Can you make sense of it?
I look back now incredulous,

unable to believe we could have been so false, so fickle,
one day protesting our undying loyalty,
and the next baying for his blood like a pack of wolves.
Yet that's what we did,
    our cries of 'Hosanna!' in just a few days turning to 'Crucify!',
    our shouts of welcome to jeers of rejection.
It was partly, I suppose, borne of disappointment,
    the truth slowly dawning on us
    that Jesus wasn't the sort of Messiah we expected,
    his kingdom of an altogether different nature
    from the one we looked for.
That was a blow, undoubtedly,
    for many of us, me included, really believed
    he was the one we waited for,
    the promised deliverer who would set us free
    from the yoke of Roman oppression.
Then, of course, there was fear,
    for we were well aware that the Pharisees were watching us,
    their beady eyes on the lookout
    for anyone less than enthusiastic in their cause –
    we all knew it wouldn't take much
    for us to suffer the same fate as Jesus.
Yet deep down those are only excuses,
    incidental to the main cause.
The ugly fact is this:
    we followed the crowd,
    caught up in the hysteria of the moment,
    until we blindly followed the one next to us
    like a bunch of sheep.
It all happened so quickly, that's the chilling thing –
    one moment we were sane, rational human beings,
    and the next no longer people at all,
    simply part of a faceless crowd,
    a senseless, soulless mob,
    all reason forgotten,
    all sanity suspended.
I thought I was different –
    able to think for myself,
    make my own decisions,
    resist the pressure to compromise –
    but I learned the hard way that I wasn't;
    I caught a glimpse of the person I really am,

and I'm still struggling to take it in.
Do you know what bothers me most, though?
It's how Jesus must have felt as he stood there,
    listening to our shouts,
    and the truth dawned on him
    that he was wasting his life on people like us –
    it must have all but finished him.
The only surprise is he didn't realise it sooner,
    for he saw everything else so clearly;
    but he couldn't have done, could he,
    or he'd have called a halt somewhere –
    it stands to reason.
Yes, I know he was special, no question about it,
    but no one in their right mind
    would have gone to their death for us
    had they seen us that day,
    had they witnessed what we were really like –
    not even Jesus would do that,
    surely?

Prayer

Gracious God,
    despite our resolve to serve you
    we are so easily led astray.
Like sheep, we blindly follow the example of the crowd.
We congratulate ourselves on resisting the latest trend or fashion,
    but the pressures to conform are more subtle than that;
    often unseen, unrecognised.
Help us to listen to you
    rather than the voices which surround us.
Help us to stay close by your side
    and respond to your guidance.
And on those occasions when we find ourselves lost,
    seek us in Christ, the Good Shepherd,
    and restore us to your fold,
    for his name's sake.
Amen.

57

IT WAS HEARTBREAKING TO SEE HIM

One of the crowd on the way to Golgotha

Reading: Luke 23:26-31

As they led him away, they seized a man, Simon of Cyrene, who was coming from the country, and they laid the cross on him, and made him carry it behind Jesus. A great number of the people followed him, and among them were women who were beating their breasts and wailing for him. But Jesus turned to them and said, 'Daughters of Jerusalem, do not weep for me, but weep for yourselves and for your children. For the days are surely coming when they will say, "Blessed are the barren, and the wombs that never bore, and the breasts that never nursed." Then they will begin to say to the mountains, "Fall on us"; and to the hills, "Cover us." For if they do this when the wood is green, what will happen when it is dry?'

Meditation

It was heartbreaking to see him,
    to watch the man we'd come to love collapsing in agony,
    to witness our dreams founder with him,
    lying broken in the dust.
Suddenly our world was in pieces,
    for it was impossible not to look back
    and remember his words in happier days,
    words which had seemed so full of promise.
'Come to me,' he had said, 'all you that are weary
    and are carrying heavy burdens,
    and I will give rest.
    Take my yoke upon you, and learn from me;
    for I am gentle and humble in heart,
    and you will find rest for your souls.
    For my yoke is easy,
    and my burden is light.'
What could we make of that now
    as he staggered under the weight of that cross,
    crushed by the burden,
    scarcely able to stand,

finally able to carry it no longer?
It challenged everything,
   all we had seen and heard,
   all we'd come to believe,
   for how could it be –
   the man who'd healed the sick,
   broken beyond recognition,
   the one who'd forgiven sins,
   convicted as a common criminal,
   the Messiah, who'd promised life,
   facing the darkness of death?
We stood there, horrified,
   unable to make sense of what was happening.
'Why doesn't he do something?' we asked.
   'He has the power, so why not use it?'
Surely now, of all times, called for one of his signs and wonders,
   another of those miracles
   which had captivated the multitudes throughout his ministry.
What was he waiting for?
Why the delay?
We just couldn't work it out.
Only then he turned and looked at us,
   a slow, sad smile touching his face,
   and I could see the sorrow he felt was not for him
   but for us –
   the pain *we* had yet to bear,
   the sorrow we had still to endure
   as part of this bleeding broken world;
   a world he had come to heal through his dying.
It was *still* heartbreaking to watch, despite that knowledge,
   more awful than I can ever tell you,
   but it was no longer a mystery, not to me anyway.
He could have walked away as I'd hoped he might do,
   sparing himself the agony and degradation,
   but he didn't –
   he took the way of the cross,
   bearing our burdens,
   carrying our punishment,
   enduring our darkness,
   dying our death –
   and I understood that he'd produced a miracle after all –
   the greatest sign and wonder we could ever ask for!

Prayer

Sovereign God,
    we cannot always make sense of your purposes
    but that doesn't mean you aren't at work.
The way may be hidden, the path may appear dark,
    but sometimes when you seem distant
    you are in fact at your most near.
You take what seems to be bad and use it for good.
You transform what looks hopeless
    into new beginnings full of promise.
You turn sorrow into laughter, weakness into strength,
    darkness into light, death into life.
Teach us, then, never to despair of any moment,
    however bleak it may seem,
    for you have shown us
    that there is nothing in heaven or earth
    beyond your renewing power.
To you be praise and glory, now and always.
Amen.

58

HE WAS TIRED

Simon of Cyrene

Reading: Mark 15:21-24

They compelled a passer-by, who was coming in from the country, to carry his cross; it was Simon of Cyrene, the father of Alexander and Rufus. Then they brought Jesus to the place called Golgotha (which means the place of a skull). And they offered him wine mixed with myrrh; but he did not take it. And they crucified him, and divided his clothes among them, casting lots to decide what each should take.

Meditation

He was tired,
    just about dead on his feet,
    and it wasn't just due to that cross he was carrying.
No, that was the easy bit –
    it was the other burdens he'd been bearing for so long,
    and the load he still had to endure
    that was getting to him.
Oh, the cross was heavy, don't get me wrong –
    if anyone knows that, it's me –
    and the beating he'd taken was enough to break any man,
    even the strongest of us.
Yet I still say there was more to it than that,
    far more.
You only had to look into his eyes, as I did,
    and see the agony there –
    an agony not of body but soul,
    not of flesh but spirit.
He was used to physical pain by then –
    ready for anything else they might throw at him –
    so when they hammered the nails into his hands and feet,
    when they hauled the cross into position,
    despite turning down the wine and myrrh they offered him,
    he scarcely flinched,

204 NO ORDINARY MAN

barely giving them the satisfaction of a groan.
But he was suffering, no question,
    suffering more deeply,
    more hellishly,
    than I'd imagined possible before.
It was as though a light went out within,
    as though he were being crushed by some extraordinary weight,
    as though he were enduring such torment
    that physical pain seemed trivial by comparison.
I was mystified at first,
    unable to imagine what could be more terrible than crucifixion.
But then suddenly,
    just before he died,
    he looked up
    and the eyes were bright,
    the face radiant,
    all sign of pain vanished.
'It is finished!' he shouted,
    and I understood then
    that he'd carried a burden beyond all imagining,
    almost, you might say,
    the weight of the whole world on his shoulders;
    and at last now,
    having been faithful to the end
    he could put it down,
    knowing the struggle was over,
    the job was done,
    mission completed!

Prayer

Lord,
    we talk glibly about all you suffered,
    but we rarely stop to consider what it involved.
It is hard enough to imagine the physical torment
    and mental anguish you went through,
    yet those must have seemed as nothing
    compared to the spiritual torture you endured.
Having walked in daily communion with the Father,
    suddenly there, as you took our sins upon you,
    you felt isolated even from him,

abandoned, totally alone
    as you stared into the dark chasm of death.
We will never be able to grasp what that was like,
    how awful it must have felt –
    yet even the little we can glimpse
    gives us an insight into the full wonder
    of your astonishing sacrifice.
For love so amazing, so divine,
    Lord Jesus Christ, receive our praise.
Amen.

59
HE WAS GASPING

Mary Magdalene

Reading: Mark 15:33-36, 40-41

When it was noon, darkness came over the whole land until three in the afternoon. At three o'clock Jesus cried out with a loud voice, 'Eloi, Eloi, lema sabachthani?' which means, 'My God, my God, why have you forsaken me?' When some of the bystanders heard it, they said, 'Listen, he is calling for Elijah.' And someone ran, filled a sponge with sour wine, put it on a stick, and gave it to him to drink, saying 'Wait, let us see whether Elijah will come to take him down.'

There were also women looking on from a distance; among them were Mary Magdalene, and Mary the mother of James the younger and of Joses, and Salome. These used to follow him and provided for him when he was in Galilee; and there were many other women who had come up with him to Jerusalem.

Meditation

He was gasping,
   his breath coming short and sharp,
   his body contorted in agony,
   and I could scarcely bring myself to watch.
It's a dreadful business, crucifixion, at the best of times,
   even when the poor wretch up there deserves to die,
   but when it's a friend,
   a loved one,
   somebody who's been special to you,
   then, I'm telling you, it's indescribable.
To stand by helpless as the pain takes hold,
   as the muscles tear and the tendons snap,
   as life ebbs out of the body –
   to see the misery,
   the torment,
   the despair,
   and to know it must get worse

before finally, in the sweet embrace of death, it gets better;
   you just can't imagine what that feels like,
   not unless you've been there.
And we *were* there, more's the pity,
   each one of us enduring our own private hell.
We wanted to run, God knows! –
   to close our eyes and pretend it wasn't happening.
But we couldn't, could we?
For he needed us then more than ever,
      simply to know we were there,
      that we cared,
      that he wasn't alone.
It wasn't much, I grant you,
      the few of us huddled together,
      watching nervously from the shadows,
      fearful of recognition,
      but it was enough,
      one ray of sunshine in a wilderness of darkness;
      for he knew that despite our faults,
      the weakness of our faith and feebleness of our commitment,
      we were risking something,
      sticking our necks out for love of him.
He was gasping,
      and we prayed it wouldn't be much longer
      before release finally came.
But however long it took,
      and whatever it might cost us,
      we were resolved to stay to the bitter end –
      it was the very least we could do.

Prayer

Lord Jesus Christ,
   we know we can never repay
   the love you showed us on the cross,
   however we might try,
   but what we *can* do is show how much it means to us.
And we can do that most of all through staying close to you,
   seeking your will and obeying your voice.
It is this which will breathe life into our faith and worship;
   this which will prove the words on our lips

through the light in our lives –
your purpose guiding our footsteps,
your love shining from our hearts.
Lord Jesus Christ, it may not be easy,
it may even be costly,
but help us to stay true to you,
just as you stayed true to us.
Amen.

60
HE WAS THINKING OF ME, EVEN THEN!

Mary, mother of Jesus

Reading: John 19:25-27

Meanwhile, standing near the cross of Jesus were his mother, and his mother's sister, Mary the wife of Clopas, and Mary Magdalene. When Jesus saw his mother and the disciple whom he loved standing beside her, he said to his mother, 'Woman, here is your son.' Then he said to the disciple, 'Here is your mother.' And from that hour the disciple took her into his own home.

Meditation

He was thinking of me, even then!
I couldn't believe it –
    despite everything he was going through,
    the awful, stomach-churning agony
    which seemed to pierce my very soul,
    he was concerned more about my welfare than his.
Yet I shouldn't have been surprised –
    it was so like Jesus,
    the way he'd been from a boy,
    always putting others before himself.
I'd dared to hope that just this once it would be different,
    that for the first time in his life he'd look after number one.
Why not?
Would it have been so wrong?
He'd given enough already, hadn't he?
Scarcely a moment to himself,
    the crowds always with him,
    clamouring,
    calling,
    pleading,
    demanding –
    enough to break any lesser man.
And, as if that wasn't enough,

his enemies had been there stalking him,
    unable to conceal their hatred,
    watching his every move,
    waiting for their moment.
He knew what they were up to,
    yet he'd continued without a murmur of complaint –
    always having time,
    always ready to respond,
    nothing and no one outside his concern.
I saw him so many times just about all in,
    drained to the point of exhaustion,
    and I can't tell you how much it troubled me,
    to see my wonderful lad pouring himself out
    in a constant act of sacrifice,
    pushing himself to the very limit.
But it was useless to argue –
    I tried it sometimes and he simply smiled at me
    in that gentle way of his,
    knowing I understood full well that there was no other way.
He was right, I knew that,
    and I knew equally there was no way
    he'd come down from that cross,
    but I could still hope, couldn't I,
    still pray I might be wrong?
He was thinking of others even then,
    not only me, but a common thief hanging there beside him,
    my fellow-women, sobbing their hearts out,
    even those who'd hounded him to his death –
    thinking, in fact, of everyone
    except himself.

Prayer

Lord Jesus,
    throughout your life you were the man for others,
    always ready to listen,
    always prepared to respond,
    whatever the cost to yourself.
At your death it was the same –
    still you poured yourself out,
    thinking of others to the last.

Forgive us that we are the opposite,
>more often than not our thoughts only for self,
>rarely willing to listen,
>even less so to respond,
>fearful of what it all might cost us.

Lord Jesus, forgive us and teach us your way,
>for until we learn to be the servant of all
>we will continue to be the slave of self.

Help us to give freely,
>and in a life of service to find true freedom.

Amen.

61

IT WAS DARK

The centurion at the foot of the cross

Reading: Luke 23:44-49

It was now about noon, and darkness came over the whole land until three in the afternoon, while the sun's light failed; and the curtain of the temple was torn in two. Then Jesus, crying with a loud voice, said, 'Father, into your hands I commend my spirit.' Having said this, he breathed his last. When the centurion saw what had taken place, he praised God and said, 'Certainly this man was innocent.' And when all the crowds who had gathered there for this spectacle saw what had taken place, they returned home, beating their breasts. But all his acquaintances, including the women who had followed him from Galilee, stood at a distance, watching these things.

Meditation

It was dark,
    so very, very dark,
    like the dead of night,
    as black as sin.
Nothing strange in that, of course,
    except that it was noon,
    the sun having blazed out of a cloudless sky just a moment before!
It was simply another ordinary day, up till then,
    the usual routine executions to get through,
    and we'd watched impassively
    as the latest batch of ne'er-do-wells had suffered in the heat,
    crying out for water as they squirmed and writhed in agony.
Did I feel anything for them?
Not a thing –
    you get used to the screams after a time.
But there was something about one of them this time
    which couldn't help but catch my attention,
    for there was a calmness about him,

even, you might say, an air of authority,
which left me flabbergasted,
unable to believe quite what I was seeing.
He was in a terrible state,
his back an ugly mass of lacerations
where the whip had bitten into him,
and blood oozing from his head, his hands, his feet;
yet some, it seemed, felt even then he hadn't endured enough.
They mocked, insulted, rebuked, tormented him,
enough to make any ordinary man return their curses,
yet, can you believe this, I heard him with my own ears cry out,
asking God to forgive them.
Amazing!
And when he died, it was more uncanny still,
for I'd swear as he drew his final breath
there was a look of triumph in his eyes,
for all the world as though he believed
that ghastly death of his had some meaning,
some hidden purpose –
heaven knows what that could have been!
Yet it was the darkness which got to me most,
the way, without warning,
literally out of the blue,
the skies closed in as he hung there,
and a cold and eerie hush seemed to cover the world.
Coincidence, some called it,
but not me;
I saw enough to convince me that this man was special,
innocent, without question,
almost, you might say, the Son of God.
It's not like me to say that, for I'm not a sentimental type –
no time usually for all that nonsense –
but as I watched the man suffer,
and when I saw him finally die,
it was *then* that the light went out for me,
the world suddenly more black
than it had ever seemed before.
It was dark,
so very, very dark.

Prayer

Living God,
    there could hardly have been a darker time
    than that day when Jesus hung on a cross.
Hatred, resentment, prejudice and fear
    combined to do their worst,
    and as your Son suffered there in agony,
    as they cut him down and laid him in a tomb,
    they seemed to be triumphant.
Living God,
    there could hardly have been a brighter time
    than that day when Jesus hung on a cross.
Love, forgiveness, acceptance and peace
    combined to do their best,
    and as your child writhed there in torment,
    as he cried out and breathed his last,
    they won the final victory.
Living God, on this day of all days
    you showed that to you even the darkness is as light
    and the night as day.
In that assurance may we live every moment,
    knowing that whatever we may face
    your love will continue to shine;
    through Jesus Christ our Lord.
Amen.

EASTER

62

YOU'D HAVE THOUGHT WE'D BE PLEASED, WOULDN'T YOU?

Salome

Reading: Mark 16:1-8

When the sabbath was over, Mary Magdalene, and Mary the mother of James, and Salome bought spices, so that they might go and anoint him. And very early on the first day of the week, when the sun had risen, they went to the tomb. They had been saying to one another, 'Who will roll away the stone for us from the entrance to the tomb?' When they looked up, they saw that the stone, which was very large, had already been rolled back. As they entered the tomb, they saw a young man, dressed in a white robe, sitting on the right side; and they were alarmed. But he said to them, 'Do not be alarmed; you are looking for Jesus of Nazareth, who was crucified. He has been raised; he is not here. Look, there is the place they laid him. But go, tell his disciples and Peter that he is going ahead of you to Galilee; there you will see him, just as he told you.' So they went out and fled from the tomb, for terror and amazement had seized them; and they said nothing to anyone, for they were afraid.

Meditation

You'd have thought we'd be pleased, wouldn't you? –
    over the moon at the news that he had risen.
And we were, later,
    once we finally took it all in.
But at the time it wasn't pleasure we felt,
    it was sheer, unadulterated fear.
Can you blame us?
I don't think so,
    for it's not every day you find a tomb empty, is it? –
    not often that you go to anoint a body
    only to find it's disappeared!
Yet that's what happened to us –
    early that morning,
    the dew still wet on the grass,

mist still rising,
the three of us making our way to the tomb,
suspecting nothing,
expecting nothing,
simply going to pay our last respects.
It was shock enough finding the stone rolled away,
our stomachs lurching at the sight of it,
and when we finally plucked up the courage to look inside,
to find not Jesus but this man we didn't know from Adam,
well, we could scarcely suppress a scream!
Who was he?
Why was he there?
What did he want?
And, most important of all, where had he taken our Lord?
The questions crowded in upon us,
our minds reeling in confusion.
He may have been calm
but *we* weren't!
We felt faint with disbelief,
dizziness growing by the second,
wanting only to get out and as far away as possible;
so when he told us to go back to the disciples,
believe me, we were only too happy to oblige.
Did we tell them what we'd seen?
Well, what do you think? Would *you* have done?
We knew all too well the response we'd get,
our words dismissed as so much nonsense –
and that's just what happened
when they finally forced it out of us,
for, try as we might, we simply couldn't hide our confusion.
We weren't just scared,
we were terrified,
trembling as though we'd seen a ghost,
and with good reason,
for we honestly thought we had!

Prayer

Lord Jesus Christ,
    we forget sometimes the sheer wonder of your resurrection.
We have heard the accounts so often that we fail to appreciate
    the enormity of what took place and the effect it had.
You were dead and buried, your body sealed in a tomb,
    and for your followers that was it,
    the end of a glorious dream.
When the women went to anoint your body
    they expected nothing more than to perform that last act of love.
But the tomb was found empty, your body gone,
    the grave clothes discarded there
    the only sign of where you had lain –
    and for a time it was too much to take in.
The women returned in shock;
    Mary broke down in tears;
    the apostles laughed in derision,
    for by all human reckoning it simply could not be.
Only it was!
You had broken the hold of death,
    turned the world upside-down,
    transformed the cost of history in one magnificent moment!
Lord Jesus Christ, as we celebrate today your victory over death
    give us that same sense of awe and wonder
    felt by those who first learned the truth.
Come alive in our hearts,
    so that *our* minds too will reel in wonder,
    and *our* spirits dance in joyous celebration
    to the glory of your name.
Amen.

63

I'LL NEVER BE ABLE TO SAY WHAT IT MEANT TO ME

Mary Magdalene

Reading: Matthew 28:1-10

After the sabbath, as the first day of the week was dawning, Mary Magdalene and the other Mary went to see the tomb. And suddenly there was a great earthquake; for an angel of the Lord, descending from heaven, came and rolled back the stone and sat on it. His appearance was like lightning, and his clothing white as snow. For fear of him the guards shook and became like dead men. But the angel said to the women, 'Do not be afraid; I know that you are looking for Jesus who was crucified. He is not here; for he has been raised, as he said. Come, see the place where he lay. Then go quickly and tell his disciples, "He has been raised from the dead, and indeed he is going ahead of you to Galilee; there you will see him." This is my message for you.' So they left the tomb quickly with fear and great joy, and ran to tell his disciples. Suddenly Jesus met them and said, 'Greetings!' And they came to him, took hold of his feet, and worshipped him. Then Jesus said to them, 'Do not be afraid; go and tell my brothers to go to Galilee; there they will see me.'

Meditation

I'll never be able to say what it meant to me,
    after the horror and the heartache,
    the darkness and the despair,
    to hear that wonderful, astonishing news –
    Jesus, alive!
I'd lived in a daze until then,
    unable to take in the horror of what I'd seen,
    the anguish and the agony which he'd borne
    with such quiet dignity and awesome courage.
He'd warned us to expect the worst,
    and I suppose in our hearts we'd known what was coming
    but we'd refused to accept it,
    hoping against hope there might be some other way,
    a path less costly, less awful for us all.
But as we walked that morning to the tomb,

all such thoughts were gone,
buried along with our Lord,
life dark, cold, empty,
bereft of meaning.
We were blind to everything in our grief,
scarcely aware even of the ground starting to shake
or light flooding around us,
but when we reached the stone, rolled away from the tomb,
we saw that all right,
and for a moment we just stood there gazing in confusion,
not knowing where to turn or what to say.
That's when it came, the news that took our breath away:
'He is not here.
He has been raised.
Come, see the place where he lay.'
We scarcely dared to look at first, afraid it might all be a dream,
but finally we found the courage,
and it was true,
he was gone! –
just the grave clothes left to show he'd been there.
You can imagine how we felt,
our hearts pounding with excitement;
but there was more to come,
things yet more wonderful,
for even as we ran to tell the news,
skipping with sheer delight,
we saw him ahead of us –
Jesus, the man we knew and loved,
arms outstretched in welcome,
waiting to greet us in his old familiar way.
He had risen, just as we'd been told,
death unable to hold him!
Only it wasn't just Jesus who rose that day,
it was all of us:
for there in the garden life began again,
life which we thought had died in us for ever –
hope reborn,
faith renewed,
love rekindled,
joy restored –
and we knew now these could never be destroyed –
the proof was there before us!

Prayer

Gracious God,
    through the resurrection of your Son
    you not only raised him to life;
    you brought also renewal and restoration
    to his broken disciples.
From the depths of misery you brought jubilation;
    from the pit of despair you brought hope;
    from the trough of doubt you brought faith.
Life which had seemed without meaning
    suddenly pulsated with purpose again,
    the future rich with promise as never before.
It is a miracle which has been re-enacted
    in countless lives across the centuries
    and which continues to be repeated today;
    for you are at work still in the world and in our own lives,
    reaching out wherever there is need,
    wherever people are broken,
    wherever hope has died,
    bringing afresh your gift of life.
Gracious God, work within us now,
    refresh our hearts and revive our spirits,
    and make us a new creation;
    through Jesus Christ our Lord.
Amen.

64

IT SEEMED TOO GOOD TO BE TRUE

Peter

Reading: Luke 24:1-12

But on the first day of the week, at early dawn, they came to the tomb, taking the spices that they had prepared. They found the stone rolled away from the tomb, but when they went in, they did not find the body. While they were perplexed about this, suddenly two men in dazzling clothes stood beside them. The women were terrified and bowed their faces to the ground, but the men said to them, 'Why do you look for the living among the dead? He is not here, but has risen. Remember how he told you, while he was still in Galilee, that the Son of Man must be handed over to sinners, and be crucified, and on the third day rise again.' Then they remembered his words, and returning from the tomb, they told all this to the eleven and to all the rest. Now it was Mary Magdalene, Joanna, Mary the mother of James, and the other women with them who told this to the apostles. But these words seemed to them an idle tale, and they did not believe them. But Peter got up and ran to the tomb; stooping and looking in, he saw the linen cloths by themselves; then he went home, amazed at what had happened.

Meditation

It seemed too good to be true,
    too wonderful even to contemplate he might be alive again –
    so we shook our heads,
    raised our eyebrows,
    and laughed between our tears.
We wanted to believe it, of course we did,
    more than anything else in the world,
    but how could we after all we'd seen,
    everything we'd been through?
Oh, it's all right for *you* –
    anyone can be wise after the event –
    but put yourself in our shoes;
    imagine what it must have been like

having seen Jesus die as we did,
  and then ask yourself honestly:
  would you have felt any different?
Our faith was in tatters,
  life seeming an empty void,
  for how could God have let it happen,
  how could he have allowed a man like that
  to endure such a terrible end?
Yet he had,
  and we just couldn't get that knowledge out of our minds.
It had been different when Jesus was with us –
  we'd looked forward then,
  confident,
  full of hope,
  no promise too wonderful,
  no vision beyond fulfilment;
  for in those few short years of his ministry
  he'd shown us another way –
  the way of love, goodness, mercy –
  and we'd actually believed
  such things could finally triumph over evil,
  no matter how impossible it seemed.
Not any more, though.
It was back to the cold harsh world of reality
  where hopes are dashed and dreams lie broken,
  where goodness is trampled underfoot
  and love tossed back in your face,
  and this time we were resolved
  to keep our feet firmly on the ground,
  the thought of another disappointment, another let-down,
  too much to bear.
And yet, despite it all, I had to be sure,
  that flicker of hope their words had kindled
  either fanned into life or laid to rest once and for all;
  so I ran to the tomb, scarcely knowing what I did,
  and found the stone rolled away just as they had said,
  the grave clothes cast aside,
  the tomb, empty!
Can it really be,
  our Lord risen, alive?
I want to believe it so much,
  more than you'll ever know,

but dare I take the risk of faith again?
What do you think –
   is it too good to be true?

Prayer

Sovereign God,
   in a world where evil so often triumphs
   and good is tossed casually aside,
   where hatred is rampant and love taken advantage of,
   it is difficult not to become cynical.
The cutting edge of our faith is remorselessly blunted
   by the blows life deals it,
   to the point that, though we may continue to say the right words,
   in our hearts we no longer believe them.
We must live in the real world, so we are told;
   and as we reluctantly come to accept that,
   so we lose sight of the kingdom of heaven
   and our ability to trust in your transforming power.
Rekindle our faith through the message of Easter.
Remind us of all you have done
   and all you are yet able to do.
Assure us, through experiencing again
   the presence of the risen Christ in our hearts,
   that with you nothing is too good to be true,
   for you are able to do more
   than we could ever ask for or imagine.
To you be praise and glory, now and for evermore.
Amen.

65
ONE LOOK, THAT'S ALL IT TOOK!

John

Reading: John 20:1-10

Early on the first day of the week, while it was still dark, Mary Magdalene came to the tomb and saw that the stone had been removed from the tomb. So she ran and went to Simon Peter and the other disciple, the one whom Jesus loved, and said to them, 'They have taken the Lord out of the tomb, and we do not know where they have laid him.' Then Peter and the other disciple set out and went towards the tomb. The two were running together, but the other disciple outran Peter and reached the tomb first. He bent down to look in and saw the linen wrappings lying there, but he did not go in. Then Simon Peter came, following him, and went into the tomb. He saw the linen wrappings lying there, and the cloth that had been on Jesus' head, not lying with the linen wrappings but rolled up in a place by itself. Then the other disciple, who reached the tomb first, also went in, and he saw and believed; for as yet they did not understand the scripture, that he must rise from the dead. Then the disciples returned to their homes.

Meditation

One look, that's all it took!
One look,
    and I knew beyond all doubt that God was at work,
    that Jesus was alive!
I should have known it sooner, of course,
    for he'd told us what to expect often enough,
    but when the hammer blow fell
    we simply couldn't see beyond it,
    tears blinding our minds as well as our eyes.
It was when Mary came bursting in,
    beside herself with excitement,
    that the mist started to clear,
    that his words about death and resurrection
    came flooding back,

rekindling a flame that had all but been extinguished.
I ran then as I've never run before,
    hope lending wings to my feet,
    heart pounding within me,
    not just from the exertion
    but from the emotion that had taken hold of me,
    the curious mixture of fear and exhilaration.
I wanted so much to believe it was true,
    only I was afraid it might be some cruel hoax
    or fancy of the imagination,
    a trick of the mind or, worse still, of our enemies.
But when I went in to the tomb
    and found the abandoned grave clothes,
    then I knew,
    and my spirit soared in jubilation.
He was not there:
    he had risen just as he promised,
    death not able to have the final word.
And suddenly everything fitted into place,
    the heartache, the hurt, the humiliation –
    it was all meant to be,
    all a part of God's sovereign purpose!
Where we had seen darkness, he had brought light!
Where there had been death, now there was life!
Everything was turned around,
    transformed,
    renewed,
    sharing in the wonder of resurrection.
One look, that's all it took –
    one look, and life was changed for ever!

Prayer

Gracious God,
    we thank you that our faith
    is not founded on theory or speculation –
    on the ideas of theologians or the musings of philosophers.
It is rooted in what individuals have seen and heard,
    in the living testimony of ordinary people like us,
    in the testimony of countless generations of believers
    who have encountered the risen Christ for themselves

through his Spirit.
In him, you came, you lived, you died, you rose again,
   making yourself known through the concrete events of history.
For all who saw for themselves and passed the message on,
   receive our thanks.
And for all that we experience today
   of your continuing love and your life-giving purpose,
   we give you our praise in joyful worship;
   through Jesus Christ, our risen, victorious Saviour.
Amen.

66

WE MET HIM, THERE ON THE EMMAUS ROAD

Cleopas

Reading: Luke 24:13-35

Now on that same day two of them were going to a village called
Emmaus, about seven miles from Jerusalem, and talking with each other
about all these things that had happened. While they were talking and
discussing, Jesus himself came near and went with them, but their eyes
were kept from recognising him. And he said to them, 'What are you discussing with each other while you walk along?' They stood still, looking
sad. Then one of them, whose name was Cleopas, answered him, 'Are
you the only stranger in Jerusalem who does not know the things that
have taken place there in these days?' He asked them, 'What things?'
They replied, 'The things about Jesus of Nazareth, who was a prophet
mighty in deed and word before God and all the people, and how our
chief priests and leaders handed him over to be condemned to death and
crucified him. But we had hoped that he was the one to redeem Israel.
Yes, and besides all this, it is now the third day since these things took
place. Moreover, some women of our group astounded us. They were at
the tomb early this morning, and when they did not find his body there,
they came back and told us that they had indeed seen a vision of angels
who said that he was alive. Some of those who were with us went to the
tomb and found it just as the women had said; but they did not see him.'
Then he said to them, 'Oh, how foolish you are, and how slow of heart to
believe all that the prophets have declared! Was it not necessary that the
Messiah should suffer these things and then enter into his glory?' Then
beginning with Moses and all the prophets, he interpreted to them the
things about himself in all the scriptures.

As they came near the village to which they were going, he walked
ahead as if he were going on. But they urged him strongly, saying, 'Stay
with us, because it is almost evening and the day is now nearly over.' So
he went in to stay with them. When he was at the table with them, he
took bread, blessed and broke it, and gave it to them. Then their eyes
were opened, and they recognised him; and he vanished from their sight.
They said to each other, 'Were not our hearts burning within us while he
was talking to us on the road, while he was opening the scriptures to
us?' That same hour they got up and returned to Jerusalem; and they

found the eleven and their companions gathered together. They were saying, 'The Lord has risen indeed, and he has appeared to Simon!' Then they told what had happened on the road, and how he had been made known to them in the breaking of the bread.

Meditation

We met him, there on the Emmaus road,
    and still we didn't understand –
    can you believe that?
Despite the testimony of the women and the apostles,
    the empty tomb,
    the vision of angels,
    still we couldn't take it in!
I suppose we'd made up our minds that it was finished,
    come to terms with the fact that our hopes had been dashed,
    and we just couldn't bring ourselves to think any different
    for fear of yet more disappointment,
    yet more broken dreams.
Condemn us, if you like,
    but remember this:
    we'd seen him hanging there on the cross,
    contorted in agony,
    we'd watched in desolation as he drew his final breath,
    and we'd been there, tears streaming from our eyes,
    as they cut him down and laid him in the tomb.
You don't forget that in a hurry, I can tell you.
So when this stranger appeared out of the blue
    we thought nothing of it –
    why should we? –
    the possibility of him being Jesus was the last thing on our minds.
Even when he interpreted the scriptures for us,
    explaining why the Messiah had to suffer and die,
    still we didn't suspect anything –
    even though our hearts burned within us with inexplicable joy.
But when we sat together at table,
    and he took bread and broke it,
    then even *we* couldn't miss it,
    the extraordinary, incredible truth –
    it *was* Jesus,

Christ crucified and risen,
    there by our sides!
We'd thought the adventure was over,
    but it had only just begun.
We'd thought there was nothing left to us but memories,
    but suddenly the future beckoned, rich with promise.
The night had ended,
    a new day was dawning,
    life was beginning again –
    and we marvelled at the sheer wonder of his grace,
    for, of course, *we* didn't meet *him* that day,
    despite what we'd thought;
    he met *us*!

Prayer

Lord Jesus Christ,
    you speak your word to us
    as you spoke it to the Apostles long ago:
    'Come, follow me.'
You call us as you have called so many over the years:
    'Come to me, all you that are weary
    and are carrying heavy burdens,
    and I will give you rest.'
You offer us, as you offer all your people,
    refreshment for our souls:
    'Let anyone who is thirsty come to me,
    and let the one who believes in me drink.'
Lord, we thank you for that invitation,
    and gladly we respond.
But, more than that, we thank you
    for the fact that before anyone comes to you,
    you come first to them.
You came to Peter, James and John by the lakeside;
    to the hungry, the sick and the outcasts in the streets of Galilee;
    to Mary Magdalene weeping in the garden;
    to two weary disciples walking the Emmaus road;
    to the Apostles trembling behind locked doors;
    to Saul breathing murder on the road to Damascus;
    and so to countless others since.

Always it is you who makes the first approach,
    calling your people to faith,
    and still you come through your Spirit to meet with us.
Open our eyes to your presence
    and lead us forward in your service
    until that day when, with all your people,
    we enter your kingdom and meet with you face to face.
Amen.

67

HE WAS BACK!

Peter

Reading: Luke 24:36-43

While they were talking, Jesus himself stood among them and said, 'Peace be with you.' They were startled and terrified, and thought that they were seeing a ghost. He said to them, 'Why are you frightened, and why do doubts arise in your hearts? Look at my hands and my feet; see that it is I myself. Touch me and see; for a ghost does not have flesh and bones as you see that I have. And when he had said this, he showed them his hands and his feet. While in their joy they were disbelieving and still wondering, he said to them, 'Have you anything here to eat?' They gave him a piece of broiled fish, and he took it and ate in their presence.

Meditation

He was back!
Back in the land of the living,
   just when we'd given up hope!
Three days it had been,
   three days of dark despair as slowly the truth sank home –
   our Lord, laid in a tomb,
   dead and buried,
   never to walk this earth again.
We couldn't believe it at first,
   none of us,
   even though we'd seen it for ourselves.
We expected to wake up any moment to find it was all a dream,
   a dreadful mistake that had somehow taken us in.
But as the numbness passed, so the reality hit us,
   and the pain began in earnest.
It was an end to everything –
   our plans,
   our hopes,
   our dreams.
There was nothing left to live for,

that's how we felt –
we'd pinned our hopes on him,
and he was gone.
Only he wasn't!
He was there,
meeting Mary in the garden as her heart broke beside the tomb.
He was there,
on the Emmaus road as two followers trudged slowly home,
their world in tatters.
He was there,
speaking to Thomas, breaking through his disbelief!
He was there,
standing among us in the upper room!
He was back in the land of the living,
and suddenly so were we –
faith rekindled,
hope renewed,
joy reborn,
life beginning again!

Prayer

Lord Jesus Christ,
just when it looked all over,
when the world had written you off
and even your disciples had given up on you,
you came back – defeat revealed as victory.
Teach us what that means for us today;
not only the promise of eternal life,
but good news for life here and now.
Help us to understand that, whatever tragedies we may suffer,
whatever obstacles we may face,
whatever disappointments we may experience,
we can bounce back from them with your help,
for you are a God able to transform even the darkest moments
and lead us through them into the light of your love.
Gladly, then, we put our hand in yours,
knowing that in life or death
you will never fail us or forsake us.
Amen.

68

WE STILL HADN'T SEEN IT, YOU KNOW

Andrew

Reading: Luke 24:44-49

Then he said to them, 'These are my words that I spoke to you while I was still with you – that everything written about me in the law of Moses, the prophets, and the psalms must be fulfilled.' Then he opened their minds to understand the scriptures, and he said to them, 'Thus it is written, that the Messiah is to suffer and to rise from the dead on the third day, and that repentance and forgiveness of sins is to be proclaimed in his name to all nations, beginning from Jerusalem. You are witnesses of these things. And see, I am sending upon you what my Father promised; so stay here in the city until you have been clothed with power from on high.'

Meditation

We still hadn't seen it, you know,
    not even after he stood there among us, alive and well.
We still imagined that his death had been a ghastly mistake,
    an unforeseen catastrophe,
    which somehow, miraculously, God had put right,
    salvaging triumph from disaster.
Perhaps some of us had an inkling –
    Peter, James, John –
    but not me, I'm afraid;
    I was convinced he'd snatched victory from the jaws of defeat.
Only, of course, I couldn't have been more wrong,
    as I learned that day when Jesus opened the scriptures,
    and opened, along with them, our minds.
It took some doing, believe me,
    for I was a slow learner,
    but slowly it sunk in –
    the mind-boggling truth that it was all there:
    suffering,
    death,
    resurrection,

each foretold,
    each purposed long before,
    each part of God's saving plan.
I was staggered,
    overwhelmed,
    for it was everywhere,
    the words leaping out at me from the pages –
    the prophets,
    the psalms,
    the law,
    all pointing to him –
    and I marvelled at the realisation that for so long,
    so many years,
    God had been building up to that one moment,
    that astonishing expression of his love –
    his Son on a cross!
The shadow of death had been the cradle of life,
    the descent into darkness the dawning of light!
Unseen,
    unnoticed,
    our God had been there,
    in the worst of moments as well as the best,
    enfolding all in his mighty hand.
And I glimpsed for a moment the awesome truth:
    that he'd brought us joy,
    not despite the sorrow
    but through it –
    the only way such joy could be.

Prayer

Sovereign God,
    we are so used to clearing up after our mistakes,
    making the best of a bad job,
    that we can sometimes mistakenly interpret the resurrection
    in those terms –
    your putting right what had gone so badly wrong
    in the suffering and death of Jesus.
Yet to think this is to misunderstand the wonder of your purpose,
    for at Easter we celebrate not the reversal of a disaster

but the culmination of your divine purpose
in which both death and resurrection were integral components.
Before the crown of glory there had to come the crown of thorns;
before *your* hands could raise him from the tomb,
his hands had to be pierced on the cross –
the two went together, one without the other impossible.
Teach us that it is only through giving that we receive,
through letting go that we find,
through dying to self that we shall rise to eternal life,
and, in understanding that, may we celebrate
the true wonder of Christ crucified and risen!
Amen.

69

THEY DON'T KNOW WHEN THEY'RE BEATEN, DO THEY?

Caiaphas

Reading: Matthew 28:11-15

While they were going, some of the guard went into the city and told the chief priests everything that had happened. After the priests had assembled with the elders, they devised a plan to give a large sum of money to the soldiers, telling them, 'You must say, "His disciples came by night and stole him away while we were asleep." If this comes to the governor's ears, we will satisfy him and keep you out of trouble.' So they took the money and did as they were directed. And this story is still told among the Jews to this day.

Meditation

They don't know when they're beaten, do they,
    those followers of Jesus?
I really thought we'd put a stop to their nonsense, once and for all.
When we dragged that so-called Christ of theirs before Pilate,
    when we saw them hammer the nails into his hands and feet,
    when we watched as they sealed the tomb,
    I was convinced that, at last, it was over,
    the whole unfortunate business at an end.
After all, who wants a dead Messiah? –
    what use could he be to anyone?
Preposterous, isn't it.
And yet, apparently not,
    for I've received news this morning
    that the body has vanished,
    spirited away during the night.
God knows how it happened,
    but it's the last thing we need right now –
    you can just imagine the sort of stories
    his followers will come up with,
    even that he's been raised from the dead, I shouldn't wonder.
Absurd, I know,

but you'd be surprised what some people
are gullible enough to believe,
and if even a few are taken in who can say how many might follow?
So you'll understand, won't you, if we mould the truth a little? –
nothing patently false, of course;
just a little fine tuning here and there to fit the facts –
we've got it off to a fine art over the years.
Let's face it, it's obvious who's behind this charade –
I've no idea how they did it,
but somehow those wretched followers of his
must have got past the guards –
no doubt sleeping on the job, the good-for-nothing layabouts.
Anyway, that's the line we're taking,
and a few greased palms should ensure a united front,
enough to dispel any rumours.
There are a few points which trouble me, I must confess:
how they shifted that stone, for one thing,
and why they left behind his grave clothes, for another –
or was that all designed to add to the illusion?
Yet what I *really* can't understand is this:
why keep his name alive? –
what do they hope to prove? –
for they must know in their hearts that they're beaten,
the game over.
Even supposing some do fall for their trick,
it can't achieve anything,
for as the months pass without sight or sound of him
they're bound to question eventually,
and what a let-down it will all seem then.
You still have your doubts, even now?
Well, let me ask you this,
one question which should settle it for good:
twenty years from now,
a hundred,
a thousand,
who will talk about Jesus then? –
will anyone remember some obscure carpenter from Nazareth?
Need I say more?

Prayer

Sovereign God,
   there is much that conspires against your purpose
   and much that frustrates your will,
   so much so that we can lose heart
   and stop believing in the coming of your kingdom.
The same must have seemed all the more true
   for the followers of Jesus in the days following his death,
   but they were to learn through the resurrection
   that your purpose can never be defeated,
   for you are always at work in the good and the bad.
Give to us that same sense of conviction
   as we respond to your calling today,
   and help us, no matter how hopeless a situation may seem,
   to persevere in faith
   until our course is completed and the race is won;
   through Jesus Christ our Lord.
Amen.

70

I JUST CAN'T UNDERSTAND WHAT HAPPENED

One of the guards at the tomb

Reading: Matthew 28:11-15

While they were going, some of the guard went into the city and told the chief priests everything that had happened. After the priests had assembled with the elders, they devised a plan to give a large sum of money to the soldiers, telling them, 'You must say, "His disciples came by night and stole him away while we were asleep." If this comes to the governor's ears, we will satisfy him and keep you out of trouble.' So they took the money and did as they were directed. And this story is still told among the Jews to this day.

Meditation

I just can't understand what happened,
   how that body could have disappeared like that
   from under our very noses.
Oh, I know what some have suggested –
   that his disciples stole him away while we were asleep,
   that we took bribes to look the other way,
   even that we nipped off for a spot of refreshment,
   but take it from me, it's nonsense,
   for we were there the whole time,
   each watching like a hawk,
   on the lookout for any suspicious goings-on,
   and I can tell you that no one came near the place all night,
   not until those women arrived early the next morning,
   and discovered that the tomb was empty.
You think *they* were shocked?
How about *us*!
We just stood there, gawping in amazement,
   unable to believe our eyes.
It couldn't be,
   that's what we kept saying,
   no way –

but it was,
    no doubt about it.
We should have come clean there and then,
    told the world what we knew even though it made no sense,
    but it wasn't that easy,
    for we knew that our jobs,
    even perhaps our lives were on the line –
    the penalty for failure.
So when those priests sidled up with their offer of money –
    a generous bonus to keep our mouths shut,
    and the promise to square things with the governor –
    well, understandably we took it;
    we'd have been fools not to.
Yet it still rankled,
    still stuck in the craw –
    not just the dressing-down we received, fierce though that was,
    but the stain on our reputation,
    the stigma of supposedly having fallen down on the job –
    so I'm taking the chance, at last, to put the record straight.
There was no foul-up that night –
    we knew our job and we stuck to it faithfully.
Don't forget we were Roman soldiers,
    proud of our legion,
    dedicated to our job –
    we'd a reputation to keep up,
    and there was no way we were going to let the side down.
No, don't look at us, we weren't to blame.
But if not us, then who?
And, more important, how?
For one thing's for certain:
    that body was there when they sealed the tomb –
    we saw it for ourselves –
    but next morning it was gone,
    vanished apparently into thin air!
Something happened that night,
    something quite extraordinary.
Can you explain it?
I wish I could.

Prayer

Sovereign God,
    we don't understand how you raised Jesus from the dead –
    how you breathed life into his broken body,
    how you rolled the stone away from the tomb,
    how he appeared unrecognised to Mary in the garden
    and to disciples on the Emmaus road;
    how he walked through locked doors to be with the Apostles;
    how repeatedly he appeared from nowhere
    to stand among his followers.
What we do understand is this –
    that he changed the lives of all who met him,
    turning their sorrow into celebration,
    their despair into hope and their doubt into faith;
    and that he is with us now through his life-giving Spirit,
    remaking our lives in turn,
    giving us joy, peace and a sense of purpose
    such as we never imagined possible before.
We do not understand, but we believe,
    we rejoice and we offer you our grateful worship
    in the name of that same Jesus,
    our risen Lord and Saviour.
Amen.

71

I WANTED TO KNOW, THAT'S ALL

Thomas

Reading: John 20:19-29

When it was evening on that day, the first day of the week, and the doors of the house where the disciples had met were locked for fear of the Jews, Jesus came and stood among them and said, 'Peace be with you.' After he said this, he showed them his hands and his side. Then the disciples rejoiced when they saw the Lord. Jesus said to them again, 'Peace be with you. As the Father has sent me, so I send you.' When he had said this, he breathed on them and said to them, 'Receive the Holy Spirit. If you forgive the sins of any, they are forgiven them; if you retain the sins of any, they are retained.'

But Thomas (who was called the Twin), one of the twelve, was not with them when Jesus came. So the other disciples told him, 'We have seen the Lord.' But he said to them, 'Unless I see the mark of the nails in his hands, and put my finger in the mark of the nails and my hand in his side, I will not believe.'

A week later his disciples were again in the house, and Thomas was with them. Although the doors were shut, Jesus came and stood among them and said, 'Peace be with you.' Then he said to Thomas, 'Put your finger here and see my hands. Reach out your hand and put it in my side. Do not doubt but believe.' Thomas answered him, 'My Lord and my God!' Jesus said to him, 'Have you believed because you have seen me? Blessed are those who have not seen and yet have come to believe.'

Meditation

I wanted to know, that's all,
  to see for myself if it could possibly be true –
  was that so awful?
Remember, we'd *all* doubted at first,
  when the women came back that morning,
  dismissing their story of the empty tomb as so much nonsense,
  so why point the finger at me,
  as though *I* questioned and *they* didn't?

All right, the situation had changed since then, I accept that,
    for they all claimed to have seen him in the meantime,
    and not just them, but others,
    each adamant the Lord had risen,
    yet as much as I wanted to believe it, I simply couldn't,
    not unless the proof was spelt out for me in black and white.
That was me all over, I'm afraid,
    the way I'd been since a boy,
    struggling to accept anything I couldn't touch for myself
    or see with my own eyes,
    and I'd said as much to Jesus before he died,
    that day he spoke about his Father's house,
    and his going there to prepare a place for us.
'Believe in God,' he'd said,
    'believe also in me.'
A wonderful promise, yes,
    only to me he was talking in riddles,
    and I made no bones about it:
    'Lord, we do not know where you are going.
    How can we know the way?'
He wasn't angry with me,
    though he could have been,
    for after all that time, all he'd said, I should have known,
    just as I should have understood
    he would rise from the tomb and return among us.
He'd spoken of it, often enough,
    done his best to prepare us not simply for his death
    but his resurrection to follow,
    but, as so often happens, we dwelt on the bad
    and forgot the good,
    unable to see beyond the demands of the present moment.
So despite it all I refused to believe,
    convinced there were still too many questions
    and not enough answers.
And I'd be doing that still,
    still wondering if it ever could be,
    but for his grace.
For suddenly he was there again, standing among us,
    arms outstretched in welcome,
    those pierced hands reaching out to me, Thomas,
    and I knew I'd been wrong –
    he was alive, just as they'd said,

risen and victorious –
and I knelt down in worship,
my heart overflowing with thanksgiving,
for he'd come, despite me,
despite my lack of faith –
though I had doubted him,
still he believed in me!

Prayer

Lord,
    we do not always believe as we should.
We try our hardest, but our faith is weak
    and we lose sight of all you have promised
    and all you are able to do.
There is so much in life which is a mystery,
    and there are so many things
    which seem to deny everything we believe about you.
Despite our good intentions,
    doubt sometimes gets the upper hand
    so that we begin to question even those things most precious to us.
Yet though we are faithless to you,
    always you are faithful to us,
    refusing to let us go.
Come to us now, we pray,
    and help us to glimpse a little more of your glory,
    so that we may confess you again
    as our Lord and our God,
    in this time of worship and in the days ahead.
Amen.

72

WHAT'S DONE CANNOT BE UNDONE, ISN'T THAT WHAT THEY SAY?

Bartholomew

Reading: Mark 16:14-18

Later he appeared to the eleven themselves as they were sitting at the table; and he upbraided them for their lack of faith and stubbornness, because they had not believed those who saw him after he had risen. And he said to them, 'Go into all the world and proclaim the good news to the whole creation. The one who believes and is baptised will be saved; but the one who does not believe will be condemned. And these signs will accompany those who believe: by using my name they will cast out demons; they will speak in new tongues; they will pick up snakes in their hands, and if they drink any deadly thing, it will not hurt them; they will lay their hands on the sick, and they will recover.'

Meditation

What's done cannot be undone, isn't that what they say?
As much as we might wish otherwise,
    it's impossible to turn the clock back.
And that's exactly what we'd thought just a few days before,
    as we stood in desolation
    and watched the Master suffer on that cross,
    as we watched him breathe his last,
    as we saw him cut down, limp and lifeless,
    and carried to the tomb.
It was over,
    finished,
    those three wonderful years we'd spent with him at an end,
    never to be repeated.
What possible reason was there to think otherwise?
So when the women burst in on us,
    babbling about the tomb being empty,
    the stone rolled away,
    well, I hate to say it, but we didn't pay much attention.

It just couldn't be, could it?
At least that's what the theory said;
    the facts told a different story –
    and what a story it was!
For the next thing we knew he was there amongst us,
    the one they thought they'd destroyed, back from the grave,
    the one we all believed dead and buried, alive!
And in that moment the world itself was turned upside down,
    for suddenly we knew beyond doubt
    that what's done *can* be undone,
    the proof right there, before our very eyes.
Defeat had become victory,
    despair, hope,
    sorrow, joy,
    darkness, light,
    tears, laughter!
The forces of evil had conspired to do their worst,
    only for the havoc they'd wreaked
    to be wiped away in a moment,
    rolled back, as surely as the stone from the tomb,
    by the power of love!
Do you realise what that means?
That no situation is too hopeless,
    no person too dreadful,
    to be beyond redemption.
That no matter who we are or what we do,
    however much we fail,
    however far we stray,
    still he can turn us round and transform our lives.
That there is nothing in heaven or earth,
    in life or in death,
    that can finally separate us
    from the love of God revealed in Christ!
He'd been to the cross,
    he'd carried our sins,
    he'd wrestled with the powers of darkness,
    and he triumphed over it all.
Life was beginning again,
    for you,
    for me,
    for everyone willing to receive it.
That, and that alone, cannot be undone!

Prayer

Lord,
    we live in a world in which nothing seems to change
    and yet in which nothing remains the same.
We look around us,
    and we see the same old mistakes being made
    as those which have littered the course of history.
We look at ourselves,
    and though the appearance may have altered a little,
    we see the same old person staring out at us,
    beset still by familiar faults and weaknesses.
For all our hopes of progress, all our efforts at improvement,
    human nature seldom varies.
It is a depressing and frustrating thought.
And yet it is only half the story,
    for in Christ you died and rose again,
    and in so doing transformed the world.
Though the old lives on, the new is here,
    at work in the world, at work in our lives,
    taking what is and shaping it into what shall be.
Through him we have forgiveness,
    the invitation to put our former selves behind us
    and to be born again, life truly different.
Lord, though all else may change,
    we know that you will not.
What you have done for us is done for ever!
Thanks be to God!
Amen.

73

THREE TIMES HE ASKED ME

Peter

Reading: John 21:15-19

When they had finished breakfast, Jesus said to Simon Peter, 'Simon son of John, do you love me more than these?' He said to him, 'Yes, Lord; you know that I love you.' Jesus said to him, 'Feed my lambs.' A second time he said to him, 'Simon son of John, do you love me?' He said to him, 'Yes, Lord; you know that I love you.' Jesus said to him, 'Tend my sheep.' He said to him the third time, 'Simon son of John, do you love me?' Peter felt hurt because he said to him the third time, 'Do you love me?' And he said to him, 'Lord, you know everything; you know that I love you.' Jesus said to him, 'Feed my sheep. Very truly, I tell you, when you were younger, you used to fasten your own belt and to go wherever you wished. But when you grow old, you will stretch out your hands, and someone else will fasten a belt around you and take you where you do not wish to go.' (He said this to indicate the kind of death by which he would glorify God.) After this he said to him, 'Follow me.'

Meditation

Three times he asked me,
    three times the same simple yet searching question:
    'Do you love me, Peter?'
And I was getting fed up with it,
    not to say a little hurt.
After all, he should have known by then, surely?
I'd followed him for three years,
    and I thought we'd become close –
    he gave that impression, anyway.
The 'Rock', he'd called me,
    the one on whom he'd build his Church –
    an expression of trust, if ever there was one –
    so how could he doubt me now,
    let alone question my love?
But then, of course, I remembered that bold, brash promise of mine:

'Though all become deserters because of you,
 I will never desert you' –
 and suddenly I understood.
He'd known I would fail, even as I said it,
 not only abandon but deny him,
 and he knew too how sick I'd felt,
 how wretched and ashamed
 when the knowledge of my failure finally sunk home.
But there was no anger from him,
 no recriminations,
 no rebuke.
His concern was for me, not himself,
 his sole desire to wipe the slate clean and start again,
 and this was my chance to deal with the guilt,
 to exorcise the demon once and for all.
Three times I'd denied him,
 three times he put the question,
 and at last I could put the record straight,
 declare to him what I should have declared to others:
 'Yes, Lord; you know that I love you.'
We couldn't change the past, we both knew that,
 but with his help we could put it behind us and change the future,
 and that's what he offered me that day;
 a new beginning,
 a fresh chapter,
 life dawning for me as surely as it had dawned again for him.
I was restored,
 cleansed,
 forgiven,
 the ghost finally laid to rest,
 and I owed it all to him,
 the man whom I abandoned so freely,
 yet who refused to abandon me!

Prayer

Gracious God,
 we try so hard to put the past behind us,
 to let go and start again,
 but all too often mistakes we imagined long buried
 return to haunt us.

We do our best to make amends,
    but there are times
    when even if *we* can learn to live with the wounds,
    others can't, scars running deep and hurts hard to forget.
But you are always ready to offer us a new beginning,
    no matter how foolish we have been
    or how many opportunities we have wasted.
Whatever we may have done,
    you grant us free and total forgiveness,
    a new page on which to start a fresh chapter.
The past is done with, the future before us –
    and nothing can ever change that.
Receive our thanks and lead us forward,
    in the name of Christ our Saviour.
Amen.

74

WE HAD COME, JUST AS HE'D TOLD US TO

Matthew

Reading: Matthew 28:16-20

Now the eleven disciples went to Galilee, to the mountain to which Jesus had directed them. When they saw him, they worshipped him; but some doubted. And Jesus came and said to them, 'All authority in heaven and on earth has been given to me. Go therefore and make disciples of all nations, baptising them in the name of the Father and of the Son and of the Holy Spirit, and teaching them to obey everything that I have commanded you. And remember, I am with you always, to the end of the age.'

Meditation

We had come, just as he'd told us to –
    up on to the mountains of Galilee where we'd walked so often,
    where we'd sat at the Master's feet,
    where we'd watched as he taught the crowds
    and marvelled as he fed the multitude –
    and suddenly it was just like old times,
    for he was there once more,
    standing by our side,
    that old familiar smile,
    that warm, comforting presence,
    Jesus, alive and well.
Can you imagine what it felt like,
    after the shock, the horror, the disbelief at his death?
We'd been crushed,
    distraught,
    everything we'd lived and worked for turned to ashes,
    and there had seemed no point to anything,
    no future,
    no hope,
    nothing to lift the pall of misery that overwhelmed us.
Do you wonder we fell down and worshipped him!
It was as though we had awoken from some dreadful dream

to find the sun burning bright,
and we were terrified of closing our eyes even for a moment
in case darkness should return and the nightmare begin again.
I know it was foolish, but we actually hoped nothing had changed,
that we could pick up where we'd left off,
and follow once more in the Master's footsteps.
But, of course, we couldn't,
for it *had* changed –
not just him,
but us,
and everything.
They'd laid him in a tomb,
and he'd emerged victorious.
They'd tried to destroy him,
but he could not be defeated.
And it was a message the whole world needed to hear –
the victory of love,
his triumph over evil,
good news not just for us but for all.
Yes, the work *would* continue, just as we'd hoped,
only it needed *us* to carry it forward,
our willingness to speak,
our faith to respond,
our courage to go out and make disciples of all nations,
so that they too might know the risen Christ
and respond in turn.
It could no longer simply be us and him,
much though we might have wished it –
there was work to be done,
a message to share,
a kingdom to build,
and he needed our help to build it.
We'd come and met him, just as he had told us to –
now it was time to go!

Prayer

God of all,
   we talk much about witness, evangelism, mission;
   about sharing the good news,
   being a light to the nations;
   but when it comes to it our words are rarely backed up by actions.
We focus instead on worship, prayer, private devotion;
   on personal growth and times of fellowship;
   our minds turned in on the Church
   rather than out to the world.
Forgive us for our lack of faith,
   our lack of courage and our lack of vision.
Give us the words to say and the will to speak them;
   and, above all, grant us a life
   which in every part proclaims your glory and tells of your love;
   through Jesus Christ our Lord.
Amen.

75

WE STOOD THERE, SPEECHLESS FOR A MOMENT

James

Reading: Acts 1:6-11

When they had come together, they asked him, 'Lord, is this the time when you will restore the kingdom to Israel?' He replied, 'It is not for you to know the times or periods that the Father has set by his own authority. But you will receive power when the Holy Spirit has come upon you; and you will be my witnesses in Jerusalem, in all Judea and Samaria, and to the ends of the earth.' When he had said this, as they were watching, he was lifted up, and a cloud took him out of their sight. While he was going and they were gazing up towards heaven, suddenly two men in white robes stood by them. They said, 'Men of Galilee, why do you stand looking up toward heaven? This Jesus, who has been taken up from you into heaven, will come in the same way as you saw him go into heaven.'

Meditation

We stood there, speechless for a moment,
    struck dumb by the enormity of it all,
    for he was gone,
    plucked away from before our very eyes
    and, quite simply, we were lost for words,
    stunned into silence.
It wasn't the first time, you see;
    we'd lost him once already –
    watched in horror as he was nailed to a cross, sealed in a tomb,
    and we'd been devastated,
    convinced we could never bounce back from such a blow.
We wouldn't have, either,
    not by ourselves,
    but suddenly he was back,
    there in the garden,
    there on the roadside,
    there in the upper room –

our Lord, alive, risen, victorious,
    death unable to hold him!
I just can't tell you how wonderful that was,
    how our hearts skipped and our spirits soared
    each time we saw him.
We felt certain nothing could ever again destroy our happiness,
    for he had taken on the last enemy
    and emerged triumphant!
Life, all at once, pulsated with promise,
    no problem too great for us,
    no challenge too daunting,
    for, with Christ by our side, what had we to fear?
Yet suddenly, as we stood there that day gazing into heaven,
    he was by our side no longer,
    and for an awful moment
    it seemed as though all our hopes had disappeared again,
    vanishing with him like a bubble on the wind.
Only, of course, this time was different,
    for we'd made time to listen,
    paid heed to his warnings,
    and we understood that, as he had departed,
    so finally he would return.
You should see us now,
    our faith, if anything, stronger today than it's ever been!
We've spoken more boldly and witnessed more powerfully
    than I thought possible –
    preaching the word,
    healing the sick,
    renewing the weak,
    uplifting the broken-hearted,
    carrying the good news of Jesus far and wide.
And I'll tell you why:
    because his going that day
    has somehow brought him closer than he's ever been before,
    filling our whole being – body, mind and soul –
    transforming our every thought and word and deed.
He's here,
    he's there,
    he's everywhere,
    no person beyond his love,
    no situation beyond his purpose,
    for he has not simply risen,

he has ascended –
Jesus, the man who lived and died amongst us,
who shared our flesh and blood,
one with the Father,
Lord of lords and King of kings,
nothing in heaven or earth able to separate us
from the wonder of his love.
And sometimes when I think of all that means,
once more I'm struck dumb,
stunned into silence by the enormity of it all,
for it's wonderful, isn't it? –
almost too wonderful for words!

Prayer

Lord Jesus Christ,
you were brought low,
yet you have been lifted high.
You were the servant of all,
yet you are above all and beyond all.
You were despised and rejected,
yet your name is exalted above all names.
You were fully human,
yet you are divine.
You were taken into heaven,
yet you are here by our sides.
You are higher than our highest thoughts,
greater than our minds can ever grasp.
So, with all your people in every age,
we bow before you and confess you as our risen Saviour,
the King of kings and Lord of lords,
to the glory of God the Father.
Amen.

PENTECOST

76

DID IT GO TO MY HEAD, BECOMING AN APOSTLE LIKE THAT?

Matthias

Reading: Acts 1:15-26

In those days Peter stood up among the believers (together the crowd numbered about one hundred and twenty persons) and said, 'Friends, the scripture had to be fulfilled, which the Holy Spirit through David foretold concerning Judas, who became a guide for those who arrested Jesus – for he was numbered among us and was allotted his share in this ministry.' (Now this man acquired a field with the reward of his wickedness; and falling headlong, he burst open in the middle and all his bowels gushed out. This became known to all the residents of Jerusalem, so that the field was called in their language Hakeldama, that is, Field of Blood.) 'For it is written in the book of Psalms, "Let his homestead become desolate, and let there be no one to live in it"; and "Let another take his position of overseer". So one of the men who have accompanied us throughout the time that the Lord Jesus went in and out among us, beginning from the baptism of John until the day when he was taken up from us – one of these must become a witness with us to his resurrection.' So they proposed two, Joseph called Barsabbas, who was also known as Justus, and Matthias. Then they prayed and said, 'Lord, you know everyone's heart. Show us which one of these two you have chosen to take the place in this ministry and apostleship from which Judas turned aside to go to his own place.' And they cast lots for them, and the lot fell on Matthias; and he was added to the eleven apostles.

Meditation

Did it go to my head, becoming an apostle like that?
Well, yes, I think it possibly did,
   for a time anyway.
It was a rare honour, after all,
   the ultimate accolade,
   so undoubtedly there was a certain swagger in my step
   for those first few days;
   I'd hardly have been human if there hadn't been.

But it didn't last long,
    for I soon came to realise that, if *I* had my role,
    others had theirs,
    just as important,
    just as necessary to the work of the kingdom.
It wasn't a question of us and them,
    the select few lording it over the many –
    we were part of a team,
    each with our own gifts to contribute,
    our own strengths and our own weaknesses,
    each depending on the other, as Christ depended on us.
We did try putting labels on people for a time, it's true –
    deacons, teachers, prophets, apostles –
    but it didn't work,
    for though the ministries were real enough,
    the Spirit couldn't be tied down to them,
    neatly pigeon-holed for our convenience.
He was working through all, irrespective of our boundaries,
    now here,
    now there,
    each day new surprises forcing us to think again,
    new evidence of his power
    compelling us to take stock and broaden our horizons.
It was true for me as much as anyone,
    perhaps more than most,
    for I had imagined that day when the lot fell on me
    that I was someone special,
    my name destined to go down in history alongside the greats,
    but the truth was soon to dawn
    that through Christ times had changed.
We were all special, every one of us,
    all called to share in his ministry
    to continue his work –
    a priesthood of believers,
    a company of saints,
    the body of Christ.
I wasn't to be a star after all,
    but it didn't matter –
    how could it, so long as Christ was proclaimed
    and his love made known?
What counted, then as now, is that I did my bit,
    and that you do yours.

Prayer

Lord,
    it is easy to overvalue our gifts
    and equally easy to undervalue them;
    to have too high or too low an opinion of ourselves.
Help us to recognise that you value us all equally,
    each having something to contribute *to* others
    and something to receive *from* them.
Teach us, then, to appreciate our own worth
    and to recognise that of those around us,
    and so may we learn to use the various gifts you have given
    wisely and with humility
    in the service of your kingdom;
    through Jesus Christ our Lord.
Amen.

77

'YOU WILL BE MY WITNESSES'

John

Reading: Acts 1:1-5, 8, 12-14

In the first book, Theophilus, I wrote about all that Jesus did and taught from the beginning until the day when he was taken up to heaven, after giving instructions through the Holy Spirit to the apostles whom he had chosen. After his suffering he presented himself alive to them by many convincing proofs, appearing to them during forty days and speaking about the kingdom of God. While staying with them, he ordered them not to leave Jerusalem, but to wait there for the promise of the Father. 'This,' he said, 'is what you have heard from me; for John baptised with water, but you will be baptised with the Holy Spirit not many days from now. . . . You will receive power when the Holy Spirit comes upon you; and you will be my witnesses in Jerusalem, in all Judea and Samaria, and to the ends of the earth.' Then they returned to Jerusalem from the mount called Olivet, which is near Jerusalem, a sabbath day's journey away. When they had entered the city, they went to the room upstairs where they were staying, Peter, and John, and James, and Andrew, Philip and Thomas, Bartholomew and Matthew, James son of Alphaeus, and Simon the Zealot, and Judas son of James. All these were constantly devoting themselves to prayer, together with certain women, including Mary the mother of Jesus, as well as his brothers.

Meditation

'You will be my witnesses
   in Jerusalem,
   in all Judea and Samaria,
   and to the ends of the earth.'
Quite a picture, isn't it,
   a prospect to stir the heart and fire the imagination.
But I tell you what,
   huddled there together in that upper room,
   those words seemed a long way off,
   a beautiful but rapidly fading memory.

We were terrified of going out, if the truth be told,
    despite our prayers,
    despite his promise,
    scared stiff our enemies would come for us
    as they'd come for him,
    and send us off to some equally ghastly death.
We wished it were different, of course we did –
    we longed for courage to get out there
    and proclaim the good news,
    to tell the world what Christ had done,
    but, even if we had found that courage,
    it wouldn't have counted for much,
    for we had no idea what to say or how to say it.
We were twelve men with a mission –
    and none of us had the first idea where to start,
    let alone where it all might finish!
So we just sat there,
    and waited,
    and hoped,
    longing to believe it might be true
    but in our heart of hearts wondering if it ever could be –
    for who were we,
    ordinary folk like us,
    to set the world on fire?
It was an unlikely prospect, to say the least.
Only, suddenly, out of the blue, it happened,
    a sound like a mighty rushing wind filling the room,
    tongues of fire leaping and dancing upon us,
    and, all at once, an ecstasy beyond words,
    a peace, a joy and a confidence that defied description.
No more fear or doubt,
    no more hesitation –
    our mouths were opened and we spoke boldly,
    moving out among the multitude that had gathered,
    the words flowing freely as we needed them,
    and each heard us,
    amazed,
    bewildered to hear us speaking in their own tongue.
A one-minute wonder?
Don't you believe it!
It was the beginning of an astonishing adventure,
    a lifetime of witness,

an incredible journey of discipleship,
out into Jerusalem,
on to Judea and Samaria,
and beyond to the ends of the earth.
As I say, quite a picture, isn't it?
One to stir even the coldest heart
and fire the poorest of imaginations.
At least I hope it does,
for the job's not over, not by a long way,
nor, praise God, is the promise.
The call is there, and the offer is there,
for you and anyone who believes –
the promise of power to be witnesses to the risen Christ.
Wait patiently,
trust in the promise of the Father,
and you, like us, will receive.

Prayer

Lord,
it is hard to share our faith with a few,
let alone many.
When we listen to your call
to be witnesses to the ends of the earth
we feel that the task is hopelessly beyond us,
our resources feebly inadequate to meet the challenge.
Yet that is to view things from our perspective
rather than yours,
for you do not leave us dependent on our strength
but rather equip us with the power of the Holy Spirit
who is able to work in ways far exceeding our expectations.
Move within us,
as you have moved in your people across the centuries,
and teach us to trust you for the help we need,
when we need it.
In the name of Christ we pray.
Amen.

78

I DON'T KNOW WHO WAS THE MORE SURPRISED

Peter

Reading: Acts 2:1-21

When the day of Pentecost had come, they were all together in one place. And suddenly from heaven there came a sound like the rush of a violent wind, and it filled the entire house where they were sitting. Divided tongues, as of fire, appeared among them, and a tongue rested on each of them. All of them were filled with the Holy Spirit and began to speak in other languages, as the Spirit gave them ability.

Now there were devout Jews from every nation under heaven living in Jerusalem. And at this sound the crowd gathered and was bewildered, because each one heard them speaking in the native language of each. Amazed and astonished, they asked, 'Are not all these who are speaking Galileans? And how is it that we hear, each of us, in our own native language? Parthians, Medes, Elamites, and residents of Mesopotamia, Judea and Cappadocia, Pontus and Asia, Phrygia and Pamphylia, Egypt and the parts of Libya belonging to Cyrene, and visitors from Rome, both Jews and proselytes, Cretans and Arabs – in our own languages we hear them speaking about God's deeds of power.' All were amazed and perplexed, saying to one another, 'What does this mean?' But others sneered and said, 'They are filled with new wine.'

But Peter, standing with the eleven, raised his voice and addressed them: 'Men of Judea and all who live in Jerusalem, let this be known to you, and listen to what I say. Indeed, these are not drunk, as you suppose, for it is only nine o'clock in the morning. No, this is what was spoken through the prophet Joel: "In the last days it will be, God declares, that I will pour out my Spirit upon all flesh, and your sons and your daughters shall prophesy, and your young men shall see visions, and your old men shall dream dreams. Even upon my slaves, both men and women, in those days I will pour out my Spirit; and they shall prophesy. And I will show portents in the heaven above and signs on the earth below: blood, and fire, and smoky mist. The sun shall be turned to darkness and the moon to blood, before the coming of the Lord's great and glorious day. Then everyone who calls on the name of the Lord shall be saved."'

Meditation

I don't know who was the more surprised,
    us, or them?
They were bewildered, certainly,
    unable to make head or tail of what was going on,
    amazed to hear us speaking to them in their own language
    and wondering what on earth it all could mean.
But if anything, our astonishment was the greater,
    each of us scarcely able to believe what was happening.
Yes, I know we'd been told to expect it,
    the promise given by Christ himself,
    but as to what it meant,
    what it actually involved,
    we'd no idea until that incredible moment
    when the Spirit came.
No warning,
    no tell-tale signs,
    just bang! –
    and our lives were changed for ever.
Truthfully, I never thought I had it in me,
    to get out there and speak fearlessly for Christ –
    and as for sharing in his ministry,
    continuing where he had left off,
    the very idea seemed ridiculous.
Only that's what happened –
    gifts beyond our wildest imagining,
    power beyond our most fantastic dreams,
    a joy that burned unquenchably within us
    and a sense of purpose which nothing could contain.
We were no longer on our own, gazing wistfully to the heavens –
    Christ was with us,
    and in a way more wonderful than he'd ever been before;
    not just by our side,
    but in our hearts,
    filling our whole being with his presence.
It was more than we'd ever expected,
    more than any of us had dared hope for,
    and we had to pinch ourselves to be sure it was true.
But it was,
    and I tell you what,
    impossible though it seems,

I shouldn't wonder if God has more yet in store,
new experiences of his love,
new expressions of his purpose,
not just for us but for everyone,
his Spirit poured out on all, just as the prophet said –
nothing will surprise us now!

Prayer

Gracious God,
    we are reminded today
    of the renewing, transforming power of your Holy Spirit,
    through which you have fired
    ordinary people like us across the years
    to live and work for you
    in joyful faith and fearless service.
Help us to know today, through that same Spirit,
    that you are able to take any person, any place,
    any moment, any situation,
    and achieve within each one things far more wonderful
    than we can ever begin to imagine.
In Christ's name we pray.
Amen.

79

THEY WERE STILL AT IT!

Annas

Reading: Acts 4:1-18

While Peter and John were speaking to the people, the priests, the captain of the temple, and the Sadducees came to them, much annoyed because they were teaching the people and proclaiming that in Jesus there is the resurrection of the dead. So they arrested them and put them in custody until the next day, for it was already evening. But many of those who heard the word believed; and they numbered about five thousand.

The next day their rulers, elders, and scribes assembled in Jerusalem, with Annas the high priest, Caiaphas, John, and Alexander, and all who were of the high-priestly family. When they had made the prisoners stand in their midst, they inquired, 'By what power or by what name did you do this?' Then Peter, filled with the Holy Spirit, said to them, 'Rulers of the people and elders, if we are questioned today because of a good deed done to someone who was sick and are asked how this man has been healed, let it be known to all of you, and to all the people of Israel, that this man is standing before you in good health by the name of Jesus Christ of Nazareth, whom you crucified, whom God has raised from the dead. This Jesus is 'the stone that was rejected by you, the builders; it has become the cornerstone.' There is salvation in no one else, for there is no other name under heaven given among mortals by which we must be saved.'

Now when they saw the boldness of Peter and John and realised that they were uneducated and ordinary men, they were amazed and recognised them as companions of Jesus. When they saw the man who had been cured standing beside them, they had nothing to say in opposition. So they ordered them to leave the council while they discussed the matter with one another. They said, 'What will we do with them? For it is obvious to all who live in Jerusalem that a notable sign has been done through them; we cannot deny it. But to keep it from spreading further among the people, let us warn them to speak no more to anyone in this name.' So they called them and ordered them not to speak or teach at all in the name of Jesus.

Meditation

They were still at it! –
    despite everything we'd thrown at them,
    our every attempt to keep them quiet,
    they were back again,
    proclaiming that so-called Messiah of theirs,
    and, would you believe it,
    claiming he'd been raised from the dead,
    just as we'd been afraid they would.
It was our worst nightmare come true,
    and, quite frankly, we were at a loss what to do next.
It had been bad enough before with Jesus on the loose,
    he alone more than a handful,
    but now they were *all* at it,
    teaching,
    preaching,
    healing the sick –
    who could say where it all might end?
We'd removed one problem, only to stir up a hornet's nest,
    and the whole business was spiralling out of control.
So we called together the best brains in the land –
    rulers, elders, chief priests, scribes –
    determined to sort things out once and for all.
Surely if anyone could put a stop to the affair it was us?
At least that's what we thought,
    but what did we finally come up with?
Nothing, that's what!
Oh, we tried all right, believe me,
    dragging in their leaders,
    expecting to humiliate them publicly,
    but it was us who ended up with egg on our faces,
    struggling in vain to conceal our embarrassment.
You see, *something* had happened, there could be no denying it,
    something we couldn't explain away no matter how we tried.
They were ordinary, everyday men,
    unschooled, uneducated,
    yet they spoke with a conviction we could never hope to match.
They had no priestly background,
    no religious qualifications,
    yet they displayed a power we'd never even contemplated.
What did we do?

We made the best of a bad job,
 sent them away with strict orders to keep silent,
 to say nothing and do nothing in the name of Christ,
 but we knew it wouldn't work,
 for we were up against a force which we didn't understand
 but which we were powerless to resist.
It can't have been God, surely,
 and yet if it wasn't, tell me this:
 who was it?

Prayer

Sovereign God,
 there is so much in our world that conspires against you,
 that seeks to frustrate your will
 and deny your love.
Yet, despite it all, your purpose cannot and will not be defeated.
Remind us each day of that wonderful truth.
Give us an inner assurance that, come what may,
 there is nothing in life or death, heaven or earth,
 which shall finally be able to separate us from your love,
 and so may we walk in faith,
 confident that in the fullness of time your will shall triumph;
 through Jesus Christ our Lord.
Amen.

80

I DIDN'T KNOW WHAT HE WAS
ON ABOUT AT THE TIME

John

Reading: John 15:12-27

This is my commandment, that you love one another as I have loved you. No one has greater love than this, to lay down one's life for one's friends. You are my friends if you do what I command you. I do not call you servants any longer, because the servant does not know what the master is doing; but I have called you friends, because I have made known to you everything that I have heard from my Father. You did not choose me but I chose you. And I appointed you to go and bear fruit, fruit that will last, so that the Father will give you whatever you ask him in my name. I am giving you these commands so that you may love one another.

If the world hates you, be aware that it hated me before it hated you. If you belonged to the world, the world would love you as its own. Because you do not belong to the world, but I have chosen you out of the world – therefore the world hates you. Remember the word that I said to you, 'Servants are not greater than their master.' If they persecuted me, they will persecute you; if they kept my word, they will keep yours also. But they will do all these things to you on account of my name, because they do not know him who sent me. If I had not come and spoken to them, they would not have sin; but now they have no excuse for their sin. Whoever hates me hates my Father also. If I had not done among them the works that no one else did, they would not have sin. But now they have seen and hated both me and my Father. It was to fulfil the word that is written in their law, 'They hated me without a cause.'

When the Advocate comes, whom I will send to you from the Father, the Spirit of truth who comes from the Father, he will testify on my behalf. You also are to testify because you have been with me from the beginning.

Meditation

I didn't know what he was on about at the time,
    not the faintest idea,
    despite the way I nodded

and attempted to smile in the right places.
The Advocate?
The Son who comes from the Father?
What did it all mean?
We believed he was sent by God, yes –
      called to reveal his will,
      build his kingdom –
      but was he saying more,
      pointing to a closer relationship?
It seemed so,
      yet, try as we might, we just couldn't get our heads round it.
'The Lord our God is one' –
      isn't that what we'd always been told?
Indeed, he said it himself,
      made no bones about it,
      so how could he also tell us, 'He who has seen me
      has seen the Father'?
We were baffled, there's no other word for it,
      and when he went on to talk about the Spirit of truth,
      the one his Father would send in his name,
      quite simply, by then, we were reeling,
      unable to make head or tail of what he was getting at.
'Do we understand now, though?' you ask.
Well, no, we don't actually –
      funnily enough if we try to explain it
      we still struggle as much as ever;
      the more we try, the worse the knots we tie ourselves in.
Yet, strange though it may sound, it makes sense despite that –
      for day after day, year after year, we've tasted the truth,
      the reality of Father, Son and Holy Spirit.
We look up,
      to the stars and the sky,
      the wonder of the heavens,
      and God is there, enthroned in splendour,
      sovereign over all.
We look around,
      at the world he's given –
      its awesome beauty,
      its endless interest,
      its bountiful provision –
      and he is there,
      stretching out his hand in love,

inviting us to share in its wonder.
We look nearby,
    at family and friends,
    beyond, to the nameless faces of the multitude,
    and he is there,
    giving and receiving,
    waiting to feed and to be fed.
We look within,
    at our aching souls,
    our pleading hearts,
    and he is there,
    breathing new life,
    new purpose within us.
One God, yes,
    but a God we meet in different guises,
    different ways,
    three in one and one in three.
It sounds odd, I know,
    and take it from me, you'll never explain it,
    no matter how you try,
    yet don't worry, for what finally matters is this:
    though words may fail you, the experience never will!

Prayer

Almighty God,
    there are no words able to sum up your nature,
    to say everything about you that needs to be said.
We do our best to express our faith,
    but inevitably we fall short,
    for you are greater than our minds can fathom,
    ultimately defying human understanding.
Yet we experience your love day after day
    in a multitude of ways:
    we glimpse your glory in the wonder of the heavens
    and the beauty of the earth;
    we see everything we believe to be true about you
    revealed in Jesus Christ,
    his life, death and resurrection;
    and we feel your power at work deep within us

through what we call your Spirit.
Each reveals different aspects of your character,
    yet it is only when we take them together,
    recognising them as facets of one being, one truth,
    that we begin to understand something of your wonder.
Our intellects reel at the mystery of it all,
    yet in our heart and soul we know that you are with us,
    and we rejoice.
Almighty God, Father, Son and Holy Spirit,
    receive our praise.
Amen!

81
WHAT A FOOL I WAS!

Simon the sorcerer

Reading: Acts 8:9-24

Now a certain man named Simon had previously practised magic in the city and amazed the people of Samaria, saying that he was someone great. All of them, from the least to the greatest, listened to him eagerly, saying, 'This man is the power of God that is called Great.' And they listened eagerly to him because for a long time he had amazed them with his magic. But when they believed Philip, who was proclaiming the good news about the kingdom of God and the name of Jesus Christ, they were baptised, both men and women. Even Simon himself believed. After being baptised, he stayed constantly with Philip and was amazed when he saw the signs and great miracles that took place.

Now when the apostles at Jerusalem heard that Samaria had accepted the word of God, they sent Peter and John to them. The two went down and prayed for them that they might receive the Holy Spirit (for as yet the Spirit had not come upon any of them; they had only been baptised in the name of the Lord Jesus). Then Peter and John laid their hands on them, and they received the Holy Spirit. Now when Simon saw that the Spirit was given through the laying on of the apostles' hands, he offered them money, saying, 'Give me also this power so that anyone on whom I lay my hands may receive the Holy Spirit.' But Peter said to him, 'May your silver perish with you, because you thought you could obtain God's gift with money! You have no part or share in this, for your heart is not right before God. Repent therefore of this wickedness of yours, and pray to the Lord that, if possible, the intent of your heart may be forgiven you. For I see that you are in the gall of bitterness and the chains of wickedness.' Simon answered, 'Pray for me to the Lord, that nothing of what you have said may happen to me.'

Meditation

What a fool I was!
I thought that money could buy me everything –
    power,

friendship,
success,
happiness –
whatever I cared to name.
It always had, you see,
not one person I'd ever met able to withstand its lure.
Oh, there were some who withstood for a time –
a matter of principle, you know the kind of thing –
but in my experience everyone had their price eventually,
and I mean *everyone*.
So when I saw the gift of the Spirit being handed out that day
it seemed the most natural thing to make my pitch,
an appropriate gesture of appreciation
to secure my share of the pickings.
I meant no harm, truly.
But you wouldn't have thought so the response I got –
I'll never forget it as long as live,
not just anger but disgust, outrage –
honestly, you'd have thought I'd killed someone.
Yet they were right – I saw that afterwards –
for, well-intentioned though it may have been,
that act of mine was an act of desecration,
even, you might say, blasphemy.
I was trying to buy what could not be bought,
to put a price on what by nature was priceless,
and nothing could more eloquently have betrayed my own poverty;
for the experience I coveted,
this blessing of God,
was not an item to haggle over
but a gift graciously bestowed,
a sign of God's presence,
a seal of his love.
It was a hard lesson for me,
the most humiliating experience of my life,
but I'm trying to learn,
trying to change.
Don't make my mistake,
don't confuse the things of earth for the things of heaven.
There are some things in life which money can't buy,
and the blessing of God is one of them.
Remember that or, like me, it may cost you dear.

Prayer

Gracious God,
    your love can never be bought;
    only received as a gift.
There is nothing we could ever offer you
    which would ever merit your love,
    for it is beyond price.
Yet still we imagine sometimes
    that we can earn our salvation or deserve your blessing,
    not through money or other inducements,
    but through words and deeds,
    through offering lives which might somehow be pleasing to you.
Forgive us the lack of understanding this reveals,
    and teach us to give of ourselves
    not in payment for your love but in joyful response to it;
    as a joyful expression of gratitude for your goodness
    which gives and goes on giving
    to all who recognise their need
    and throw themselves entirely on your grace.
In the name of Christ we ask it.
Amen.

82

Jesus? The very name filled me with fury

Paul

Reading: Acts 9:1-9

Saul, still breathing threats and murder against the disciples of the Lord, went to the high priest and asked him for letters to the synagogues at Damascus, so that if he found any who belonged to the Way, men or women, he might bring them bound to Jerusalem. Now as he was going along and approaching Damascus, suddenly a light from heaven flashed around him. He fell to the ground and heard a voice saying to him, 'Saul, Saul, why do you persecute me?' He asked, 'Who are you, Lord?' The reply came, 'I am Jesus, whom you are persecuting. But get up and enter the city, and you will be told what you are to do.' The men who were travelling with him stood speechless because they heard the voice but saw no one. Saul got up from the ground, and though his eyes were open, he could see nothing; so they led him by the hand and brought him into Damascus. For three days he was without sight, and neither ate nor drank.

Meditation

Jesus? The very name filled me with fury –
    not just anger but a blind, all-consuming rage.
To think that some were calling him the Messiah,
    this man who had wilfully flouted the law,
    desecrated the temple,
    blasphemed against God himself,
    and finally suffered the fate due to all his kind,
    death on a cross –
    how could anyone look up to a person like that?
Yet there were plenty only too willing,
    and as if that weren't enough,
    they actually claimed he was alive,
    that somehow he'd cheated death itself
    and risen from the tomb.
Ridiculous!
Well, they could swallow such nonsense if they wanted to,

but not me, you could be sure of that.
I knew exactly what I stood for,
    precisely what I believed,
    and no one was going to shake me from it,
    least of all some misguided crank from Galilee.
But if I was secure, others weren't,
    and it was my duty to protect them from possible contagion,
    so I set about his followers with a vengeance,
    determined to wipe away every last trace of their heresy
    by whatever means necessary.
Let Jesus show himself now, I sneered!
Only that's where I came unstuck,
    for he did,
    there on the Damascus road –
    a blinding flash and a voice from heaven:
    'Saul, Saul, why do you persecute me?'
It couldn't be, I thought, surely?
But it was,
    the man I believed dead and buried, all too clearly alive!
I expected immediate retribution,
    to be struck down on the spot as a lesson to all –
    let's be clear, I deserved it.
But, instead, something very different and completely unexpected –
    the call to service,
    to carry his name to the Gentiles,
    to help build his kingdom.
Me! Paul!
I couldn't believe it,
    nor anyone else, come to that,
    the last thing anyone would have imagined possible
    in their wildest dreams.
Yet that's how it worked out,
    the results there to be seen by anyone who cares to question.
God, in his mercy, saw fit to use me,
    the greatest of sinners,
    the least of disciples,
    to proclaim the good news of Christ crucified and risen.
I thought I knew just where I stood,
    that I understood precisely who I was and what I was doing,
    but I learned that day a truth which still fills me with wonder:
    the fact that Jesus knew me better than I knew myself,
    and still loved me, despite it all!

Prayer

Gracious God,
    you are under no illusions about us.
You do not imagine we are better than we really are,
    nor are you taken in by the mask we wear for the world.
You see us in all our shabbiness and shame,
    and you reach out in love.
But you are under no illusions either about our unworthiness.
You do not consider that we are worse than we really are,
    nor are you swayed
    by the way we can sometimes do ourselves down.
You see us in all our potential and all our weakness,
    and you find a place in your heart for both.
You see the bad *and* the good,
    the worst *and* the best,
    and you recognise not only what we are
    but what we might become through your grace.
Come to us now, as we come to you,
    and use us for your glory,
    in the name of Jesus Christ our Lord.
Amen.

83

You must be joking, Lord!

Peter

Reading: Acts 10:1-6, 9-20, 23a, 24-28, 34b-35, 44-48

In Caesarea there was a man named Cornelius, a centurion of the Italian Cohort, as it was called. He was a devout man who feared God with all his household; he gave alms generously to the people and prayed constantly to God. One afternoon at about three o'clock he had a vision in which he clearly saw an angel of God coming in and saying to him, 'Cornelius.' He stared at him in terror and said, 'What is it, Lord?' He answered, 'Your prayers and your alms have ascended as a memorial before God. Now send men to Joppa for a certain Simon who is called Peter; he is lodging with Simon, a tanner, whose house is by the seaside.'

About noon the next day . . . Peter went up on the roof to pray. He became hungry and wanted something to eat; and while it was being prepared, he fell into a trance. He saw the heaven opened and something like a large sheet coming down, being lowered to the ground by its four corners. In it were all kinds of four-footed creatures and reptiles and birds of the air. Then he heard a voice saying, 'Get up, Peter; kill and eat.' But Peter said, 'By no means, Lord; for I have never eaten anything that is profane or unclean.' The voice said to him again, a second time, 'What God has made clean, you must not call profane.' This happened three times, and the thing was suddenly taken up to heaven.

Now while Peter was greatly puzzled about what to make of the vision that he had seen, suddenly the men sent by Cornelius appeared. They were asking for Simon's house and were standing by the gate. They called out to ask whether Simon, who was called Peter, was staying there. While Peter was still thinking about the vision, the Spirit said to him, 'Look, three men are searching for you. Now get up, go down, and go with them without hesitation; for I have sent them.' . . . So Peter invited them in and gave them lodging.

The following day they came to Caesarea. Cornelius was expecting them and had called together his relatives and close friends. On Peter's arrival Cornelius met him, and falling at his feet, worshipped him. But Peter made him get up, saying, 'Stand up; I am only a mortal.' And as he talked with him, he went in and found that many had assembled; and he said to them, 'You yourselves know that it is unlawful for a Jew to associate with or to visit a Gentile; but God has shown me that I should not call anyone profane or unclean . . . I truly understand that God shows no partiality, but in every nation anyone who fears him and does what is right is acceptable to him . . .'

While Peter was still speaking, the Holy Spirit fell upon all who heard the word. The circumcised believers who had come with Peter were astounded that the gift of the Holy Spirit had been poured out even on the Gentiles, for they heard them speaking in tongues and extolling God. Then Peter said, 'Can anyone withhold the water for baptising these people who have received the Holy Spirit just as we have?' So he ordered them to be baptised in the name of Jesus Christ. Then they invited him to stay for several days.

Meditation

You must be joking, Lord!
That's what I told him,
    and I was deadly serious,
    for the very idea of eating such unclean gentile food
    filled me with revulsion,
    my stomach heaving at the prospect.
Even if I'd been starving I wouldn't have touched it –
    no way!
Yet this voice went on and on, ringing in my ears:
    'Get up, Peter. Kill and eat.'
And each time afterwards, despite my protestations,
    the same message:
    'What God has made clean, you must not call profane.'
I was thankful to wake up and find it was all a dream,
    yet my relief was short-lived
    for the picture still haunted me,
    hovering in my mind's eye,
    and, try as I might, I could not remove it.
I was baffled,
    mystified,
    and a touch ashamed at even entertaining such thoughts,
    for they went against everything I believed,
    everything I'd been taught from my mother's arms.
But there was no time for brooding
    for suddenly these strangers appeared, calling my name,

and to their voices was added another –
    that voice of my dream:
    'Get up,
    go down,
    go with them.'
So I went,
    and found that God had gone before me –
    a man waiting there expectantly,
    a Roman centurion,
    and all at once, it made sense,
    the mystery resolved.
He was a Gentile, you see,
    according to our law unclean, impure,
    someone I was bound, as a Jew, to refuse –
    and just a day earlier I'd have done just that,
    the alternative unthinkable.
Only that was yesterday,
    this was today –
    God had shown me different,
    his love open to any,
    whatever their culture, colour or creed.
I left him rejoicing,
    singing God's praises and filled with the Holy Spirit,
    that man I'd have passed by without a thought,
    impervious to his pleas.
But while *I* saw the barriers which kept us apart,
    God through his love brought us together,
    and at last, for the first time in my life,
    I saw not the outside but the person within,
    the life beneath –
    the child of God for whom Christ died,
    as he died for you,
    for me,
    for everyone!

Prayer

Mighty God,
    we imagine that we are open to those around us,
    but in reality we are not.
Our attitudes are coloured by a host of preconceptions

which subconsciously create deep-rooted prejudices within us.
We pass judgement without even realising it
    and close our minds to anyone or anything
    which dares to challenge our narrow horizons.
Forgive us,
    and help us to realise that truth is far bigger
    than any one of us can grasp alone.
Teach us to be open to all the ways you are at work
    and everything we can learn from the experiences
    and insights of others.
Sweep away the bias and bigotry
    which can so easily come to dominate our lives,
    and so may we grasp the height, length, depth and breadth
    of your purpose which transcends all our expectations;
    through Jesus Christ our Lord.
Amen.

84

I WAS SENT OUT TO INVESTIGATE

Barnabas

Reading: Acts 11:19-26

Now those who were scattered because of the persecution that took place over Stephen travelled as far as Phoenicia, Cyprus, and Antioch, and they spoke the word to no one except Jews. But among them were some men of Cyprus and Cyrene who, on coming to Antioch, spoke to the Hellenists also, proclaiming the Lord Jesus. The hand of the Lord was with them, and a great number became believers and turned to the Lord. News of this came to the ears of the church in Jerusalem, and they sent Barnabas to Antioch. When he came and saw the grace of God, he rejoiced, and he exhorted them all to remain faithful to the Lord with steadfast devotion; for he was a good man, full of the Holy Spirit and of faith. And a great many people were brought to the Lord. Then Barnabas went to Tarsus to look for Saul, and when he had found him, he brought him to Antioch. So it was that for an entire year they met with the church and taught a great many people, and it was in Antioch that the disciples were first called 'Christians'.

Meditation

I was sent out to investigate,
    do you realise that?
To find out exactly what was going on amongst the Gentiles,
    whether the rumours we'd heard
    about the gospel being preached to them were true.
And if they were, then my brief was plain enough –
    to ensure they toed the official line without exception,
    that they followed the law down to the very last letter.
Oh, it wasn't put like that, of course,
    nothing quite so transparent,
    but we all knew the purpose of my visit –
    those who sent me,
    those I went to,
    those I worked with –

the reason for my being there was plain enough.
Yet if I went out with that in mind,
    it very soon changed when I arrived,
    for straightaway I could tell God was at work,
    his Spirit moving in a wonderful way.
You should have seen it,
    day after day more people coming to faith –
    not just the odd one here and there,
    the occasional cluster responding in dribs and drabs,
    but a constant flow,
    a great multitude joyfully committing their lives to Christ.
It was a revelation to me,
    turning my world upside down,
    for, like my fellow apostles,
    I'd never looked further than my own people until then,
    beyond those who were Jews as we were.
What place did the Gentiles have in our faith?
God had chosen *us* as his people, not them,
    sent Jesus to *our* nation as *our* Messiah,
    the fulfilment of promises made in *our* Scriptures,
    so why go spreading it about further?
Only there in Antioch I realised that this simply wouldn't do,
    for I could see the evidence of God's blessing with my own eyes –
    the transformation in people's lives,
    the joy, the peace, the love, the power –
    and I knew then that the message of Christ was for the many,
    not just the few,
    glad tidings for everyone, everywhere.
It hurt to admit it, but it had to be said:
    we'd become too comfortable,
    too narrow,
    too concerned with our own affairs,
    and God was saying, loud and clear: think again!
A world was out there, waiting to respond,
    hungry and thirsty,
    and for too long we had deprived them
    of the opportunity to hear the message.
We had the word of life,
    the good news,
    the gospel of salvation,
    and we'd hidden it away like some closely guarded secret.
Don't make the mistake we did,

looking inwards rather than out.
Rejoice in what Christ has done, yes,
　　celebrate his love for you,
　　but then, please, whatever else,
　　don't keep it to yourselves!

Prayer

Eternal God,
　　for all our claims to be a pilgrim people
　　the fact is we are often anything but.
We like what is well known, tried and trusted, familiar,
　　and we find change hard to deal with,
　　resenting anything which jogs us out of our comfortable routine.
Far from encouraging new blood and new ideas,
　　we react with hostility and suspicion,
　　even to the point that we keep our faith to ourselves
　　rather than risk outsiders coming in
　　and upsetting the apple-cart.
We may not do it consciously,
　　but it is true nonetheless,
　　and the result is to frustrate your will
　　and deny your purpose.
Help us to remember that there was a time once
　　when *we* had no place among your people
　　and that any part we may have in your kingdom now
　　is down to the way *you* have changed *our* lives.
So teach us not to fear change,
　　but to welcome it as the agent of your transforming purpose
　　which is constantly at work in the world,
　　shaping not just us but all;
　　through Jesus Christ our Lord.
Amen.

85

OUR PRAYERS WERE ANSWERED THAT NIGHT

Mary, the mother of John Mark

Reading: Acts 12:1-17

About that time King Herod laid violent hands upon some who belonged to the church. He had James, the brother of John, killed with the sword. After he saw that it pleased the Jews, he proceeded to arrest Peter also. (This was during the festival of Unleavened Bread.) When he had seized him, he put him in prison and handed him over to four squads of soldiers to guard him, intending to bring him out to the people after the Passover. While Peter was kept in prison, the church prayed fervently to God for him.

The very night before Herod was going to bring him out, Peter, bound with two chains, was sleeping between two soldiers while guards in front of the door were keeping watch over the prison. Suddenly an angel of the Lord appeared and a light shone in the cell. He tapped Peter on the side and woke him, saying, 'Get up quickly.' And the chains fell off his wrists. The angel said to him, 'Fasten your belt and put on your sandals.' He did so. Then he said to him, 'Wrap your cloak around you and follow me.' Peter went out and followed him; he did not realise that what was happening with the angel's help was real; he thought he was seeing a vision. After they had passed the first and the second guard, they came before the iron gate leading into the city. It opened for them of its own accord, and they went outside and walked along a lane, when suddenly the angel left him. Then Peter came to himself and said, 'Now I am sure that the Lord has sent his angel and rescued me from the hands of Herod and from all that the Jewish people were expecting.'

As soon as he realised this, he went to the house of Mary, the mother of John whose other name was Mark, where many had gathered and were praying. When he knocked at the outer gate, a maid named Rhoda came to answer. On recognising Peter's voice, she was so overjoyed that, instead of opening the gate, she ran in and announced that Peter was standing at the gate. They said to her, 'You are out of your mind!' But she insisted that it was so. They said, 'It is his angel.' Meanwhile Peter continued knocking; and when they opened the gate, they saw him and were amazed. He motioned to them with his hand to be silent, and described for them how the Lord had brought him out of the prison.

And he added, 'Tell this to James and to the believers.' Then he left and went to another place.

Meditation

Our prayers were answered that night,
    wonderfully, sensationally answered –
    and you could have knocked us over with a feather.
We never expected it, you see –
    despite everything God had done among us,
    the astonishing signs,
    the awesome wonders,
    not one of us believed our prayers would make
    the slightest scrap of difference.
Does that shock you?
It did us when we finally realised it.
But what shocked us more was that we'd no idea it was the case,
    no inkling whatsoever
    that we were simply going through the motions.
We thought we trusted completely,
    and, believe me, had you heard us praying
    you'd have thought so too,
    but when our maid Rhoda burst in upon us,
    eyes wide with wonder,
    tripping over her words in her haste to get them out,
    that's when our lack of trust was laid bare.
'It's Peter!' she told us.
    'Here!
    Outside!
    Knocking at the door!'
And, do you know what? –
    we just sat there and looked at her, as though she were mad.
'Pull yourself together,' we told her.
    'Get a grip!
    You know where Peter is.
    We all do.'
Poor girl, she tried to argue,
    beside herself with frustration,
    but we just wouldn't listen,
    wouldn't even countenance the possibility
    that we might be mistaken.

So much for faith!
In the end she did what she should have done sooner –
    opened the door! –
    and there he was, just as she'd said,
    wondering what on earth had taken us so long.
He told us the whole story –
    his initial despair,
    the sudden burst of light,
    the mysterious deliverer,
    the joy of freedom –
    and then, before he left, he added one last thing:
    'Tell this to James and to the believers.'
Was it a gentle dig at our lack of faith?
I don't think so,
    yet it might as well have been,
    for it brought home again how little we'd trusted.
We'd believed him doomed,
    lost to us for ever this side of eternity,
    but God showed us otherwise –
    a glorious reminder that, though the well of faith runs dry,
    his faithfulness continues to flow
    in a never-failing stream!

Prayer

Gracious God,
    we do not find prayer easy,
    for there are many times when you do not seem to answer
    or when the answer you give is not quite what we hoped for.
Faith tells us one thing, experience another,
    and eventually it is experience, often all too painful,
    which wins the day.
There was a time, perhaps,
    when we would have asked for something
    fully confident you would grant,
    but, as the years pass and that fails to happen,
    it becomes hard to keep on believing,
    and slowly our prayers become mechanical,
    offered more out of duty than expectation.
Yet you *do* hear, and you *do* respond;

and, did we but know it, our failure to recognise your answer
    is often due to our failure to listen,
    or to the strait-jacket we subconsciously set upon you.
Teach us to recognise that you may say no, you may say yes,
    but you will always say something,
    and so may we pray with renewed confidence,
    trusting in your eternal purpose;
    through Jesus Christ our Lord.
Amen.

86

WAS I HURT BY PAUL'S ATTITUDE?

Mark

Reading: Acts 15:36-41

After some days Paul said to Barnabas, 'Come, let us return and visit the believers in every city where we proclaimed the word of the Lord and see how they are doing.' Barnabas wanted to take with them John called Mark. But Paul decided not to take with them one who had deserted them in Pamphylia and had not accompanied them in the work. The disagreement became so sharp that they parted company; Barnabas took Mark with him and sailed away to Cyprus. But Paul chose Silas and set out, the believers commending him to the grace of the Lord. He went through Syria and Cilicia, strengthening the churches.

Meditation

Was I hurt by Paul's attitude,
   his refusal to let me share again in his ministry?
Not really, no,
   for I knew that I'd let him down when he needed me most,
   walked away when I couldn't stand the heat.
I hadn't been well, admittedly,
   the demands of our journey having told on me
   more than I'd anticipated –
   not just the physical toll, though that was testing enough,
   but the mental and spiritual exhaustion,
   the pressure of constantly giving out
   with scarcely a moment's respite –
   yet whatever strain *I* was under,
   Paul was wrestling with far worse,
   only he never once complained,
   the idea of taking a break
   not even crossing his mind for a moment.
He had a mission to fulfil,
   a calling to honour,

and he wasn't going to rest until he'd completed it,
    however much it cost him.
Me, I took the first opportunity to cut and run.
So no, I couldn't blame him –
    I'd made my bed,
    now I could lie on it.
Yet thankfully that wasn't the end of the story,
    for, though I didn't deserve it,
    there was someone else ready to give me another chance –
    good old Barnabas.
It was typical of the man, really –
    no wonder we'd called him 'son of encouragement' –
    always ready to see the best,
    to make allowances,
    to draw out the good instead of dwell on the bad.
He may not have made the headlines like the others did,
    but to many of us he was the star of the show,
    his gentle prompting the secret behind so much of our success.
It was true for me, that's for sure –
    while some like Paul were writing me off,
    he stepped in with a word of welcome,
    and I needed no second bidding –
    this time I would not fail.
I was right too,
    for I can look back now on a life of service,
    years of rich fulfilment in the cause of the kingdom,
    and I thank God from the bottom of my heart
    for that man who made it possible,
    my friend Barnabas.
Only, as he never ceases to tell me, it isn't him I owe it to,
    not finally;
    it's Christ,
    the one who is always there, however much we've failed,
    however little we deserve it,
    ready to put the past behind us
    and help us start again!

Prayer

Lord,
   it's not easy to give someone a second chance,
   especially when they've let us down personally.
It's hard to overcome our feelings of hurt and anger,
   and harder still to trust that person in the way we used to.
Yet *you* go on giving us another chance day after day,
   and despite our repeated failure
   you are willing still to entrust us
   with the work of your kingdom.
Teach us, then,
   instead of finding fault to look for strengths,
   and instead of putting people down to lift them up.
Help us to forgive others as you forgive us,
   and so may we offer a ministry of encouragement
   to all we meet;
   through Jesus Christ our Lord.
Amen.

87

Have you ever tried turning over a new leaf?

Paul

Reading: Romans 7:14-25

For we know that the law is spiritual; but I am of the flesh, sold into slavery under sin. I do not understand my own actions. For I do not do what I want, but I do the very thing I hate. Now if I do what I do not want, I agree that the law is good. But in fact it is no longer I that do it, but sin that dwells within me. For I know that nothing good dwells within me, that is, in my flesh. I can will what is right, but I cannot do it. For I do not do the good I want, but the evil I do not want is what I do. Now if I do what I do not want, it is no longer I that do it, but sin that dwells within me.

So I find it to be a law that when I want to do what is good, evil lies close at hand. For I delight in the law of God in my inmost self, but I see in my members another law at war with the law of my mind, making me captive to the law of sin that dwells in my members. Wretched man that I am! Who will rescue me from this body of death? Thanks be to God through Jesus Christ our Lord!

So then, with my mind I am a slave to the law of God, but with my flesh I am a slave to the law of sin.

Meditation

Have you ever tried turning over a new leaf?
I have,
    again,
    and again,
    and again.
Every morning I wake up and say,
    'Today is going to be different!'
And every night I lie down with the knowledge that is wasn't.
For all my good intentions
    I make the same mistakes I've always made,
    display the same old weaknesses,
    succumb to the same old temptations –
    a constant cycle of failure.

Why does it happen?
I just can't work it out,
    for I want so much to be faithful –
    more than anything else in the world –
    yet somehow, before I know it, I find I've fallen again,
    unable to do even my own will,
    let alone God's.
It's as though there are two selves at war within me,
    one intent on good and the other on evil,
    and you don't need me to tell you which one emerges the victor.
Can it ever change?
I'd like to think so,
    but I honestly don't think it will,
    for though the spirit is willing, the flesh is weak,
    rushing, like a moth before a candle,
    towards its own destruction.
Do you wonder that I despair sometimes?
It's impossible not to.
Yet I shouldn't lose heart,
    because despite it all God still loves me,
    not for what one day I might be,
    but for what I am now,
    with all my sin sticking to me.
That's why he sent his Son into the world –
    not to save the righteous,
    but to rescue people like you and me,
    weak, foolish, faithless,
    unable to help ourselves.
It doesn't mean I'll stop trying,
    I'll never do that until my dying day.
But it *does* mean, however many times I fail,
    however often he finds me lying in the gutter,
    he'll be there to pick me up and set me on my way again,
    cleansed, restored, forgiven,
    the slate wiped clean, ready to start afresh –
    through his grace, a new creation!

Prayer

Merciful God,
  unlike us you don't dwell on our failures.
Instead, you invite us to acknowledge them openly before you,
  to receive your pardon and then to move on.
Teach us to do just that –
  to accept your offer for what it is
  and, rather than wallow in our guilt,
  to rejoice in your mercy.
Help us not simply to *talk* about new life
  but to *live* it joyfully,
  receiving each moment as your gracious gift;
  through Jesus Christ our Lord.
Amen.

88

IT WAS ALL SO UNNECESSARY

Paul

Reading: 1 Corinthians 11:17-22; 12:1, 4-6, 12, 27-31

Now in the following instructions I do not commend you, because when you come together it is not for the better but for the worse. For, to begin with, when you come together as a church, I hear that there are divisions among you, and to some extent I believe it. Indeed, there have to be factions among you, for only so will it become clear who among you are genuine. When you come together, it is not really to eat the Lord's supper. For when the time comes to eat, each of you goes ahead with your own supper, and one goes hungry and another becomes drunk. What! Do you not have homes to eat and drink in? Or do you show contempt for the church of God and humiliate those who have nothing? What should I say to you? Should I commend you? In this matter I do not commend you!

Now, concerning spiritual gifts, brothers and sisters, I do not want you to be uninformed . . . There are varieties of gifts, but the same Spirit; and there are varieties of services, but the same Lord; and there are varieties of activities, but it is the same God who activates all of them in everyone . . . For just as the body is one and has many members, and all the members of the body, though many, are one body, so it is with Christ . . . Now you are the body of Christ and individually members of it. And God has appointed in the church first apostles, second prophets, third teachers; then deeds of power, then gifts of healing, forms of assistance, forms of leadership, various kinds of tongues. Are all apostles? Are all prophets? Are all teachers? Do all work miracles? Do all possess gifts of healing? Do all speak in tongues? Do all interpret? But strive for the greater gifts. And I will show you a still more excellent way.

Meditation

It was all so unnecessary,
  such a senseless stupid waste –
  grown men and women who should have known better,
  arguing amongst each other,
  almost coming to blows,

and all over so-called gifts of the Spirit.
Well, some gifts they turned out to be!
I could hardly believe it –
    so much anger,
    so much bitterness,
    just because people experienced God differently.
Why couldn't they see the other's point of view,
    recognise that some need to express themselves one way,
    some another;
    some have this gift,
    others one completely different?
Why turn it into a competition,
    a test of spiritual blessing?
It wouldn't have been so bad had it been over something important –
    our failure to love,
    our inability to forgive,
    our weakness in discipleship.
But this –
    it was all finally so trivial,
    the whole business peripheral
    to what should really have concerned us.
Oh, I don't deny such things have their place –
    a time and a season for everything –
    but when they divide rather than bring together,
    upset rather than uplift,
    surely something has to be wrong somewhere?
Yet they just wouldn't have it,
    each vying to outdo the other,
    jostling to claim the most spectacular gift,
    the profoundest blessing.
Couldn't they see the damage they were doing,
    the message they broadcast to the world?
Didn't they realise that every dispute, every division,
    broke again the body of Christ,
    inflicting yet more suffering upon him?
Apparently not.
They were tearing themselves apart,
    slowly but surely destroying the unity
    which he had suffered such agony to bring them,
    and all in the name of his Spirit.
Don't think I blame one above the other;
    I don't.

They were all to blame,
   each as intolerant as the next,
   denying through their deeds what they claimed with their lips.
It's up to them now;
   I've done my best,
   tried to get the message home.
They can go on feuding if they want to,
   no place for anyone but themselves,
   but when the day comes when they're finally called to account,
   and they find then that there's no place
   for anyone *like* themselves,
   don't say I didn't warn them!

Prayer

Lord,
   we each have *some* gifts,
   but none of us has them *all*.
We each have something to contribute to others,
   and equally something to receive from them in turn.
We each need one another,
   and our lives are impoverished
   if we attempt to go it alone.
You call us all to be part of your body
   with a unique role to play within that,
   but by the same token we belong to an interdependent whole
   in which every member is of vital importance.
Teach us, then,
   not only to exercise our own gifts wisely
   but at the same time to appreciate those of others,
   and so may we grow together,
   building one another up in love,
   to the glory of your name.
Amen.

89

'WHAT WILL IT BE LIKE?' THEY ASK ME

Paul

Reading: 1 Corinthians 15:12-22, 35-6; 42-44a, 50-57

Now if Christ is proclaimed as raised from the dead, how can some of you say there is no resurrection of the dead? If there is no resurrection of the dead, then Christ has not been raised; and if Christ has not been raised, then our proclamation has been in vain and your faith has been in vain. We are even found to be misrepresenting God, because we testified of God that he raised Christ – whom he did not raise if it is true that the dead are not raised. For if the dead are not raised, then Christ has not been raised. If Christ has not been raised, your faith is futile and you are still in your sins. Then those also who have died in Christ have perished. If for this life only we have hoped in Christ, we are of all people most to be pitied. But in fact Christ has been raised from the dead, the first fruits of those who have died. For since death came through a human being, the resurrection of the dead also came through a human being; for as all die in Adam, so all will be made alive in Christ.

But someone will ask, 'How are the dead raised? With what kind of body do they come?' Fool! What you sow does not come to life unless it dies . . . So it is with the resurrection of the dead. What is sown is perishable, what is raised is imperishable. It is sown in dishonour, it is raised in glory. It is sown in weakness, it is raised in power. It is sown a physical body, it is raised a spiritual body.

What I am saying, brothers and sisters, is this: flesh and blood cannot inherit the kingdom of God, nor does the perishable inherit the imperishable. Listen, I will tell you a mystery! We will not all die, but we will all be changed, in a moment, in the twinkling of an eye, at the last trumpet. For the trumpet will sound, and the dead will be raised imperishable, and we will be changed. For this perishable body must put on imperishability, and this mortal body must put on immortality. When this perishable body puts on imperishability, and this mortal body puts on immortality, then the saying that is written will be fulfilled:

'Death has been swallowed up in victory.'

Where, O death, is your victory?

Where, O death, is your sting?'

The sting of death is sin, and the power of sin is the law. But thanks be to God, who gives us the victory, through our Lord Jesus Christ.

Meditation

'What will it be like?' they ask me.
   'What sort of body will we have?
   What sort of clothes?
   What sort of food?'
And then, as if that weren't enough,
   'When will it be?
   Where will we go?
   How will it happen?'
As if *I* should know!
All right, so maybe I did catch a glimpse of life outside the body,
   but that doesn't make me an expert, does it –
   an authority on the life to come?
Yet admit that to some people
   and they start to question everything,
   as though the whole idea of resurrection
   hinges on our ability to understand it.
I know why they ask, of course I do,
   for it's not easy living with mystery,
   accepting claims one cannot fathom or even begin to picture;
   yet is that really anything new
   when it comes to the things of God?
'My thoughts are not your thoughts,
   nor are your ways my ways' –
   isn't that what he told us,
   so why presume they are?
I realised long ago just because we don't understand something
   doesn't mean it isn't true.
The trouble is we start in the wrong place,
   looking to what's yet to be rather than what's been already,
   but it's there that our faith rests –
   in the wonder of the empty tomb, the folded grave clothes,
   the risen Lord,
   in the glorious message of his victory over death,
   his final triumph over evil.
Isn't that enough for you?
It is for me.
I can't explain how it happened, but I know it's real,
   for I've met him myself,
   experienced his presence,
   died, through his power, to the old self and risen to the new.

Take away that, and you take away everything.
We'd all like to know more, I accept that,
    to end, once and for all, the guessing and speculation,
    but we wouldn't understand even if it was spelt out for us,
    for the things God has in store
    are beyond the human eye to see or heart to conceive.
So no more brooding about the future –
    what *may* be,
    what *could* be.
Think rather of Christ –
    what he's *done*,
    what he's *doing*,
    and then you will learn to take on trust
    the things he's yet to do,
    and the life which yet *shall* be.

Prayer

Sovereign God,
    you do not ask us to base our faith on what might be
    but on what *has* been and what *is*.
You came to our world in Christ and lived among us,
    demonstrating your commitment to humankind.
Through him you suffered and died on a cross,
    but in triumph you rose again,
    testifying to your victory over death.
And now, through that same Jesus,
    we experience the daily reality of your presence
    and the constant wonder of your love.
May all you have done and continue to do
    inspire us to trust in the future you hold for us,
    confident that as you are with us now
    so you shall be for all eternity;
    through Jesus Christ our Lord.
Amen.

90

I COULD THINK ABOUT NOTHING ELSE AT THE TIME

Paul

Reading: 2 Corinthians 12:7b-10

To keep me from being too elated, a thorn was given to me in the flesh, a messenger of Satan to torment me . . . Three times I appealed to the Lord about this, that it would leave me, but he said to me, 'My grace is sufficient for you, for power is made perfect in weakness.' So, I will boast all the more gladly of my weaknesses, so that the power of Christ may dwell in me. Therefore I am content with weaknesses, insults, hardships, persecutions, and calamities for the sake of Christ; for whenever I am weak, then I am strong.

Meditation

I could think about nothing else at the time
    but that affliction of mine,
    that thorn in the flesh, as I finally came to call it.
It dominated my whole life, and very nearly destroyed me,
    sapping my strength,
    destroying my confidence,
    eating into the very fabric of my faith.
Try as I might, I just couldn't get it out of my head –
    it was always there,
    preying on my mind,
    lurking in the shadows,
    waiting to devour me.
When I woke up in the morning it was waiting to meet me,
    a constant reminder of my weakness.
When I walked in the street it pursued me,
    striking me down when I least expected.
When I talked with friends it was there too,
    breaking into our conversation.
When I turned to God in prayer, even there it turned up,
    insinuating itself between us.
And I was getting desperate,

sucked ever deeper into a dark pit of despair,
   the laughter, the love, the life being drained from me.
Why? I asked.
Why me?
What sin had I committed?
What penance did I have to do
   before God would have pity and set me free?
I'd make it worth it, I told him,
   not just for me but for both our sakes.
I could do so much more,
   serve him so much better,
   if only he'd hear my prayer.
But there was no answer,
   no release,
   nothing.
I begged him again,
   angry,
   disappointed,
   resentful.
But it made no difference –
   still nothing.
So I left off for a while,
   until my patience could take it no longer,
   the frustration too much to bear.
And then once more I asked,
   grovelling this time,
   begging,
   pleading.
But yet again, nothing,
   just a blank, empty silence.
Or so I thought,
   until suddenly this picture of Jesus came to me,
   his eyes filled with pain, his body broken,
   and on his head a crown of thorns;
   the blood trickling down his tortured face,
   the hands outstretched in agony –
   and all at once I knew I was wrong.
He'd heard me all right,
   and answered,
   only I hadn't been ready to listen.
For it was there,
   in the sorrow and suffering of the Cross,

that God fulfilled his eternal purpose;
there,
in what the world counts weakness,
that God showed us true greatness!
So have I finally come to terms with this problem of mine,
exorcised the demon that's haunted me for so long?
No, I can't claim that,
for I still have my moments,
still sometimes ask why,
and still hope some day it might be different.
But when I catch myself feeling like that
I stop and think of Jesus,
and I realise again
that in my weakness is God's strength.

Prayer

Loving God,
we do not like living with weakness.
We want to feel strong, in control of our destiny,
able to stand up against whatever life might throw at us,
and we resent anything which threatens that sense of security.
Yet time and again across the years
you have turned this world's expectations upside-down,
your values totally different from our own.
You humble the proud, you bring down the mighty,
you reduce the powerful to nothing,
choosing instead to work through those
who seem insignificant and vulnerable.
Teach us, then, when we find our weaknesses hard to accept,
to recognise that you are able to use them
in ways beyond our imagining,
and to understand that in those very weaknesses
your strength is most perfectly seen;
through Jesus Christ our Lord.
Amen.

91

I SHOULD HAVE KNOWN BETTER,
A MAN IN MY POSITION

Felix

Reading: Acts 24:1-26

The high priest Ananias came down (to Caesarea) with some elders and an attorney, a certain Tertullus, and they reported their case against Paul to the governor. When Paul had been summoned, Tertullus began to accuse him, saying: 'Your Excellency, because of you we have long enjoyed peace, and reforms have been made for this people because of your foresight. We welcome this in every way, and everywhere with utmost gratitude. But, to detain you no further, I beg you to hear us briefly with your customary graciousness. We have, in fact, found this man a pestilent fellow, an agitator among all the Jews throughout the world, and a ringleader of the sect of the Nazarenes. He even tried to profane the temple, and so we seized him. By examining him yourself you will be able to learn from him concerning everything of which we accuse him.' The Jews also joined in the charge by asserting that all this was true.

When the governor motioned to him to speak, Paul replied: 'I cheerfully make my defence, knowing that for many years you have been a judge over this nation. As you can find out, it is not more than twelve days since I went up to worship in Jerusalem. They did not find me disputing with anyone in the temple or stirring up a crowd, either in the synagogues or throughout the city. Neither can they prove to you the charge that they now bring against me. But this I admit to you, that according to the Way, which they call a sect, I worship the God of our ancestors, believing everything laid down according to the law or written in the prophets. I have a hope in God – a hope that they themselves also accept – that there will be a resurrection of both the righteous and the unrighteous. Therefore I do my best always to have a clear conscience toward God and all people. Now after some years I came to bring alms to my nation and to offer sacrifices. While I was doing this, they found me in the temple, completing the rite of purification, without any crowd or disturbance. But there were some Jews from Asia – they ought to be here before you to make an accusation, if they have anything against me. Or let these men here tell what crime they had found when I stood before the council, unless it was this one sentence that I called out while standing before them, "It is about the resurrection of the dead that I am on trial before you today."'

But Felix, who was rather well informed about the Way, adjourned the hearing with the comment, 'When Lysias the tribune comes down, I will decide your case.' Then he ordered the centurion to keep Paul in custody, but to let him have some liberty and not to prevent any of his friends from taking care of his needs.

Some days later when Felix came with his wife Drusilla, who was Jewish, he sent for Paul and heard him speak concerning faith in Christ Jesus. And as he discussed justice, self-control, and the coming judgement, Felix became frightened and said, 'Go away for the present; when I have an opportunity, I will send for you.' At the same time he hoped that money would be given him by Paul, and for that reason he used to send for him very often and converse with him.

Meditation

I should have known better, a man in my position,
    to dither like that,
    postpone a decision,
    and all for the hope of personal gain.
It was inexcusable, even had the man been guilty,
    but I knew full well that he wasn't;
    the only reason for his presence there before me
    was the sheer malice of his accusers.
They wanted him out of the way,
    silenced once and for all,
    and, just as it had been with that fellow Jesus,
    they wanted someone else to do their dirty work for them,
    to save them soiling their holy hands with blood.
I should have dismissed the case there and then,
    but I didn't, did I?
I kept Paul dangling on a string,
    hanging in limbo,
    in the vain hope he might slip me a little incentive
    to swing the case his way.
What was I thinking of?
He had nothing to give anyway,
    not a penny to his name,
    but, more important, there was no way

he was going to stoop to corruption,
   however just his cause –
   unlike me, the man was as straight as the day is long.
I should have known that, and done the decent thing,
      got the action right for a change
      even if the motive was still wrong.
It was a chance for once in my life to make a stand of principle,
      and, true to form, I let it slip through my fingers.
You think that bad,
      well, there's worse,
      for what shames me most
      is that I knew all about the followers of the Way,
      and it was crystal clear they were on to something special.
One look at them told you that –
      a serenity,
      a confidence,
      an inner joy about them which I yearned to share.
It didn't matter what we put them through;
      still they held firm,
      their faith and courage quite frankly staggering –
      and of all of them Paul exemplified those qualities.
I ached to find out more,
      but I was afraid –
      scared of what it might cost,
      scared of the inner secrets it might reveal –
      so I backed away when the truth began to hurt.
The opportunity was there to find true and lasting wealth,
      not riches on earth but treasure in heaven,
      and I threw it away for what offered little
      and yielded less.

Prayer

Lord,
      we know that money can't buy happiness,
      or at least we say we do,
      but we find it hard to resist its lure.
Though we hate to admit it,
      few of us are above temptation if the price is right.
It is not that we would wilfully do wrong
      so much as that we slowly succumb

to the pressure to compromise our convictions,
   imperceptibly bending the rules
   until we have lost sight of the things we stand for.
The spirit says one thing, the flesh another,
   craving the trappings of success and security
   which wealth apparently offers.
We know that it profits us nothing to gain the world itself
   if, in the process, we forfeit our soul,
   but we cannot seem to help ourselves.
Forgive us the inner poverty which this betrays,
   and teach us to set our hearts
   on the true riches which only you give;
   through Jesus Christ our Lord.
Amen.

92

I'M ASHAMED NOW, LOOKING BACK

Euodia

Reading: Philippians 4:2-3

I urge Euodia and I urge Syntyche to be of the same mind in the Lord. Yes,
and I ask you also, my loyal companion, help these women, for they have
struggled beside me in the work of the gospel, together with Clement and
the rest of my co-workers, whose names are in the book of life.

Meditation

I'm ashamed now, looking back.
It was all so stupid,
   so unnecessary,
   so childish.
I really don't know what came over me,
   how I could have let myself get so carried away.
Yet at the time it seemed important, that's the thing –
   a minor disagreement in some ways,
   but a matter of principle –
   or so at least I told myself.
If I gave in once, who could say what would follow,
   what other errors might creep in if the door was left ajar?
So I dug my heels in deep and stood firm,
   determined not to give an inch no matter what.
The only problem was Syntyche did the same,
   equally convinced she was in the right,
   and before we knew it we were at each other's throats,
   spitting and snarling like two alley cats.
We'd been the best of friends until then – that's what made it worse –
   working together all those years,
   preaching the Gospel,
   nurturing young Christians,
   leading by example.
Well, some example!
I wince now at the very thought of it –

how I blew things out of all proportion,
never listening to a word she said,
closed to every viewpoint but my own.
And to make it worse I went round canvassing support,
subtly doing her down,
sowing the seeds of mistrust.
It was completely out of hand,
threatening to tear us apart.
But it wasn't just our friendship that was under threat,
it was the members of our fellowship –
those dear trusting friends who looked to us for guidance,
who needed our support –
the longer our dispute went on,
the more damage it was doing to them.
Thank God Paul made us see sense.
Not that he said much, mind you!
He knew a lecture would only have got our backs up further.
So he simply urged us to stop
and think
and listen;
and, in a brief aside, asked our brothers and sisters in Christ
to help us as best they could.
I think that's what did it, finally,
the sheer shock of realising
that we were the ones needing counsel,
that we, more than any, had gone astray.
Remember that, next time you disagree.
Before the hackles rise and the claws come out,
pause for a moment,
and ask yourself this:
what's it all about?
For, whatever it may be,
can anything truly matter more
than the love which has brought us together in Christ?

Prayer

Gracious God,
    forgive us the foolish divisions we allow to come between us,
    the petty disputes which grow out of all proportion
    until they destroy the fellowship we share.
We recognise there will always be occasions when we disagree
    for we are all different,
    each having our own ideas,
    our own way of looking at the world
    and our own unique experience of life,
    but in Christ we should be able to see such diversity
    as a blessing rather than a threat,
    a source of strength instead of a cause of weakness.
Forgive us the pride and insecurity which prevents that,
    leading us instead to nurse anger, bitterness
    and resentment in our hearts.
Teach us to admit our mistakes whenever we are in the wrong,
    and, when the fault lies with others,
    to forgive freely as you have forgiven us.
Grant us the mind of Christ
    so that we may live in harmony,
    for his name's sake.
Amen.

93

WAS I HAPPY WITH MY LOT?

Paul

Reading: Philippians 4:4-7, 10-12

Rejoice in the Lord always; again I will say, Rejoice. Let your gentleness be known to everyone. The Lord is near. Do not worry about anything, but in everything by prayer and supplication with thanksgiving let your requests be made known to God. And the peace of God, which surpasses all understanding, will guard your hearts and your minds in Christ Jesus.

I rejoice in the Lord greatly that now at last you have revived your concern for me; indeed, you were concerned for me, but had no opportunity to show it. Not that I am referring to being in need; for I have learned to be content with whatever I have. I know what it is to have little, and I know what it is to have plenty. In any and all circumstances I have learned the secret of being well-fed and of going hungry, of having plenty and of being in need.

Meditation

Was I happy with my lot?
Well, as a matter of fact, I wasn't,
   not at first, anyway.
Oh, I gave thanks, don't get me wrong –
   I marvelled each day at the love of Christ
   and rejoiced constantly at the awesome grace he'd shown to me,
   but for all that there was much I found difficult,
   far more than I'd ever bargained for.
It wasn't the weariness,
   the endless travel,
   the days, weeks, even months without a rest –
   I could cope with those, despite my infirmities.
But when the hostility began,
   the beatings,
   the stone-throwing,
   the interminable hours rotting in a prison cell,
   that's when it became hard to bear,

when I began to wonder just what I'd got myself into.
You wouldn't believe the things I endured,
    the hunger,
    the pain,
    the privations –
    enough to break anyone,
    crush the strongest of spirits.
And yet, somehow, they weren't able to do that,
    for in my darkest moments I always found the strength I needed –
    a word of encouragement,
    a sign of hope,
    a light dawning –
    and I knew that Christ was with me even there,
    especially there,
    in my time of need.
I may have been hungry,
    but I had food in plenty for my soul.
I may have been broken in body,
    but my spirit had been made whole.
I may have been poor in the things of this world,
    but I was rich in the things of God.
It didn't take away the pain, I can't claim that –
    the hardship, the fear and the suffering were just as real,
    just as terrible –
    but it changed the way I saw them,
    my perspective on life, on death, on everything
    transformed for ever.
I had joy in my heart,
    peace which passed all understanding,
    and the promise of treasure in heaven –
    whatever else might be taken from me,
    nothing could take away those.
It was enough, and more than enough!

Prayer

Loving God,
    you do not promise those who follow you
    a life in which everything will go smoothly.
You do not guarantee success or prosperity,
    nor do you offer immunity from the trials

and tribulations of this world.
Indeed, true service may involve us in sacrifice and self-denial,
    more demands rather than *less*,
    greater and more testing challenges
    than we may ever have faced without you.
But what you *do* promise us is fulfilment in Christ.
Through him you are able to satisfy our spiritual hunger and thirst,
    to meet our deepest needs,
    to give us inner peace and an enduring contentment
    in each and every circumstance.
Such peace does not come overnight –
    it matures gradually as day by day we learn to let go
    and put our trust in you.
Reach out then, and draw us ever closer to your side,
    so that we may learn the secret
    of being content with whatever we have;
    through Jesus Christ our Lord.
Amen.

94

IT LOOKED IMPOSSIBLE AT THE BEGINNING

Paul

Reading: Galatians 1:13-24

You have heard, no doubt, of my earlier life in Judaism. I was violently persecuting the church of God and was trying to destroy it. I advanced in Judaism beyond many among my people of the same age, for I was far more zealous for the traditions of my ancestors. But when God, who had set me apart before I was born and called me through his grace, was pleased to reveal his Son to me, so that I might proclaim him among the Gentiles, I did not confer with any human being, nor did I go up to Jerusalem to those who were already apostles before me, but I went away at once into Arabia, and afterwards I returned to Damascus.

Then after three years I did go up to Jerusalem to visit Cephas and stayed with him fifteen days; but I did not see any other apostle except James, the Lord's brother. In what I am writing to you, before God, I do not lie! Then I went into the regions of Syria and Cilicia, and I was still unknown by sight to the churches of Judea that are in Christ; they only heard it said, 'The one who formerly was persecuting us is now proclaiming the faith he once tried to destroy.' And they glorified God because of me.

Meditation

It looked impossible at the beginning,
    utterly beyond me.
And I don't mind confessing there were many times
    when I felt like giving up,
    throwing in the towel and cutting my losses.
Surprised?
You shouldn't be.
After all, just look what I was up against –
    me, Paul, called to take the gospel beyond Jerusalem,
    beyond Judea,
    out to the ends of the earth!
It was a tall order by anyone's reckoning,
    and when you remember how the Jews felt about the Gentiles,

and how the Gentiles felt in return,
    well, you can begin to understand the scale of the problem, can't you!
I was up against it from the very start,
    doing my best to keep a foot in both camps to avoid causing offence,
    trying to share the good news,
    but forever keeping one eye over my shoulder,
    knowing the snipers wouldn't be far away.
It didn't help I suppose, with my own people anyway,
    me being a Jew myself,
    schooled as a Pharisee and expert in the law to boot!
They thought I was betraying my roots,
    reneging on my convictions,
    denying the faith of our fathers.
And as for the Gentiles, many simply wondered what I was doing,
    pushing my nose into their affairs.
So, yes, I had my doubts, to put it mildly!
Wouldn't you have felt the same?
Who was I to overcome that sort of prejudice,
    to break down the barriers between us,
    to bring people of such contrasting backgrounds together
    into one family of humankind?
Who was I to talk of a new way of thinking,
    of building a different sort of kingdom,
    of sharing a different sort of love?
Someone else perhaps – but me?
No way!
And yet the mystery is, I did!
Somehow, in a way I'll never understand,
    I found the strength and the words I needed
    when I needed them most.
I found energy to begin new tasks,
    courage to meet new people,
    faith to dream new dreams.
I unearthed reserves I never knew existed,
    and achieved results I never imagined possible –
    all kinds of people
    in all kinds of ways,
    discovering the joy of sharing and working together,
    discovering a faith that answered their deepest needs –
    a faith to live by.
It looked impossible, you can't argue with that –
    wonderful yet altogether ridiculous.

But it wasn't,
 for I've discovered since then,
 much to my amazement,
 much to my relief,
 that I can do all things
 through him who strengthens me.
Thanks be to God!

Prayer

Sovereign God,
 the challenges you set before us may be very modest
 compared with those faced by others over the years,
 but they can seem daunting nonetheless.
We feel inadequate to meet the task,
 acutely conscious of our lack of faith,
 the limitations of our gifts
 and our inability to serve you as we would wish.
Yet time and again throughout history
 you have taken the most unpromising of material
 and used it in ways defying all expectations.
You have turned doubt into faith,
 weakness into strength,
 timid service into fearless discipleship,
 and you go on doing that today
 through the power of your Holy Spirit.
Give us, then, the faith to respond to your call,
 trusting that, whatever you ask of us,
 you will be by our side to help us see it through,
 to the glory of your name.
Amen.

95

IT'S BEEN GOOD TO SHARE WITH YOU

Paul

Reading: Philippians 1:3-8

I thank my God every time I remember you, constantly praying with joy in every one of my prayers for all of you, because of your sharing in the gospel from the first day until now. I am confident of this, that the one who began a good work among you will bring it to completion by the day of Jesus Christ. It is right for me to think this way about all of you, because you hold me in your heart, for all of you share in God's grace with me, both in my imprisonment and in the defence and confirmation of the gospel. For God is my witness, how I long for all of you with the compassion of Jesus Christ.

Meditation

It's been good to share with you,
    more than you'll ever know.
The times we've been through,
    the experiences we've faced,
    they've gone together,
    little by little,
    bit by bit,
    to weave a web between us –
    our lives inextricably entwined.
I've preached the word to you,
    led your prayers and guided your thoughts.
I've visited your homes,
    heard your problems,
    witnessed your joys.
But more than that,
    we've laughed together,
    learned together,
    grieved together,
    grown together –

this time that's passed as much about your ministry to me
    as mine to you.
And they will live with me, the moments we've shared –
    the good times,
    the bad,
    the times of joy,
    the times of sorrow –
    remembered or unremembered, they have all been special,
    every one of them –
    a part of the person I am,
    a symbol of all that we have been together.
It's been good to share,
    more than words can quite express;
    and it's hard to part,
    more difficult that you may ever think.
But it's not goodbye,
    not for us or anyone who holds dear the name of Christ –
    simply farewell, until that day we meet again,
    in this life or the next.
Whatever the future,
    whatever we face,
    come rain or sunshine,
    pleasure or pain,
    we are one with each other, always,
    through being one together in him.

Prayer

Lord Jesus Christ,
    we thank you for all those
    with whom we have walked on the journey of faith,
    those who have been part of our family in Jesus Christ.
We praise you for the gift of fellowship
    which continues to mean so much to us –
    for all the strength and support we receive through it;
    the love, comfort, inspiration and encouragement it brings us
    in such abundance.
You do not leave us to travel alone
    but bind us together through your Spirit,
    granting us a unity of faith and purpose

which transcends those things which keep us apart.
Forgive us those times we have failed to share as we ought to,
    neglecting each other's needs
    and forgetting our mutual responsibilities.
Forgive us the divisions we have allowed to come between us;
    the thoughtless words and careless actions
    which have broken your body.
Teach us to open our hearts to one another,
    to grow together in love
    and to celebrate the privilege of belonging to your people;
    through Jesus Christ our Lord.
Amen.

96

I WAS READY TO GIVE UP, IF I'M HONEST

Writer to the Hebrews

Reading: Hebrews 11:32-12:2

And what more should I say? For time would fail me to tell of Gideon, Barak, Samson, Jephthah, of David and Samuel and the prophets – who through faith conquered kingdoms, administered justice, obtained promises, shut the mouths of lions, quenched raging fire, escaped the edge of the sword, won strength out of weakness, became mighty in war, put foreign armies to flight. Women received their dead by resurrection. Others were tortured, refusing to accept release in order to obtain a better resurrection. Others suffered mocking and flogging, and even chains and imprisonment. They were stoned to death, they were sawn in two, they were killed by the sword; they went about in skins of sheep and goats, destitute, persecuted, tormented – of whom the world was not worthy. They wandered in deserts and mountains, and in caves and holes in the ground.

Yet all these, though they were commended for their faith, did not receive what was promised, since God had provided something better so that they would not, apart from us, be made perfect.

Therefore, since we are surrounded by so great a cloud of witnesses, let us also lay aside every weight and the sin that clings so closely, and let us run with perseverance the race that is set before us, looking to Jesus the pioneer and perfecter of our faith, who for the sake of the joy that was set before him endured the cross, disregarding its shame, and has taken his seat at the right hand of the throne of God.

Meditation

I was ready to give up, if I'm honest,
   tired, scared, disillusioned.
We all were, every last one of us,
   just about ready to call it a day.
You ask why?
Well, you wouldn't have if you'd been there with us,
   if you'd heard the screams as we did,

the cries for mercy,
the gasps of agony,
the sobs of desolation as yet more martyrs went to their death.
It was hard, I can tell you,
and, worse still, we knew that at any moment
our turn might come –
the axe,
the sword,
the stones,
the lions,
all waiting for another victim to satisfy their hunger.
We'd lost hundreds,
good honest men and women,
honest,
devout,
dedicated,
led like lambs to the slaughter,
nothing and no one able to save them,
not even our prayers.
What could I say to bring hope in such times?
What possible message of reassurance could I give
when I was troubled and confused myself?
It was a crisis for me as well as them,
every one of us struggling to make sense
of such dreadful carnage,
such appalling suffering,
but there seemed nothing to say,
no words which offered any hope or comfort.
Until suddenly I thought of Jesus,
the pain he endured for us –
gasping as the lash tore into his flesh,
as the thorns pierced his head,
as the nails smashed through his hands and feet;
groaning as the cramps convulsed his body
and the lifeblood seeped away.
He need not have faced it,
but he'd done so willingly,
faithful to the last for our sake.
And I knew then that, whatever might be asked of us,
whatever we might suffer,
it could never be worse than the agony he endured,
the terrible total desolation he was asked to bear.

It wasn't an answer, of course, I can't claim that –
    it simply rephrased the question –
    but it was enough,
    for I knew then, and I could say then with confidence,
    that God is with us in our suffering,
    by our sides, whatever we might face.

Prayer

Living Lord,
    as well as the good times, life brings the bad –
    moments of pain, fear, sorrow and suffering.
Most of the time we are able to get by,
    tested but not pushed to the limit,
    but occasionally we question our ability to continue,
    so great are the problems we face.
We feel crushed, overwhelmed,
    our strength sapped and our spirits exhausted,
    even our faith hanging by a thread.
Be with us in such moments
    and give us courage to persevere despite everything.
Though the present seems bleak and the future looks hopeless,
    though our burdens seem many and our resources few,
    help us still to walk the way of Christ,
    knowing that he has gone before us
    and is waiting to meet us at our journey's end.
Take our hand and lead us forward,
    for his name's sake.
Amen.

97

THEY'LL NOT THANK ME FOR SAYING THIS

James

Reading: James 2:14-26

What good is it, my brothers and sisters, if you say you have faith but do not have works? Can faith save you? If a brother or sister is naked and lacks daily food, and one of you says to them, 'Go in peace; keep warm and eat your fill', and yet you do not supply their bodily needs, what is the good of that? So faith by itself, if it has no works, is dead. But someone will say, 'You have faith and I have works.' Show me your faith apart from your works, and I by my works will show you my faith. You believe that God is one; you do well. Even the demons believe – and shudder. Do you want to be shown, you senseless person, that faith apart from works is barren? Was not our ancestor Abraham justified by works when he offered his son Isaac on the altar? You see that faith was active along with his works, and faith was brought to completion by the works. Thus the scripture was fulfilled that says, 'Abraham believed God, and it was reckoned to him as righteousness', and he was called the friend of God. You see that a person is justified by works and not by faith alone. Likewise, was not Rahab the prostitute also justified by works when she welcomed the messengers and sent them out by another road? For just as the body without the spirit is dead, so faith without works is also dead.

Meditation

They'll not thank me for saying this,
    I can tell you that now,
    but I'm going to say it anyway, whether they like it or not,
    for it's too important a matter to keep quiet.
This business of faith and works,
    we've made it all too easy,
    too neat,
    too comfortable,
    so concerned with one truth
    that we've lost sight of another, equally vital,
    equally part of our response to Christ.

No, I'm not saying go back to the old way
   where works were everything,
   where salvation was something to be earned –
   I know what that's like, struggling to obey the law
   in the vain hope we may deserve God's blessing,
   and I can tell you from bitter experience that it's hopeless,
   a road to nowhere.
But to veer in the opposite direction,
   as though it must be all or nothing,
   faith *or* works –
   is that really any better?
Not in my book it isn't,
   for what kind of faith is it that doesn't prove itself in action?
The proof of the pudding's in the eating, isn't that what they say?
And didn't Jesus himself teach much the same?
   'Not everyone who says to me, "Lord, Lord",
   will enter the kingdom of heaven,
   but only the one who does the will of my Father in heaven.
'For I was hungry and you gave me no food,
   I was thirsty and you gave me nothing to drink,
   I was a stranger and you did not welcome me,
   naked and you did not give me clothing,
   sick and in prison and you did not visit me.
'I never knew you;
   go away from me, you evil-doers.'
It's disturbing, I know,
   not the kind of thing we like to hear,
   but it was Jesus who said it, not me,
   so I reckon we'd do well to listen.
Of course we'll fail sometimes,
   I realise that,
   and of course we'll always finally be dependent on his grace –
   without that we'd all be sunk, no hope for any of us –
   but that doesn't mean our actions aren't important.
Think otherwise and you're in for a rude awakening.
We need faith *and* works,
   for they're two sides of the same coin,
   either of them without the other equally useless,
   a pale imitation of the truth.
Ignore me if you want to,
   it's up to you,
   only remember this:

if what you practise is different from what you preach –
your words saying one thing but your deeds another –
then it's not just the world that will see through you,
it will be God as well.

Prayer

Lord,
    to our shame we know that our deeds
    all too rarely match up to our words.
We are full of fine-sounding ideals,
    of lofty talk about serving others,
    loving our neighbour,
    taking the way of the Cross,
    but our actions put across a very different message.
The reality is that there is little in our lives
    to set us apart from anyone else,
    scant evidence of the faith we profess
    or the Christ we claim to represent.
Forgive us, for until we learn to practise what we preach
    few will take notice of the gospel.
Forgive us for making the good news seem like empty rhetoric
    rather than the word of life,
    and help us in the days ahead
    to show the truth of what we believe
    through the things we do and the people we are.
Teach us not simply to proclaim Christ,
    but to help make him real,
    to the glory of his name.
Amen.

98

SENTIMENTAL RUBBISH, THAT'S WHAT SOME WILL ACCUSE ME OF

John

Reading: 1 John 4:7-21

Beloved, let us love one another, because love is from God; everyone who loves is born of God and knows God. Whoever does not love does not know God, for God is love. God's love was revealed among us in this way: God sent his only Son into the world so that we might live through him. In this is love, not that we loved God but that he loved us and sent his Son to be the atoning sacrifice for our sins. Beloved, since God loved us so much, we also ought to love one another. No one has ever seen God; if we love one another, God lives in us, and his love is perfected in us.

By this we know that we abide in him and he in us, because he has given us of his Spirit. And we have seen and do testify that the Father has sent his Son as the Saviour of the world. God abides in those who confess that Jesus is the Son of God, and they abide in God. So we have known and believe the love that God has for us.

God is love, and those who abide in love abide in God, and God abides in them. Love has been perfected among us in this: that we may have boldness on the day of judgement, because as he is, so are we in this world. There is no fear in love, but perfect love casts out fear; for fear has to do with punishment, and whoever fears has not reached perfection in love. We love because he first loved us. Those who say, 'I love God', and hate their brothers and sisters, are liars, for those who do not love a brother or sister whom they have seen, cannot love God whom they have not seen. The commandment we have from him is this: those who love God must love their brothers and sisters also.

Meditation

Sentimental rubbish, that's what some will accuse me of,
    another airy-fairy spiel about 'love',
    whatever that's supposed to mean.
And I can see their point,

for we do use the word loosely,
   enough sometimes to cover a multitude of sins.
Yet I'm sorry, but when it comes to God
   there's no other word that will do,
     for God *is* love!
It's as simple,
   as straightforward,
   as uncomplicated as that –
   the one description that says it all,
   and if you lose that simple truth, you lose everything.
Not that you'd think it, mind you, to hear some people talk,
   the picture they paint altogether different.
A God of wrath, they say,
   of justice, righteousness, punishment,
   sometimes jealous,
   often forbidding,
   remote, holy, set apart.
He *is* those, of course –
   or at least he can be when necessary –
   but never out of malice,
   only in love.
He longs to bless, not punish,
   to give, rather than take away;
   his nature is always to have mercy,
   to show kindness,
   to fill our lives with good things.
If you see him otherwise,
   as some vengeful ogre intent on destroying you,
   then you don't know him,
   for I tell you, God *is* love –
   all the law,
   all the commandments,
   all our faith summed up in that small but wonderful word.
And though I can't put it into words,
   you'll understand what I mean if you *do* know him,
   for his love will flow in you, through you and from you,
   touching every part of your life.
No, we don't deserve such goodness,
   not for a moment,
   for we'll continue to fail him,
   our love always imperfect;
   but isn't that just the point,

the thing which makes love so special?
It *does* cover a multitude of sins! –
    cleansing,
    renewing,
    restoring,
    forgiving –
    refusing to let go come what may.
That's the God we serve,
    the sort of being he is –
    and if that isn't love, I don't know what is!

Prayer

Lord God,
    we use many words to describe you,
    many terms in an attempt sum up all you are
    and all you mean.
We speak of your power, your might, your majesty
    as we try to express your greatness.
We call you eternal, everlasting, infinite
    in an effort to convey your timelessness.
We speak of your justice, righteousness and holiness
    as we strive to give voice to your otherness.
We call you Creator, Father, Redeemer
    as we seek to articulate your goodness.
Yet always our words fall short,
    pointing to part but not all of the truth.
But we praise you that there is one word that says it all,
    which is able to encapsulate your mystery and wonder,
    your sovereignty and transcendence,
    your mercy and faithfulness –
    that little word 'love'.
Overworked, misapplied, misunderstood we know it to be,
    but with you it says it all,
    for it is your whole nature, your whole purpose
    and your whole being.
In that knowledge may we live each day,
    assured that, whatever may be, your love will always enfold us
    until it finally conquers all.
Lord God, we praise you,
    through Jesus Christ our Lord.
Amen.

99

'SHAME ON THEM!' THEY SAID

Jude

Reading: Jude 1-4, 16-25

Jude, a servant of Jesus Christ and brother of James. To those who are called, who are beloved in God the Father and kept safe for Jesus Christ: may mercy, peace, and love be yours in abundance.

Beloved, while eagerly preparing to write to you about the salvation we share, I find it necessary to write and appeal to you to contend for the faith that was once for all entrusted to the saints. For certain intruders have stolen in among you, people who long ago were designated for this condemnation as ungodly, who pervert the grace of our God into licentiousness and deny our only Master and Lord, Jesus Christ.

These are grumblers and malcontents; they indulge their own lusts; they are bombastic in speech, flattering people to their own advantage. But you, beloved, must remember the predictions of the apostles of our Lord Jesus Christ; for they said to you, 'In the last time there will be scoffers, indulging their own ungodly lusts.' It is these worldly people, devoid of the Spirit, who are causing divisions. But you, beloved, build yourselves up on your most holy faith; pray in the Holy Spirit; keep yourselves in the love of God; look forward to the mercy of our Lord Jesus Christ that leads to eternal life. And have mercy on some who are wavering; save others by snatching them out of the fire; and have mercy on still others with fear, hating even the tunic defiled by their bodies.

Now to him who is able to keep you from falling, and to make you stand without blemish in the presence of his glory with rejoicing, to the only God our Saviour, through Jesus Christ our Lord, be glory, majesty, power, and authority, before all time and now and for ever. Amen.

Meditation

'Shame on them!' they said.
   'To think that anyone could be so false, so faithless,
   as to abandon the Lord Jesus Christ.
   How *could* they do it!'
And I could see that they were thirsting for punishment,
   eager that those who had fallen from grace

should pay for it in full.
I knew why, of course.
It wasn't any malice on their part
    so much as their own sense of insecurity,
    the knowledge that it could so easily have been them in their place,
    and very well still could be.
For it wasn't easy keeping faith, not easy at all,
    the pressure to compromise,
    to follow the way of the world,
    always there –
    and the wiles of the enemy more insidious than any of us realised,
    striking through the most unlikely of people.
No, I don't mean those who were openly hostile –
    we could cope with them, for we knew where we stood,
    no reason to be caught unawares.
It's where we least suspected it that temptation invariably struck,
    lurking unseen, unrecognised,
    stealthily chipping away beneath the surface,
    a little here, a little there,
    the attack so subtle that faith was undermined
    before we even began to notice.
Never think you're exempt, for you're not.
We can all stumble, every one of us,
    the darkness much closer than we ever imagine,
    so when someone goes astray, don't set yourself up as judge and jury,
    still less point the accusing finger,
    for next time it could very well be you.
Forgive, as you have been forgiven,
    ask God to have mercy,
    and commit yourself again to Christ,
    who alone is able to keep you from falling,
    to make you stand without blemish in the presence of his glory,
    to protect you from evil, this day and for evermore.
Thanks be to God.

Prayer

Living God,
    so often we underestimate the power of temptation.
'*We* can resist,' we tell ourselves,
    '*we're* strong enough to get by.'

Even when our defences are breached,
  still we make light of the danger.
'It won't matter,' we say. 'Not just this once,
  so long as nobody gets hurt.'
And so it goes on –
  an allowance here, another there –
  until eventually we look back with horror
  to discover how far we have fallen.
Forgive us our weakness,
  and give us strength to stay faithful to you
  despite the pressures to compromise.
And save us from ever judging those
  who *have* succumbed to temptation,
  for there, but for your grace, we may easily go ourselves.
Living God, protect us from evil and keep us from falling;
  through Jesus Christ our Lord.
Amen.

100

I HAD A DREAM LAST NIGHT

John

Reading: Revelation 21:1-4; 22:5

Then I saw a new heaven and a new earth; for the first heaven and the first earth had passed away, and the sea was no more. And I saw the holy city, the new Jerusalem, coming down out of heaven from God, prepared as a bride adorned for her husband. And I heard a loud voice from the throne saying, 'See, the home of God is among mortals. He will dwell with them as their God; they will be his peoples, and God himself will be with them; he will wipe away every tear from their eyes. Death will be no more; mourning and crying and pain will be no more, for the first things have passed away.'

And there will be no more night; they need no light of lamp or sun, for the Lord God will be their light, and they will reign for ever and ever.

Meditation

I had a dream last night,
    a wonderful, astonishing dream –
    so real,
    so vivid,
    that it will live with me for the rest of my days.
I caught a glimpse of God,
    enthroned in majesty,
    encircled by the great company of heaven,
    and there at his right hand,
    exalted,
    lifted up in splendour,
    our Lord Jesus Christ,
    King of kings and Lord of lords!
It was wonderful,
    breathtaking,
    indescribable.
Yet I have to share it with you somehow –
    clutching at metaphors,

searching for the right words,
    but at least giving you some idea of what I saw.
Why? I hear you say.
What does it matter if it was only a dream?
And I take your point.
Yet I have this feeling, deep within,
    no – more than just a feeling – this certainty,
    that God was speaking to me through that dream;
    speaking to *me*,
    to *you*,
    to everyone with ears to hear and a mind to listen.
He was telling us that in all the chaos of this humdrum world;
    all the changes and chances of this uncertain life;
    despite all the pain,
    all the suffering,
    all the evil,
    all the sorrow,
    everything that seems to fight against him,
    God is there,
    slowly but surely working out his purpose.
And one day,
    in the fullness of time,
    his kingdom will come
    and his will shall be done.
Don't ask me when, for I can't tell you that.
But though we may not see it
    and though we may not feel it,
    I am assured that he will triumph.
Joy will take the place of sorrow.
Life will follow death.
Love will be victorious!

Prayer

Eternal and sovereign God,
    you have promised that one day there will be an end
    to everything that frustrates your will and denies your love.
You promise us a kingdom
    in which there will be no more hatred,
    no more sorrow and no more suffering;
    a kingdom of everlasting peace

filled with light and love and happiness.
You promise that death itself shall be overcome
    and we shall be raised to life eternal,
      one with all your people from every place and time,
      and one with you.
That great picture seems like a dream sometimes,
    faced by the cold realities of life now,
      and yet we know that what you have promised shall be done.
So may that vision burn bright in our hearts –
    a constant source of comfort and inspiration
      as we journey in faith towards that final goal.
Walk with us and see us safely through,
    until that time when your word is fulfilled,
    your will is done
    and your kingdom comes in all its glory;
    through Jesus Christ our Lord.
Amen.

SECTION TWO

SERVICES

ADVENT (1)

Suggested visual material	Jesus of Nazareth 1 In the Beginning The Life of Christ I Jesus, the Child Come, let us adore
Music	*Christmas Concerto (First movement)* Corelli
Introduction	We are here to celebrate the first Sunday in Advent; a day which is almost unique in the Christian calendar, for it calls us, in a way few other days can, to consider both past, present and future. It looks back to the coming of Jesus Christ; not just his birth in Bethlehem, but the promises of God made long before to Abraham and his people across the centuries. It looks forward to his coming again; that day when he will return in glory to establish his kingdom and reign victorious. And in the light of both these perspectives, it urges us to reflect on the present moment; to examine the life we are living, and then to ask ourselves, quite simply: have we received the joy Christ offers, and are we ready to welcome him should he return here and now? Hear then the words of Scripture and consider what God is saying about *your* past, *your* present and *your* future – in other words, what Advent is saying to *you*.
Lighting of Advent candle	
Hymn	*O come, O come, Emmanuel* *Sing we the King who is coming to reign*
Prayer	Gracious God, we come to reflect on your age-old promises, your sovereign purpose, your constant working within human history. We remember that you brought this world into being,

guiding your people across the centuries,
despite repeated rebellion and disobedience;
and we rejoice that, in love,
you took on human flesh,
coming to our world through Jesus Christ.
We remember his birth in Bethlehem,
his life and ministry,
his death and resurrection,
and we celebrate his living presence with us now,
through his Spirit.
Open our hearts to everything you would say to us
through this day and season,
so that we may understand your love
more completely,
and serve you more faithfully;
through Christ our Lord.
Amen.

Slides and music   *Gloria (Missa Ouer natus est nobis)* Tallis
during which John 1:1-5, 10-14 is read

Meditation 3   *'Where did it all start?'* – John the Apostle

Silence

Hymn   *Where do Christmas songs begin*
The light of the morning is breaking

Slides and music   *Dies irae (Requiem)* Mozart
during which Mark 13:3-13 is read

Meditation 42   *It was a chilling picture he gave us* – Andrew

Silence

Slides and music   *Trumpet Voluntary* Clarke
during which Psalm 24:7-10 is read

Meditation 2   *The Messiah – not coming?* – A Zealot

Silence

Prayer   Lord Jesus Christ,
  as you came once so you shall come again
  to establish your kingdom
  and to fulfil the purpose of the one who sent you.
Help us to learn from your first coming –
  to remember that, despite the long years
  of expectation
  and the desire of so many to see you,
  there were few who found room for you
  when you finally came.
Save us, then, from complacency,
  and teach us to live each day to your glory,
  happy at each moment to stand in your presence,
  and ready to welcome you
  on the day of your return.
In your name we pray.
Amen.

Hymn   *Hark, the glad sound*
Come, thou long-expected Jesus

Blessing

Music   *Christmas Concerto (Third movement)* Corelli

ADVENT (2)

Suggested visual material	Jesus of Nazareth 1, 3, 4 and 5 In the Beginning Jesus, the Child Come, let us adore
Music	*Sinfonia (Messiah)* Handel (excerpt)

Introduction We come today to hear again familiar words of scripture, words which pointed centuries beforehand to the coming of Jesus Christ, the Word made flesh. We come rejoicing that God still speaks today, through the same scriptures and the same Lord, able to challenge and guide, to encourage and inspire, to comfort and bless, to teach and nurture. We come, seeking to understand more of everything God has spoken across the centuries, and so asking that we may hear his voice today; his word speaking to our lives, here and now.

Lighting of Advent candles

Hymn *Of the Father's heart begotten*
There's a light upon the mountains

Prayer Gracious God,
    your word was in the beginning
    and shall continue until the end of time.
It brought life itself into existence,
    and controls the destiny
    of everything you have created.
What you have decreed shall be,
    for no word of yours returns to you empty.
Help us, then, to listen to what you would say to us
    today and throughout this season of Advent.
Open our ears,
    open our hearts,
    open our minds,

so that we may hear your voice
and respond in joyful service;
through Jesus Christ our Lord.
Amen.

Slides and music	*Il riposo – per il Santissimo Natale (Concerto for strings)* Vivaldi – during which Isaiah 9:2, 6-7 is read
Meditation 1	*'The people who walked in darkness'* – Resident of Jerusalem
Silence	
Hymn	*Thou art the everlasting Word* *Hail to the Lord's anointed*
Slides and music	*Prelude in C sharp minor* Rachmaninov during which Matthew 10:16-23, 34-39 is read
Meditation 41	*I thought he might be the one we were waiting for* – Judas Iscariot
Silence	
Slides and music	*Come, Lord (Fountain of Life)* Rizza during which Revelation 21:1-4; 22:5 is read
Meditation 100	*I had a dream last night* – John
Silence	
Prayer	Living God,

you spoke, and the world was brought
into being –
the heavens and the earth,
the sea and dry land,
night and day,
life in all its variety and abundance.
You spoke again in the book of the law,
the poetry of the psalms,
the wisdom of the teacher,
the chronicling of history

and the message of the prophets,
revealing your will,
proclaiming your purpose.
You spoke through Jesus Christ,
the Word made flesh,
through those who witnessed
to his life and ministry
and those who shared in the building
of his Church.
You have spoken throughout history,
through preaching and teaching,
through study and quiet devotion,
through prayer and fellowship,
through the wonder of this world,
and still you speak today,
your word ever old but always new,
able to redeem, renew and restore.
Speak to us now, we pray.
Help us to use this season of Advent
to listen more carefully to your voice,
and so to walk with you more closely,
this and every day,
through Jesus Christ our Lord.
Amen.

Hymn   *The King shall come when morning dawns*
               Earth was waiting, spent and restless

Blessing

Music   *Sinfonia (Messiah)* Handel (excerpt)

Advent (3)

Suggested visual material	Jesus of Nazareth 1 and 2 In the Beginning The Life of Christ I Jesus, the Child Come, let us adore
Music	*Earl of Salisbury* Byrd (arranged Graves)
Introduction	We focus today, this third Sunday in Advent, on John the Baptist, the one who came to bear witness to the light. He stands as a bridge between the old and the new, his unforgettable ministry paving the way for the dawn of the kingdom which Christ was shortly to bring. And in that ministry we see exemplified the call of God to each and every member of his Church since, for the task of witnessing to Christ is as vital today as it has ever been. Many have yet to hear, still more have yet to respond – a desert of doubt and disbelief lies waiting. Are we ready to follow in John's footsteps and to be a voice in the wilderness, a witness to the light of the world?
Lighting of Advent candles	
Hymn	*Pull back the veil on the dawn of creation* *Search for the infant born in a stable*

Prayer	Loving God,
	    you called your servant John
	    to go out into the wilderness
	    to prepare the way of the Lord;
	    not to be the light you promised,
	    but to point to the one who was coming,
	    who would bring light to all.
	You call us in turn to share in this responsibility,
	    to prepare the way of Christ
	    in the wilderness of the world today.

Give us the courage, the faith and the humility
    we need to respond,
    and may our lives bear witness in word and deed
    to the life-giving power of Christ,
    in whose name we pray.
Amen.

Slides and music   *Ovysen and Kolyada Procession* Rimsky-Korsakov
during which Luke 1:5-20 is read

Meditation 4   *I wanted to believe it, honestly!* – Zechariah

Silence

Slides and music   *Schlafe, mein Liebster (Christmas Oratorio)* J. S. Bach
during which Luke 1:24-25, 39-45 is read

Meditation 5   *Was it just a coincidence?* – Elizabeth

Silence

Hymn   *A great and mighty wonder*
Behold, the mountain of the Lord

Slides and music   *Videntes stellam (Quatre motets pour le temps de Noël)*
Poulenc – during which Luke 1:57-58, 67-80 is read

Meditation 6   *How did we feel about him?* – Zechariah

Silence

Prayer   Sovereign God,
    we thank you for all those
    who have borne witness to your coming in Christ,
    all who have shared their faith
    so that others might come to know him
    and experience his love for themselves.
We thank you for those
    from whom we first heard the gospel,
    and all those who have nurtured
    and encouraged us in the years following.
Help us, now, to play our part

ADVENT (3)   351

in that continuing ministry,
sharing what Christ means with those around us,
and making known the way he has worked
in our lives.
Send us out in his name,
to his glory.
Amen.

Hymn   *On Jordan's bank the Baptist's cry*
              Born in the night

Blessing

Music   *Earl of Salisbury* Byrd (arranged Graves)

Carol Service

This service follows a traditional pattern of lessons and carols, supplemented by meditations developing the themes of the readings. No visual material is recommended for this service.

Music *Sleep, holy babe* Traditional Carol

Introduction 'Let us go now to Bethlehem and see this thing that has taken place, which the Lord has made known to us': the response of the shepherds to the good news of Christ's birth, and the beginning of a night which was to see them returning soon after 'glorifying and praising God for all they had heard and seen, as it had been told them'. We cannot, of course, see quite what they saw, even if we were able to go now to the Holy Land and visit the place where these great events unfolded, but we are here now to listen again to words of scripture which, familiar though they may be, still have the power to speak to us in new and unexpected ways. Let us step back then, and put ourselves in the shoes of those who were part of that extraordinary night of his birth, and let us hear afresh the good news of Jesus Christ, which God continues to make known to us today.

Lighting of Advent Candles

Carol *O come, all ye faithful*

Prayer Gracious God,
at this time of giving and receiving
we remember the greatest gift of all –
your coming to our world in Christ
to live and die among us,
your identifying with humankind
so that we might become your children
and know life in all its fullness.

Help us, as we hear again the Christmas message,
   to understand more fully
   the sheer magnitude of all you have given,
   and as we celebrate this glad season
   help us to receive Christ into our hearts,
   and offer to you, through him,
   our heartfelt praise and joyful service.
Amen.

Reading	Luke 1:26-34
Meditation 8	*'You've got it wrong,' I told him* – Mary
Carol	*The angel Gabriel from heaven came*
Reading	Matthew 1:18-25
Meditation 7	*It was the strangest of dreams* – Joseph
Carol	*O little town of Bethlehem*
Reading	Luke 2:1-7
Meditation 10	*He looked so tiny lying there* – Mary
Carol	*Child in the manger*
Reading	Luke 2:8-14
Meditation 11	*Don't talk to strange men* – Shepherd
Carol	*While shepherds watched their flocks by night*
Reading	Luke 2:15-20
Meditation 12	*I had mixed feelings, to tell the truth* – Mary
Carol	*The virgin Mary had a baby boy*
Reading	Matthew 2:1-12
Meditation 16	*Do you know what we gave him?* – Magi

Carol   *The first Nowell*

Reading   John 1:1-5, 10-14

Meditation 3   *'Where did it all start?'* – John

Prayer   God of Mary and Joseph,
      God of the shepherds and the magi,
      God of the baby lying in a manger,
      God with *us*,
      touch our hearts
      with the living presence of Christ,
      fill us with the love and joy
      which he alone can bring,
      and send us out to proclaim his kingdom,
      glad tidings for all.
In his name we pray.
Amen.

Carol   *Hark, the herald-angels sing*

Blessing

Music   *The Shepherds' Farewell* Berlioz

CHRISTMAS

Suggested visual material	Jesus of Nazareth 1 In the Beginning The Life of Christ I Jesus, the Child Come, let us adore
Music	*On Christmas night all Christians sing (Sussex Carol)*
Introduction	'I am bringing you good news of great joy for all the people: to you is born this day in the city of David a Saviour, who is the Messiah, the Lord' – words announcing to the shepherds the glad tidings of the birth of Jesus Christ. But they are words not only to the shepherds, nor simply confined to that day long ago, but words for us today, spoken to you, to me; to everyone – 'good news of great joy for all the people'. That is the wonder of Christmas; the one thing behind all the trivia with which we have surrounded this festival that gives it meaning – the dawn of God's kingdom through the birth of his Son, the coming of the Word made flesh; his sharing our humanity so that we may share his eternity. Come then and hear again the familiar story, for to *you* has been born in the city of David a Saviour, who is the Messiah, the Lord!
Lighting of Advent candles	
Hymn	*Good Christians all, rejoice*

Prayer	Gracious God,
	    we thank you for the good news of Jesus Christ
	    which we celebrate today,
	    the message which brought joy
	    to Mary and Joseph,
	    to shepherds and wise men,
	    and to so many others

in the years following his birth.
We thank you that this message has continued
   to be good news for successive generations,
    bringing joy, hope and meaning to untold lives.
Speak to us now and give us ears to hear.
Meet with us now and give us hearts to respond.
So may Christ be born in us today,
   to the glory of your name.
Amen.

Slides and music	*Ave Maria* Schubert during which Luke 1:26-38 is read
Meditation 9	*Was it all a dream?* – Mary
Silence	
Hymn	*Once in royal David's city* *O come, all ye faithful*
Slides and music	*L'Enfance du Christ (The Shepherds' Farewell)* Berlioz during which Luke 2:8-20 is read
Meditation 11	*Don't talk to strange men* – Shepherd
Silence	
Hymn	*God rest you merry, gentlemen* *The first Nowell*
Slides and music	*The Three Kings* Carol during which Matthew 2:1-12 is read
Meditation 15	*Well, we made it at last!* – Magi
Silence	
Reading	Matthew 2:13-18
Meditation 17	*It was as though all hell was let loose* – Mother in Bethlehem

Prayer   Lord Jesus Christ,
          you came to our world
          and it did not know you,
          you came to your own people
          and they would not accept you,
          you came to the inn
          and there was no room for you there
          as there has been no room so often
          among so many people.
Help us to make room for you this Christmas-time,
          to welcome you gladly
          at the heart of our celebrations,
          and to receive you as our Lord and Saviour
          with body, soul and mind.
Lord Jesus Christ,
          come now, and make your home within us.
Amen.

Hymn   *Angels from the realms of glory*
Joy to the world!

Blessing

Music   *For unto us a child is born (Messiah)* Handel

EPIPHANY

Suggested visual material	Jesus of Nazareth 1 and 2 The Life of Christ I Bread and Wine Jesus, the Child
Music	*Sie Werden aus Saba alle kommen* *(Cantata No. 65, Epiphany)* J. S. Bach

Introduction   After Christmas, Epiphany; after shepherds, wise men – the end of a marathon journey and an arrival long after the events of Bethlehem. But one thing was unchanged – the light which had begun to shine then was shining still, as strongly and brightly as that first day; a light which nothing, not even death itself, would ever be able to extinguish. We come to remember that journey of the magi, and to consider the meaning both of their pilgrimage and the gifts they brought. We come to give our homage to the one at the centre of it all, Jesus Christ, the light of the nations, the Saviour of the world.

Hymn   *As with gladness men of old*
Let all mortal flesh keep silence

Prayer   Light of the world,
    shine in our darkness today.
Where there is pain and sorrow
    may the brilliance of your love bring joy.
Where there is sickness and suffering,
    may sunshine come after the storm.
Where there is greed and corruption,
    may your radiance scatter the shadows.
Where there is hatred and bitterness,
    may your brightness dispel the clouds.
Lord Jesus Christ, light of the world,
    rise again upon us we pray,
    and illuminate the darkness of this world

through your life-giving grace.
In your name we ask it.
Amen.

Slides and music   *Earl of Salisbury* Byrd (arranged Graves)
during which Luke 2:21-24, 39-40 is read

Meditation 13   *There was something about that couple* – Priest

Silence

Slides and music   *Sleep, holy babe* Carol
during which Luke 2:25-35 is read

Meditation 14   *It was as though a wave of peace engulfed me* – Simeon

Silence   *I lift my eyes to the quiet hills*
Peace, perfect peace
Infant holy, infant lowly

Slides and music   *The Three Kings* Carol
during which Matthew 2:1-12 is read

Meditation 15   *Well, we made it at last* – Magi

Silence

Prayer   Loving God,
    inspire us, as you inspired the magi,
    to journey in faith,
    following where you would lead
    until we reach our goal.
Though we do not know the way ahead,
    and though the path may be hard,
    keep us walking in the light,
    travelling steadfastly to our journey's end.
Teach us to live as a pilgrim people,
    fixing our eyes on Jesus,
    and running the race with perseverance
    for the joy set before us,
    until that day when we kneel

before the throne of grace,
and offer our homage to Christ our Lord.
Amen.

Hymn   *Brightest and best are the sons of the morning*
The light of the morning is breaking

Blessing

Music   *Sie Werden aus Saba alle kommen (Epiphany)* J. S. Bach

LENT (1)

Suggested visual material	Jesus of Nazareth 2 The Life of Christ II
Music	*Comfort ye my people (Messiah)* Handel
Introduction	We are here in the season of Lent, a time which calls us to stop, take stock and reflect on the health or otherwise of our faith. It recalls the temptation of Jesus in the wilderness, and invites us to consider our own response to temptation in turn. It reminds us of his steadfast commitment to the way of the cross, and asks if we are willing to bear the cost of discipleship. It speaks of the prayer and devotion which sustained Jesus during those forty days and nights of testing, and from there urges us to make time and space for God a priority in our own lives. Today we listen to some of the accounts of that time in the desert, exploring what it meant for Jesus, what it meant for John the Baptist, and what it means for us today. We look back, asking that God might lead us forward.
Hymn	*When he was baptised in Jordan* *O love, how deep, how broad, how high*

Prayer	Loving God,
	    we try to look at ourselves openly and honestly,
	    but we find it so hard,
	    for we are so often blind to our faults,
	    closed to anything which disturbs the image
	    we have of ourselves.
	So we come to you,
	    appealing to your grace and mercy.
	Search us, we pray –
	    forgive us our sins,
	    cleanse us of our iniquities,
	    have mercy on our weakness,
	    and through your love create a clean heart

and a right spirit within us.
Remake us,
    redeem us,
    restore us,
    and grant that we may live as your people,
    a new creation in Christ,
        to the glory of your name.
Amen.

Slides and music	*O thou that tellest (Messiah)* Handel during which Mark 1:9-13 is read
Meditation 18	*It took me by surprise* – John the Baptist
Silence	
Slides and music	*Mars (The Planets)* Holst during which Luke 4:1-13 is read
Meditation 19	*I thought I had him* – The Devil
Silence	
Hymn	*Forty days and forty nights* *O changeless Christ, for ever new*
Slides and music	*And the glory of the Lord (Messiah)* Handel during which Luke 4:14-15 is read
Meditation 20	*He was back at last!* – John the Baptist
Silence	
Slides and music	*Canticle de Jean Racine* Fauré during which Luke 7:18b-19, 21-23 is read
Meditation 21	*Shall I tell you something strange?* – John the Baptist
Silence	
Prayer	Gracious God, deal mercifully with us, we pray.

Give us the courage we need
 to see ourselves as we really are,
 the faith we need to see ourselves as we can be,
 the wisdom we need to discern your will,
 the humility we need to accept your correction,
 and the commitment we need
 to respond to your guidance.
We know our faults,
 we recognise our need for help,
 and so we come to you,
 dependent on your grace.
Gracious God,
 have mercy,
 in the name of Christ.
Amen.

Hymn *It is a thing most wonderful*
     Lord Jesus, for my sake you come

Blessing

Music *Lord of my life (Fountain of Life)* Rizza

LENT (2)

Suggested visual material Jesus of Nazareth 3, 4 and 5
The Life of Christ II
The Gospel: Life of Jesus

Music *Come to me (Fountain of Life)* Rizza

Introduction Who was Jesus? What lay at the heart of his message? Why had he come? What did it all mean? These and a host of other questions must have teemed in the minds of all those who glimpsed anything of the earthly ministry of Jesus. No one who heard his words or witnessed his actions could have been untouched by the experience, for here was a man who spoke and acted with an authority no one has ever matched. The result may have been more questions than answers, as much rejection as acceptance, but one thing is clear: when people came into contact with Jesus they had to decide for themselves just who it was they were dealing with; there could be no sitting on the fence. And as we listen today to words of Scripture and reflect upon the encounters they record, the same challenge is put to us: what do we make of this man and his message?

Hymn *Jesus, name above all names*
Love divine, all love's excelling

Prayer Lord Jesus Christ,
we remember today how the crowds
listened spellbound to your teaching,
how they gazed in wonder
as you demonstrated your love in action,
how they gave thanks to God
as you transformed the lives of all
who came to you seeking your help.
Come again to our lives,
to your Church,
and to your world today.

May your power be seen,
 your love displayed,
 your forgiveness received
 and your word proclaimed.
Break through the complacency of our discipleship,
 and fire us with renewed commitment,
 restored vision
 and revitalised faith,
 so that we may live to your glory,
 and lead others to a saving knowledge of your
  love.
For your name's sake we ask it.
Amen.

Slides and music	*Träumerei* Schumann during which Matthew 5:38-45 is read
Meditation 22	*Can you believe what he told us?* – Listener to the Sermon on the Mount
Silence	
Slides and music	*Intermezzo (Carmen, Suite No 1)* Bizet during which Matthew 6:31-33; 7:7-11 is read
Meditation 23	*'Ask,' he said, 'and you will receive'* – Another listener to the Sermon on the Mount
Silence	
Hymn	*Seek ye first the kingdom of God* *Yesu, Yesu, fill us with your love*
Slides and music	*He was despised and rejected (Messiah)* Handel during which Matthew 13:54-58 is read
Meditation 36	*Do you know what they're saying about him* – Resident of Nazareth
Silence	
Slides and music	*Nocturne in B flat minor* Chopin during which Mark 12:28-31 is read

Meditation 39   *He made it all sound so easy* – The Scribe

Silence

Slides and music   *Credo (Mass in B minor)* J. S. Bach
during which Mark 9:14-24 is read

Meditation 29   *Lord, I do believe* – Father of the epileptic boy

Prayer   Loving God,
  we do not know all there is to know,
  or understand all there is to understand,
  but one thing we are sure of:
  that in Jesus Christ we have met with you,
  experiencing your love,
  rejoicing in your mercy,
  receiving your guidance,
  thrilling to your blessing.
There is much still to learn
  and much that will always be beyond us,
  but we have seen and heard enough
  to convince us of your grace,
  and we have tasted sufficient of your goodness
  to know that nothing can ever separate us
  from your love revealed in Christ.
Help us to live as he taught us,
  to love as he urged us,
  to serve as he showed us
  and to trust as he told us.
So may we live in him and he live in us,
  to the glory of your name. Amen.

Hymn   *Let there be love shared among us*
Let there be peace on earth

Blessing

Music   *Jesus, you are the way (Fountain of Life)* Rizza

LENT (3)

Suggested visual material	Jesus of Nazareth 2 and 4 The Life of Christ II The Gospel: Life of Jesus
Music	*Intermezzo (Carmen, Suite No. 1)* Bizet

Introduction

For many people Lent is associated with giving something up. It is seen as an opportunity, perhaps, for kicking that unwanted habit, for going at last on that long-intended diet, or for denying oneself those unnecessary extra luxuries. All such acts of discipline may have their place, but they give a very one-sided view of this season, for, if anything, it should be about taking something on; committing oneself, in the words of Jesus, to going the extra mile. That doesn't mean taking work on for work's sake. Rather, it is about resolving to follow Christ more faithfully, a determination to give him our wholehearted discipleship. It might mean more disciplined devotion, perhaps more practical service, maybe more effective witness, or possibly the offering of previously unused gifts. Whatever it is, it is more than giving something *up*; above all, it is giving something *back* to the one who gave us his all. Consider today what Christ has done for you; then ask what you can do for him, and use Lent as an opportunity to respond.

Hymn

O loving Lord, you are for ever seeking
Take this moment, sign and space

Prayer

God of peace,
    quieten our hearts
    and help us to be still in your presence.
We find this so hard to do,
    for our lives are full of noise and confusion,
    a host of demands and responsibilities

seeming to press in upon us from every side,
consuming our time and sapping our energy.
We run here and there,
doing this and that,
always something else to think about,
another pressing matter
demanding our attention –
and then suddenly,
in the middle of it all,
we stop and realise we have forgotten you,
the one we depend on to give us strength
and calm our spirits.
God of peace,
we offer you now this little space we have made
in the frantic scramble of life.
Meet with us,
so that we may return to our daily routine
with a new perspective,
an inner tranquillity,
and a resolve to make time for you regularly,
so that we may use all our time more effectively
in the service of your kingdom;
through Jesus Christ our Lord.
Amen.

Slides and music   *Silent, surrendered (Fountain of Life)* Rizza
during which Mark 5:25-34 is read

Meditation 27   *I was sick* – The woman who touched Jesus' cloak

Silence

Slides and music   *Lord of my life (Fountain of Life)* Rizza
during which Mark 7:24-30 is read

Meditation 28   *Was he just testing me?* – The Syrophoenician woman

Silence

Slides and music   *Libera me Domine (Requiem)* Verdi
during which John 8:2-11 is read

Meditation 32	*I expected him to condemn me like all the rest –* The woman caught in adultery
Silence	
Hymn	*I know not why God's wondrous grace* *I am trusting you, Lord Jesus*
Slides and music	*Kyrie eleison (Fountain of Life)* Rizza during which Luke 21:1-4 is read
Meditation 37	*I was ashamed, if I'm truthful –* The widow at the treasury
Silence	
Slides and music	*Jesus, you are the way (Fountain of Life)* Rizza during which Mark 14:3-9 is read
Meditation 40	*Was it guilt that made them turn on me? –* The woman who anointed Jesus' head
Silence	

Prayer   Lord Jesus Christ,
   you spoke,
   and you brought hope, joy, comfort, forgiveness;
   you touched,
   and you brought love, peace, healing, wholeness.
Come now,
   and speak again,
   bringing your word of life
   into our parched lives and our weary world.
Come now,
   and reach out again,
   bringing your touch of love to our aching hearts
   and to all who cry out for help.
Where there is despair, sorrow, hurt or guilt
   may your voice renew.
Where there is loneliness, turmoil, pain and sickness
   may your hand restore.
Lord Jesus Christ,

you came once,
you shall come again,
but we ask you: come now,
and bring your kingdom closer here on earth.
We ask it in your name.
Amen.

Hymn   *Will you come and follow me?*
            From heaven you came, helpless babe

Blessing

Music   *Intermezzo (Carmen, Suite No. 1)* Bizet

Palm Sunday

Suggested visual material

Jesus of Nazareth 5
The Life of Christ III and IV
He Carries our Cross (a)

Music

Gloria in Excelsis Deo (Gloria) Vivaldi

Introduction

Palm Sunday is one of the enigmas in the Christian calendar. It speaks of joy and celebration, and of worshipping Jesus as the King of kings, and yet of course it leads us into the events of Holy Week, the memory of sorrow and suffering, and finally death on a cross. We cannot think of one without the other, and any talk of the majesty of Jesus must be understood in the light of all that followed. The one we serve came to serve others. The Lord of life endured the darkness of death. The way to the throne involved the costly path of sacrifice. It is easy enough to sing Christ's praises and acknowledge him as Lord; it is a different matter to take up our cross and follow him. Yet that is the homage he asks of us and the challenge this day brings. As we offer today our glad hosannas let us ask ourselves if we are ready also to offer ourselves in his service.

Hymn

Listen to the shouts of praises
Make way

Prayer

Lord Jesus Christ,
    you had no interest in serving yourself,
    only in serving others;
    you did not desire your own glory,
    only the glory of him who sent you,
    and because of that God has highly exalted you,
    giving you the name that is above every name.
Teach us today the true nature
    of kingship, service and authority,
    and so help us to honour you as you desire,

through loving God with heart, mind and soul,
and loving our neighbour as ourselves.
So may we build your kingdom,
until you return in glory
and gather all things to yourself.
Amen.

Slides and music *Trumpet Voluntary* Clarke
during which Psalm 24:7-10 is read

Meditation 2 *The Messiah – not coming? –* A Zealot

Silence

Hymn *Ride on! ride on in majesty!*
Majesty, worship his majesty

Slides and music *Berceuse* Godard
during which Luke 19:29-40 is read

Meditation 43 *Hello, I thought, what's going on here? –*
One of the owners of the colt ridden by Jesus

Silence

Slides and music *Osanna in excelsis* J. S. Bach
during which Matthew 21:1-11 is read

Meditation 44 *You should have heard them –* Simon the Zealot

Silence

Prayer Lord Jesus Christ,
servant of all,
friend of all,
saviour of all,
ruler of all,
receive our worship.
To you be glory and honour,
praise and thanksgiving,
this day and for evermore.
Amen.

Hymn   *All glory, laud and honour*
         Meekness and majesty

Blessing

Music   *Rex Tremendae (Requiem)* Mozart

MONDAY OF HOLY WEEK

Suggested visual material	Jesus of Nazareth 2 and 5 The Life of Christ 2 He Carries our Cross
Music	*Adagio (Oboe Concerto)* Marcello
Introduction	Holy Monday, and already the events of Palm Sunday must have seemed both to Jesus and his disciples like some distant memory, for the atmosphere now was changing swiftly, fuelled by the fury of Jesus shown in the temple. The spectre of the cross was starting to cast its shadow. So why did Jesus act as he did? What led him to prejudice the welcome he'd so spontaneously received? How can we explain not only his apparent courting of disaster, but the fact that, within a few days, one of his own disciples would turn against him to the point of betrayal, and the hosannas of the crowd would melt away as though they had never been? To look for an answer we must go back with Jesus to the start of his ministry and the time of his temptation in the wilderness, for in the issues raised there we see foreshadowed the decisions which would shape this week leading up to the cross; decisions which Jesus had taken at the beginning, fully aware of where they all would end.
Hymn	*All you that pass by*

Prayer	Loving God,
	    through your Son you walked the way of the
	        cross,
	    each step leading you inexorably to suffering,
	    humiliation and death.
	We know it,
	    and yet we continue to marvel,
	    for such love defies human logic,
	    and transcends anything we can give in return.
	Open our hearts during this day and this week,

                    so that we might glimpse again
                    the wonder of your grace.
            Give us insight into all it involved,
                    all it cost,
                    and all it meant;
                    and through that same grace, we ask you,
                    help us to respond.
            Amen.

Slides and music   *Mars (The Planets)* Holst
                    during which Luke 4:1-13 is read

Meditation 19   *I thought I had him* – The Devil

Silence

Slides and music   *Prelude in C sharp minor* Rachmaninov
                    during which Matthew 10:16-23, 34-39 is read

Meditation 41   *I thought he might be the one we were waiting for* –
                    Judas

Silence

Slides and music   *Finlandia* Sibelius (excerpt)
                    during which Mark 11:15-19 is read

Meditation 45   *He was angry* – James

Silence

Prayer   Lord Jesus Christ,
                    you didn't take the *easy* way
                    as we would have done –
                    the path of popular acclaim,
                    of least resistance –
                    you took the *right* way,
                    the way of truth, love and service,
                    and you followed it faithfully,
                    knowingly,
                    undeterred by the consequences,
                    intent on serving others rather than yourself.

Forgive us that we are so easily led astray,
    thoughts so much for ourselves
    and so little for you.
Forgive us for our willingness to compromise,
    even when we know the way we ought to take.
Strengthen our resolve,
    increase our faith,
    and help us to stay true to our calling
    and true to you,
    to the glory of your name.
Amen.

Hymn   *Love divine, all loves excelling*

Blessing

Music   *Adagio (Oboe Concerto)* Marcello

Tuesday of Holy Week

Suggested visual material	Jesus of Nazareth 2 and 5 The Life of Christ II-IV He Carries our Cross
Music	*Meditation* Massenet
Introduction	Another day, and another step nearer the cross; the ultimate sacrifice, the enormous cost which Christ so willingly paid. But what of our response to him? Today we consider three contrasting reactions: one for whom the cost was too great, another which looked for commensurate reward, and a third representing a spontaneous outpouring of thanksgiving. We may know which of these we would most like to be, but we must ask ourselves which we actually are. In the memorable words of Isaac Watts: 'Were the whole realm of nature mine, that were an offering far too small; love so amazing, so divine, demands my soul, my life, my all.'
Hymn	*Can it be true, the things they say of you?* *Jesus is Lord! Creation's voice proclaims it*

Prayer	Lord Jesus Christ,
	    you gave so much;
	    forgive us that we give so little.
	You refused to count the cost;
	    we resent even the smallest price
	    being asked of us.
	You took the way of others;
	    we take the way of self.
	Lord Jesus,
	    all good, all loving,
	    we have no claim on your goodness,
	    no reason to expect your mercy,
	    yet, knowing all that, still you died for us.
	Have mercy, we pray,
	    and, poor though it may be,
	    accept the discipleship we offer,

and use us in the service of your kingdom,
to the glory of your name.
Amen.

Slides and music   *Pié Jesu (Requiem)* Andrew Lloyd Weber
during which Mark 12:20-27 is read

Meditation 38   *I've never been so embarrassed* – James

Silence

Slides and music   *Adagietto (L'Arlésienne, Suite No. 1) Bizet*
during which Luke 18:18-25 is read

Meditation 34   *It was a lot to ask, wasn't it?* – The rich ruler

Silence

Slides and music   *Jesus, you are the way (Fountain of Life)* Rizza
during which Mark 14:3-9 is read

Meditation 40   *Was it guilt that made them turn on me?* –
The woman who anointed Jesus' head

Silence

Prayer   Gracious God,
we know we can never repay
the love you have shown us,
but we long to show our gratitude
by loving you in return,
by serving you as you desire,
by being the sort of people you call us to be.
Set us free from our preoccupation
with the things of this world,
from our obsession with self,
from the pride, greed and envy
which blind us to all that really matters.
Teach us to live
according to the values of your kingdom,
where it is in giving that we shall receive,
in letting go that we shall find,

in being poor that we shall become rich.
Take us and use us, we pray,
    by your grace,
    through Jesus Christ our Lord.
Amen.

Hymn   *When I survey the wondrous cross*
        All for Jesus, all for Jesus!

Blessing

Music   *Meditation* Massenet

WEDNESDAY OF HOLY WEEK

Suggested visual
material
Jesus of Nazareth 5 and 6
The Life of Christ III
He Carries our Cross

Music
Agnus Dei J. S. Bach

Introduction
Wednesday of Holy Week, and by now, for Jesus, death was almost upon him, his enemies waiting greedily to seize their moment. How would we have felt in his place, knowing the agony his opponents would shortly put him through? I'm not sure we'd like our thoughts repeated! Yet Jesus had told the multitude, 'Love your enemies and pray for those who persecute you.' Could he live by those words when the moment came? The answer, of course, was yes! So how about us? Could we? To answer that, we reflect today on the words of that astonishing challenge; we go on to ask, 'Who were the enemies of Jesus and why were they so against him?'; and we think finally of the impact his life and teaching may have had on those willing to consider their implications, whether friend or foe.

Hymn
The Lord's my shepherd
The King of love my shepherd is

Prayer
Loving God,
        once more we come to worship you,
        not out of tradition or duty,
        but because we want to remember,
        to learn,
        and to understand.
For all our faith,
        all our desire to serve you,
        we are conscious of how weak
        our discipleship has been,
        and we hunger to know you better,
        to grasp more fully
        the love you have shown in Christ,

and to live more in tune
with the example he has shown.
Meet with us, we pray.
May your word of old come to life,
    the message we have heard so often
    speak with new power.
Come now, and work within us,
    that we in turn may work for you,
    through Jesus Christ our Lord.
Amen.

Slides and music   *Träumerei* Schumann
during which Matthew 5:38-45 is read

Meditation 22   *Can you believe what he told us?* –
Listener to the Sermon on the Mount

Silence

Slides and music   *Asturias (Suite Espanol)* Albéniz
during which Mark 2:23-3:6 is read

Meditation 25   *We were lost for words* – Pharisee

Silence

Slides and music   *Adagio un poco mosso (Piano Concerto No. 5)*
Beethoven – during which John 3:1-6; 19:38-42
is read

Meditation 24   *It was dark when I went to him* – Nicodemus

Silence

Prayer   Lord Jesus Christ,
    you didn't just talk about love;
    time and time again you showed it.
And you didn't just love those who loved you;
    you loved your enemies equally,
    those who you knew were intent
    on destroying you by whatever means necessary.
We stand ashamed, in contrast,

our own love so weak,
so limited,
so dependent on its object.
Even loving our friends is hard enough;
to love our enemies is beyond us;
and yet we know that only this
can break the cycle of hatred, suspicion
and fear which so divides our world.
Lord Jesus,
we cannot achieve it ourselves,
but we ask you, move within us,
touch our hearts,
and teach us to love,
for your name's sake.
Amen.

Hymn   *Man of sorrows! wondrous name*
I am trusting you, Lord Jesus

Blessing

Music   *Ave Verum* Mozart

Maundy Thursday Communion (1)

Suggested visual material
Jesus of Nazareth 5 and 6
Oberammergau 1990
The Life of Christ III and IV
He Carries our Cross
Bread and Wine
Man of the Cross

Suggested music
Rather than use separate pieces of music, I have suggested here the use of one continuous piece, excerpts faded in and out as appropriate.

Music
Adagio Albinoni (excerpt – total length 11:27)

Introduction
What must it have been like to have sat with Jesus in the upper room as he broke bread and shared wine, as he prophesied that one of those sitting there would betray him, and as he spoke of his coming death? What must it have been like to see him wrestling with his inner torment in the garden of Gethsemane, betrayed with a kiss and finally taken off before the Sandhedrin? We know the stories so well that we can read them with barely a flicker of emotion, but if we put ourselves into the shoes of those who lived through these events, we can begin to glimpse something of the pain, the shock and the disbelief they must have faced as the events of that astonishing night unfolded. As we break bread and share wine together this evening, imagine yourself there in that upper room, there in the garden watching with his disciples, there fleeing in haste as the soldiers march him away, and marvel afresh at the selfless love, the astonishing sacrifice, which lies at the centre of it all.

Hymn
Let us break bread together on our knees
Great God, your love has called us here

Prayer
Lord Jesus Christ,
    we praise you for your love

which knows no bounds,
your grace which was prepared to suffer so much
for our sakes.
Forgive us that we forget sometimes
how much it all cost you,
the inner turmoil, the sorrow,
the pain you endured to make us whole.
Speak to us afresh through all we share this
evening,
and help us to show our response
not just through these few moments' worship
but through lives offered in service to you.
In your name we pray.
Amen.

Slides and music   *Adagio* Albinoni (excerpt)
during which Matthew 10:16-23, 34-39 is read

Meditation 41   *I thought he might be the one we were waiting for –*
Judas

Silence

Slides and music   *Adagio* Albinoni (excerpt)
during which Luke 22:7-13 is read

Meditation 46   *It was ready for us, just as he'd said it would be* – Peter

**Celebration of
the Eucharist**

Slides and music   *Adagio* Albinoni (excerpt)
during which Luke 22:39-46 is read

Meditation 50   *He was unsure of himself* – Peter

Silence

Slides and music   *Adagio* Albinoni (excerpt)
during which John 18:19-24 is read

Meditation 51   *Angry? You bet I was!* – Annas

Silence

Prayer   Lord Jesus Christ,
> we have broken bread,
> we have shared wine –
> and we have done it,
> together with your people across the centuries,
> in remembrance of you.

You promise that the time will come
> when we share with you
> in your Father's kingdom;
> a time when your will shall be done
> and all things be made new.

Until then, may the memory of your great sacrifice
> shape our lives,
> and guide our footsteps,
> to the glory of your name.

Amen.

Hymn   *From heaven you came, helpless babe*
I will sing the wondrous story

Blessing

Music   *Meditation* Massenet

MAUNDY THURSDAY COMMUNION (2)

Suggested visual material
Jesus of Nazareth 5 and 6
Oberammergau 1990
The Life of Christ III and IV
He Carries our Cross
Bread and Wine
Man of the Cross

Suggested music
Rather than use separate pieces of music, I have suggested here the use of one continuous piece, excerpts faded in and out as appropriate.

Music
Adagio (Symphony No. 2 in E minor)
Rachmaninov (excerpt – total length 14:59)

Introduction
'The Lord Jesus Christ on the night when he was betrayed took a loaf of bread, and when he had given thanks, he broke it and said, "This is my body that is for you. Do this in remembrance of me." In the same way he took the cup also, after supper, saying, "This cup is the new covenant in my blood. Do this, as often as you drink it, in remembrance of me."' (1 Corinthians 11:23b-25). These are words which always have the power to move and inspire us, no matter how many times we hear them. But tonight, of all nights, they have a special poignancy, for we are here to recall that night long ago when the words were first spoken and the chain of events to which they point was to be set into motion. Events which were to reveal evil at its worst and good at its best; hatred at its most ugly and love at its most beautiful. We reflect on those events this evening through focusing on four of those most intimately involved in them – Philip, Judas Iscariot, a soldier from the cohort sent to arrest Jesus, and Annas the high priest. But above all we focus on Jesus – this man who aroused such passion for and against him, such fierce devotion yet such bitter rejection; a man whose unique character demanded a response from all he met, just as it goes on demanding a response from us today.

Hymn   *Now, Jesus, we obey your last and kindest word*
              Lord Jesus Christ, you have come to us

Prayer   Lord Jesus Christ,
              we are here at your invitation –
              here to share, as so many have shared before us,
              ⌐   supper,
                    ct which you commanded us to do
                 of you.
                    member –
                       of all you suffered

                          our love
                          our sacrifice.
                          rate –
                          ve done for us

                       all you go on doing for us
                       achieved there on the cross.

                    d,
                    a wine,
                 body broken,
              your blood shed for us.
              Help us, as we eat and drink together,
                    to receive you more completely into our hearts,
                    to welcome you more fully into our lives,
                    and so to represent you more truly
                    as your body here on earth,
                    until that day when we are wholly one with you,
                    and you are all in all.
              Amen.

Slides and music   *Adagio (Symphony No. 2 in E minor)*
                     Rachmaninov (excerpt)
                     during which Mark 14:17-25 is read

Meditation 47   *He couldn't mean me, surely!* – Philip

Silence

Slides and music	*Adagio (Symphony No. 2 in E minor)* Rachmaninov (excerpt) during which John 13:21-30 is read
Meditation 48	*'Do what you have to do,' he told me* – Judas
Silence	
Celebration of the Eucharist	
Slides and music	*Adagio (Symphony No. 2 in E minor)* Rachmaninov (excerpt) during which John 18:1-14 is read
Meditation 49	*Why didn't he escape while he had the chance?* – The Temple policeman
Silence	
Slides and music	*Adagio (Symphony No. 2 in E minor)* Rachmaninov (excerpt) during which John 18:19-24 is read
Meditation 51	*Angry? You bet I was!* – Annas
Silence	
Prayer	Lord Jesus Christ, we have eaten the bread and drunk from the cup, and so once more proclaimed your death. Now let us go back to the world and proclaim your death there, through the people we are and the lives we live. May we make known your love, make real your compassion, make clear your grace, and so make nearer your kingdom, until you come. Amen.

Hymn   *Love is his word, love is his way*
                     Come, let us sing of a wonderful love

Blessing

Music   *Adagio (Symphony No. 2 in E minor)*
                     Rachmaninov (excerpt)

GOOD FRIDAY (1)

Suggested visual material   Jesus of Nazareth 5 and 6
Oberammergau 1990
The Life of Christ III and IV
He Carries our Cross
Bread and Wine
Man of the Cross

Suggested music   Rather than use separate pieces of music, I have suggested here the use of one continuous piece, excerpts faded in and out as appropriate. For a more traditional Good Friday service, the slides and music should be omitted.

Music   *Adagietto (Symphony No. 5)* Mahler (excerpt – total length 12:10)

Introduction   How would you have acted had you been hanging on the cross in place of Jesus, listening to the sneers and shouts of your enemies as they watched you writhing there in agony? Would you have called curses down upon them from heaven? I think I might have done. Would you have cried out in anger, 'Why me? What have I done to deserve this?' Again, yes, I think I might. Or would you have been so preoccupied with your pain and misery that you had no thoughts for anyone but yourself. On reflection, that's probably most likely of all. The one thing I'm sure I wouldn't have done is say this: 'Father, forgive them, for they do not know what they are doing?' In the most appalling of suffering to think not simply of others, but of those who have brought such suffering upon you; in the throes of death to look them in the eye and seek God's forgiveness for your killers – amazing! That's why we're here today. That's the man we come to honour and the God we meet through him; the God who gives, and goes on giving; who loves, and goes on loving; who died, and goes on dying, even though he lives; until that day when each and every one of us has responded

to his grace and been gathered into his kingdom.
Come now, and worship him.

Hymn   *When I survey the wondrous cross*
Beneath the cross of Jesus
In the cross of Christ I glory

Prayer   Gracious God,
we fail you, we deny you,
we abandon and betray you,
yet still you love us, still you have mercy,
nothing able to exhaust your grace.
So we come,
with all our faults and weaknesses,
all our doubt and disobedience,
seeking again your renewing touch
upon our lives.
Help us to stand again before the cross
and to receive the forgiveness you so freely offer,
so that our lives may speak of your goodness
and honour you through all we are and all we do.
Amen.

Slides and music   *Adagietto* Mahler (excerpt)
during which John 18:33-38 is read

Meditation 52   *'Truth!' I said. 'What is truth?'* – Pilate

Silence

Slides and music   *Adagietto* Mahler (excerpt)
during which Mark 15:6-15 is read

Meditation 55   *I still can't believe my luck* – Barabbas

Silence

Slides and music   *Adagietto* Mahler (excerpt)
during which John 19:1-16 is read

Meditation 56   *What got into us that day?* – One of the mob

Silence

Slides and music	*Adagietto* Mahler (excerpt) during which Luke 23:26-31 is read
Meditation 57	*It was heartbreaking to see him –* One of the crowd on the way to Golgotha
Silence	
Slides and music	*Adagietto* Mahler (excerpt) during which Mark 15:33-36, 40-41 is read
Meditation 59	*He was gasping* – Mary Magdalene
Silence	
Slides and music	*Adagietto* Mahler (excerpt) during which Luke 23:44-49 is read
Meditation 61	*It was dark* – The centurion at the foot of the cross
Silence	

Prayer

Lord Jesus Christ,
  there are no words sufficient
  to express the wonder of your love,
  no deeds sufficient
  to express the enormity of our gratitude,
  but we come asking that you will receive
  our worship, our faith and our lives
  as a token of our thanksgiving,
  and as a sign of our love for you.
Lord Jesus Christ,
  receive this day our heartfelt praise,
  and use us to your glory,
  for your name's sake.
Amen.

Hymn
We sing the praise of him who died
Meekness and majesty
A purple robe, a crown of thorns

Blessing

Music *Lacrymosa dies illa (Requiem)* Mozart

Good Friday (2)

Suggested visual material	Jesus of Nazareth 5 and 6 Oberammergau 1990 The Life of Christ III and IV He Carries our Cross Bread and Wine Man of the Cross
Suggested music	Rather than use separate pieces of music, I have suggested here the use of one continuous piece, excerpts faded in and out as appropriate. For a more traditional Good Friday service, the slides and music should be omitted.
Music	*Adagio for Strings* Barber (excerpt – total length 8:41)
Introduction	Imagine you are one of those in the crowd that has followed the path of Jesus to the place called Golgotha. You have watched thus far in horror, but now you close your eyes, unable to look any more at the scenes unfolding before you, yet you cannot block out the sounds of what is happening; sounds which are equally if not more dreadful. The ringing of the hammer as it drives the nails mercilessly through the flesh of Jesus. The involuntary gasps of agony as the cross is lifted up and those skewered hands and feet begin to tear under his weight. The raucous jeers of the crowd as they gather round to gloat, mingled with the sobs of women close by, their hearts close to breaking. Surely it will be over soon? Nothing can be worse than this! And then it comes, the most terrible, haunting sound of all; a cry of such torment, such desolation, that your blood runs cold: 'My God, my God, why have you forsaken me?' And suddenly you realise, for the first time, just how much this man dying before you has gone through; the full extent of his suffering, the wonder of his sacrifice. Today, as best we may, we stand by that cross again. We listen, we watch, we marvel!

Hymn   *O sacred head sore wounded*
               Lord of the cross of shame
               O dearest Lord, thy sacred head

Prayer   Gracious God,
                   when you seemed furthest away
                   you were nearer than you had ever been,
                   when you seemed at your most weak
                   you were at your most strong,
                   when you seemed overwhelmed by hatred
                   you were enfolding all in love,
                   when you seemed defeated
                   you were victorious.
               Gracious God,
                   we come to you on this day
                   which seemed so full of evil,
                   yet which we can call 'Good Friday',
                   and we thank you for the proof it brings us
                   that no person, no place and no experience
                   is outside your love or beyond your purpose.
               Receive our praise,
                   accept our thanks;
                   through Jesus Christ our Lord.
               Amen.

Slides and music   *Adagio for Strings* Barber (excerpt)
                       during which John 13:21-30 is read

Meditation 48   *'Do what you have to do,' he told me* – Judas

Silence

Slides and music   *Adagio for Strings* Barber (excerpt)
                       during which Luke 23:1-12 is read

Meditation 53   *He was a fool, that's what I thought* – Herod

Silence

Slides and music   *Adagio for Strings* Barber (excerpt)
                       during which Mark 15:21-24 is read

Meditation 58   *He was tired* – Simon of Cyrene

Silence

Slides and music   *Adagio for Strings* Barber (excerpt)
during which Luke 23:39-43 is read

Meditation 54   *'Remember me,' he cried* – Mother of one of the thieves

Silence

Slides and music   *Adagio for Strings* Barber (excerpt)
during which John 19:25-27 is read

Meditation 60   *He was thinking of me, even then!* –
Mary, mother of Jesus

Silence

Slides and music   *Adagio for Strings* Barber (excerpt)
during which Luke 23:44-49 is read

Meditation 61   *It was dark* – The Centurion at the foot of the cross

Silence

Prayer   Lord Jesus Christ,
      there are many who suffer,
      many who have endured untold agony
      of body, mind and spirit,
      but there are few who do so willingly,
      fewer still who would choose that course
      as their vocation in life.
Yet you came and walked the way of the cross
      with single-minded determination,
      and you gave your life freely,
      so that one day there will be an end
      to all suffering and sorrow,
      a time when all will rejoice
      in the wonder of your love
      and experience the joy of your kingdom.
Until then, Lord, reach out
      into our world of darkness,
      into every place of need,

and bring the comfort, the strength,
the peace and the hope which you alone can
bring.
In your name we ask it.
Amen.

Hymn   *Were you there when they crucified my Lord?*
There is a green hill far away
Lift high the cross, the love of Christ proclaim

Blessing

Music   *Ave Verum* Mozart

EASTER COMMUNION (1)

Suggested Visual Material	Jesus of Nazareth 6 The Life of Christ III and IV Bread and Wine
Music	*I know that my redeemer liveth (Messiah)* Handel
Introduction	'He is not here. He has risen.' Words which were to change not only the lives of those who first went to the tomb to anoint the body of Jesus, but the very course of history. For here is the message which turns our human expectations upside down, bringing laughter out of tears and victory out of defeat. What looked to be a conclusive end turned out instead to be a new beginning, holding promise not just for one but for all; and across the centuries countless people have experienced the full wonder of that promise for themselves. Listen again, then, to the testimony of scripture to the events of that first Easter; reflect on what they meant and what they continue to mean; and open your heart again to what God is able to do in your life through Christ crucified and risen!
Hymn	*Christ is risen! alleluia!* *Come, you faithful, raise the strain*

Prayer	Sovereign God,
	    this is the day of victory –
	    a day on which we celebrate
	    the triumph of good over evil,
	    truth over falsehood,
	    light over darkness,
	    life over death.
	This is the day which changes every day –
	    which brings joy out of sorrow,
	    hope out of despair,
	    faith out of doubt,
	    love out of hatred.

This is the day which makes every day
an Easter Day,
and every moment a new beginning.
Sovereign God,
receive our praise,
in the name of the risen Christ.
Amen.

Slides and music   *Gloria in Excelsis Deo (Gloria)* Vivaldi
during which Mark 16:1-8 is read

Meditation 62   *You'd have thought we'd be pleased, wouldn't you? –*
Salome

Silence

Slides and music   *Ode to Joy* Beethoven
during which Luke 24:1-12 is read

Meditation 64   *It seemed too good to be true –* Peter

Silence

Hymn   *Led like a lamb to the slaughter*
He lives! He lives!

Slides and music   *Hallelujah (Messiah)* Handel
during which Luke 24:13-35 is read

Meditation 66   *We met him there on the Emmaus road –* Cleopas

Silence

Slides and music   *Since by man came death (Messiah)* Handel
during which Mark 16:14-18 is read

Meditation 72   *What's done cannot be undone, isn't that what they say? –*
Bartholomew

Silence

**Celebration
of the Eucharist**

Prayer   Sovereign God,
                you turned the darkest of nights
                into the brightest of days
                through the resurrection of your Son,
                our Saviour,
                Jesus Christ.
            Come now into our darkness,
                into the night-time of suffering and sickness,
                of doubt and despair,
                of hurt and heartbreak,
                of injustice and evil,
                of violence and hatred,
                of fear and death.
            May your new day dawn here,
                and the light of Christ blaze to your glory,
                as we share his resurrection life,
                and rejoice in the victory he has won.
            In his name we pray.
            Amen.

Hymn   *I know that my Redeemer lives!*
            Jesus Christ is risen today

Blessing

Music   *Worthy is the lamb that was slain (Messiah)* Handel

EASTER COMMUNION (2)

Suggested visual material   Jesus of Nazareth 6
The Life of Christ III and IV
Bread and Wine

Music   *Gloria in Excelsis Deo (Gloria)* Vivaldi

Introduction   We are here in the season which gives meaning to all seasons, for without Easter there would be no gospel, no message, no Church, no faith. We could talk still, it's true, of the birth of Jesus, his life, his ministry and his death, but without the empty tomb and the risen Christ all this would finally be a tale of tragedy rather than triumph – a mirror of this world's ultimate impermanence rather than a window into the eternal purpose of God. No wonder today we celebrate! And what better way to do that than to think again of some of those whose lives were transformed by that first Easter, and, through reflecting on their experience, to meet the risen Christ afresh and open our lives to his renewing power.

Hymn   *Jesus, stand among us*
Jesus lives! your terrors now

Prayer   Lord Jesus Christ,
it was not just you who was broken
that day you hung on a cross;
it was your disciples too,
their hearts broken just as surely,
their dreams and hopes snuffed out,
their faith cut from beneath them and laid to rest.
It was not just you who rose again
that day you emerged from the tomb;
it was your disciples too,
their hearts beating once more
with joyful anticipation,
their vision for the future reborn,

their faith rekindled,
bursting into unquenchable flame.
Come to us now where we are broken –
where love has died,
where hope has faded,
where faith has grown cold.
Reach out and touch us in body, mind and spirit,
and help us to walk in the newness of life
which you alone can bring.
In your name we ask it.
Amen.

Slides and music   *I know that my redeemer liveth (Messiah)* Handel
during which Matthew 28:1-10 is read

Meditation 63   *I'll never be able to say what it meant to me –*
Mary Magdalene

Silence

Slides and music   *Gloria (Coronation Mass)* Mozart
during which Luke 24:36-43 is read

Meditation 67   *He was back!* – Peter

Silence

Hymn   *Early on Sunday, Mary comes running*
Were you there when they crucified my Lord?

Slides and music   *Why do the nations? (Messiah)* Handel
during which Matthew 28:11-15 is read

Meditation 69   *They don't know when they're beaten, do they? –*
Caiaphas

Silence

Slides and music   *Worthy is the lamb that was slain (Messiah)* Handel
during which John 21:15-19 is read

Meditation 73   *Three times he asked me* – Peter

Silence

**Celebration
of the Eucharist**

Prayer   Loving God,
　　we praise you again for this season
　　and the assurance it brings
　　that nothing can ever finally overcome your love.
You confronted the forces of evil,
　　allowing them to throw everything
　　they could muster against you,
　　and when they had done their worst
　　you emerged victorious,
　　no power able to hold you down.
Teach us always to hold on to that truth,
　　and so to live each moment in the knowledge
　　that, whatever we may face,
　　your love will see us through.
In the name of the risen Christ we pray.
Amen.

Hymn   *Low in the grave he lay*
This joyful Eastertide

Blessing

Music   *Gloria in Excelsis Deo (Gloria)* Vivaldi

EASTER (3)

Suggested visual material	Jesus of Nazareth 6 The Life of Christ III and IV Bread and Wine
Music	*Laudamus te (Mass in C minor)* Mozart

Introduction 'They came to him, took hold of his feet, and worshipped him.' . . . 'They said to each other, "Were not our hearts burning within us while he was talking to us on the road?"' . . . 'She turned and said to him in Hebrew, "Rabbouni!" (which means Teacher).' . . . 'Thomas answered him, "My Lord and my God!"' . . . 'Jesus came and stood among them and said, "Peace be with you." . . . Then the disciples rejoiced when they saw the Lord.' The Christ who came, the Christ who comes, risen and victorious! Together, let us welcome him with thanksgiving, and join the celebration!

Hymn *This is the day, this is the day*
Christ is alive! let Christians sing

Prayer Lord Jesus Christ,
   you met with Mary in the garden,
   bringing laughter after tears;
   you met with women returning from the tomb,
   bringing confidence after confusion;
   you met with Cleopas on the Emmaus road,
   bringing hope after dismay;
   you met with the Apostles
   in a room barred against the world,
   bringing joy after sorrow;
   you met with Thomas, in his disbelief,
   bringing faith after doubt;
   you met with Paul on his way to Damascus,
   bringing love after hatred;
   you met with countless generations
   across the centuries,

bringing renewal after rejection.
Meet with us now, in this day, this moment,
    bringing light after darkness.
Fill our hearts with the new life of Easter,
    until that day when, with all your people,
    we enter your kingdom
    and rejoice in the wonder of your love
    for all eternity.
In your name we pray.
Amen.

Slides and music   *Alleluia (Exsultate, Jubilate)* Mozart
during which John 20:1-10 is read

Meditation 65   *One look, that's all it took!* – John

Silence

Slides and music   *How beautiful are the feet (Messiah)* Handel
during which Luke 24:44-49 is read

Meditation 68   *We still hadn't seen it, you know* – Andrew

Silence

Hymn   *Alleluia, alleluia, give thanks to the risen Lord*
When fear and grief had barred the door

Slides and music   *Gloria (Mass in B minor)* J. S. Bach
during which John 20:19-29 is read

Meditation 71   *I wanted to know, that's all* – Thomas

Silence

Slides and music   *Spring Song in A* Mendelssohn
during which Matthew 28:16-20 is read

Meditation 74   *We had come, as he'd told us to* – Matthew

Silence

Prayer   Jesus of Bethlehem,
    be born in us today.
Jesus of Galilee,
    touch our lives with your presence.
Jesus of Gethsemane,
    strengthen us in times of trial.
Jesus of Calvary,
    have mercy upon us,
    for we do not know what we do.
Jesus of the empty tomb,
    lead us from light into darkness,
    from death into life.
Jesus of eternity,
    the Word made flesh,
    the King of kings and Lord of lords,
    walk with us until our journey's end,
    and to you be glory this day and for evermore.
Amen.

Hymn   *Christ triumphant, ever reigning*
Thine be the glory, risen conquering Son

Blessing

Music   *Ode to Joy* Beethoven

EASTER (4)

Suggested visual material Jesus of Nazareth 6
The Life of Christ III and IV
Bread and Wine

Music *Alleluia (Exsultate, Jubilate)* Mozart

Introduction 'This is the day that the Lord has made. Let us rejoice and be glad in it.' Words which remind us of the need to let go of the past and embrace the present moment, recognising each day as a new beginning. The theory is excellent, the practice harder, for as the years pass so our ability to bounce back from life's disappointments and look forward with undiminished enthusiasm becomes ever more jaded. Yet if it seems hard sometimes for *us*, how much harder must it have seemed for the disciples of Jesus in the days following his death. How could they recover from that? How could life ever hold any meaning again? Life must have seemed bleak beyond redemption. Until suddenly it all changed! Hope reborn, joy returning as Christ was there once more, risen and victorious. And in that moment they knew it was true; life was beginning again, not just for Jesus but for them all; a fresh start, a new chapter in a story which would have no end. So it is for us – each day, each moment offering a clean break, the past forgotten, the future there for the taking. 'This is the day that the Lord has made. Let us rejoice and be glad in it.'

Hymn *The strife is o'er, the battle done*

Prayer Lord God,
we thank you for this day –
a day which brought hope after despair,
new beginnings
from what had looked like the end of everything.
Teach us that the truth of Easter goes on being true

today and every day,
your invitation to start again constantly extended,
your gift of new life always open.
So, trusting in the future,
may we rejoice in the present,
and celebrate each day that you give us,
through Jesus Christ our Lord.
Amen.

Slides and music   *Gymnopédie No. 2* Satie
during which Matthew 28:11-15 is read

Meditation 70   *I just can't understand what happened –*
One of the guards at the tomb

Silence

Slides and music   *Since by man came death (Messiah)* Handel
during which Mark 16:14-18 is read

Meditation 72   *What's done cannot be undone, isn't that what they say? –*
Bartholomew

Silence

Hymn   *Now the green blade rises*

Slides and music   *The trumpet shall sound (Messiah)* Handel
during which 1 Corinthians 15:12-22, 35-36, 42-44a,
50-57 is read

Meditation 89   *'What will it be like?' they ask me* – Paul

Silence

Slides and music   *Come, Lord (Fountain of Life)* Rizza
during which Revelation 21:1-4; 22:5 is read

Meditation 100   *I had a dream last night* – John

Silence

Prayer   Loving God,
    we catch a glimpse today
    into the mystery of this world,
    into the strange puzzle
    that there can be no life without death,
    no light without darkness,
    no joy without sorrow,
    no starting the new without ending the old.
May that truth give us strength
    when days are hard to bear.
Reassure us with the knowledge
    that in the bleakest moments you are there,
    and that it is often in such times
    that you are supremely at work.
Though we do not see or understand,
    teach us still to trust,
    confident that in Christ
    all things will be made new,
    to the glory of your name.
Amen.

Hymn   *Come and see the shining hope that Christ's apostle saw*
Thank you, Jesus, thank you, Jesus

Blessing

Music   *Hallelujah (Messiah)* Handel

Ascension

Suggested visual material	Jesus of Nazareth 6 In the Beginning The Life of Christ IV
Music	*Rex tremendae (Requiem)* Mozart

Introduction They had seen death, they had seen resurrection, and for the disciples of Jesus that sight of the risen Christ back among them must have seemed the most wonderful thing they could ever hope to witness. No wonder they asked the question which had been on each one's lips since his return: 'Lord, is this the time when you will restore the kingdom to Israel?' It had to be, surely? What more could be revealed than had been revealed to them already? The answer was just a few moments away, as suddenly Jesus was taken from them, and they were left struggling to come to terms with the unexpected once again. Whatever the precise event behind the language, one thing is clear – their picture of Christ had been far too small, their understanding of his purpose much too narrow. For he came not just to restore Israel but to redeem the world, not to rule on earth but to be enthroned in heaven. They had glimpsed the man but not the face of God beneath. They believed they saw the whole picture, when they saw but one piece of the jigsaw. Suddenly they had to think again, for Jesus was greater than they had begun to imagine. The same, I suspect, may be true for us all.

Hymn *The head that once was crowned with thorns*
Come and see the shining hope

Prayer Lord Jesus Christ,
you are greater than we can ever imagine,
before all,

beyond all,
in all,
over all.
Forgive us for losing sight of your greatness,
for underestimating the breadth of your love
and the extent of your purpose,
for tying you down to the things of earth
rather than opening our hearts
to the kingdom of heaven.
Broaden our vision,
enlarge our understanding,
deepen our faith,
kindle our imagination,
that we may glimpse your glory,
and work more faithfully for your kingdom.
In your name we ask it.
Amen.

Slides and music   *Dies irae (Requiem)* Mozart
during which Mark 13:3-13 is read

Meditation 42   *It was a chilling picture he gave us* – Andrew

Silence

Hymn   *Alleluia! sing to Jesus*
Hail the day that sees him rise

Slides and music   *On wings of song* Mendelssohn
during which Acts 1:6-11 is read

Meditation 75   *We stood there, speechless for a moment* – James

Silence

Slides and music   *Come, Lord (Fountain of Life)* Rizza
during which Revelation 21:1-4; 22:5 is read

Meditation 100   *I had a dream last night* – John

Silence

Prayer   Baby of Bethlehem, born in a stable,
            we worship you.
        Child of Nazareth, full of grace and truth,
            we acknowledge you.
        Man of Galilee, teacher, preacher, healer, redeemer,
            we praise you.
        Son of David,
            coming in humility to claim your kingdom,
            we greet you.
        Suffering servant, bruised, beaten, broken,
            we salute you.
        Lord of the empty tomb, risen and triumphant,
            we honour you.
        King of kings, exalted by the side of the Father,
            we adore you.
        Jesus Christ, our Lord and Saviour,
            receive the homage we offer,
            to the glory of your name.
        Amen.

Hymn   *Hail, thou once despised Jesus*
        Restore, O Lord, the honour of your name

Blessing

Music   *Rex tremendae (Requiem)* Mozart

Pentecost

Suggested visual material	In the Beginning Jesus of Nazareth 3, 4 and 6 The Life of Christ IV St Paul The Story of Saint Paul
Music	*Cum Sancto Spiritu (Mass in B minor)* J. S. Bach

Introduction

'I just can't do it!' How often have we claimed that, or something similar? If so, think again, for today we remember how twelve disciples, who must have said and thought much the same, were transformed in the space of a few moments into those for whom nothing apparently was beyond them. What was their secret? There wasn't one, for the change within them had nothing to do with themselves but everything to do with God. It took simply the breath of his Spirit to bring about one of the most astonishing transformations in history, and to set into motion the extraordinary events of what we call 'the day of Pentecost'. Yet Pentecost is not about *one* day but *every* day, for the gift of the Spirit is a continuous experience intended for all. You and I, like those who have gone before us, are called to be Pentecost people, living and working in ways we might once have thought beyond us to the glory of Christ. Have we risen to the challenge?

Hymn

The King is among us
This is the day
Holy Spirit, hear us

Prayer

Living God,
    we remember today
    how you transformed the lives of the Apostles,
    how, through the breath of your Spirit,
    you turned their fear and uncertainty
    into a confidence which knew no bounds.
Come to us now, through that same Spirit.

Take our weak and hesitant faith
    and fill us with unshakable trust in your purpose.
Take our stumbling discipleship,
    and grant us energy and enthusiasm
    to proclaim the gospel through word and deed.
Take our fear and anxieties,
    and give us courage
    and your peace which passes understanding.
Take our gifts and talents,
    and use them in the service of your kingdom.
Living God,
    help us to remember today
    not simply all you did *once*,
    but to rejoice in all you are doing *now*,
    and all you shall continue to do
    through your Holy Spirit.
In the name of Christ we ask it.
Amen.

Slides and music	*Veni, lumen cordium (Fountain of Life)* Rizza during which Acts 1:1-5, 8, 12-14 is read
Meditation 77	*'You will be my witnesses'* – John
Silence	
Slides and music	*Send forth your spirit, Lord (Fountain of Life)* Rizza during which Acts 2:1-21 is read
Meditation 78	*I don't know who was the more surprised* – Peter
Silence	
Slides and music	*The Ride of the Valkyries* Wagner during which Acts 4:1-18 is read
Meditation 79	*They were still at it!* – Annas
Silence	
Hymn	*O Holy Spirit breathe on me* *Away with our fears* *Spirit of the living God*

Slides and music   *Gavotte (Holberg Suite)* Grieg
during which Acts 10:1-6, 9-20, 23a, 24-28, 34b-35, 44-48 is read

Meditation 83   *You must be joking, Lord! –* Peter

Silence

Slides and music   *Danse profane (Danses sacrée et profane)* Debussy
during which 1 Corinthians 11:17-22; 12:1, 4-6, 12, 27-31 is read

Meditation 88   *It was all so unnecessary –* Paul

Silence

Prayer   Spirit of God,
refining like fire,
free as the wind,
gentle as a dove,
come among us.
Cleanse our hearts,
liberate our souls,
bring peace to our minds,
and send us out with power
to proclaim the kingdom of God,
in the name of the living Christ.
Amen.

Hymn   *Spirit of God, unseen as the wind*
There's a spirit in the air
O Spirit of the living God

Blessing

Music   *Cum Sancto Spiritu (Mass in B minor)* J. S. Bach

TRINITY

Suggested visual material	In the Beginning Come, let us adore Jesus of Nazareth 6 The Life of Christ IV
Music	*En Trinitatis Speculum (Magnificat)* Praetorius

Introduction

We are here today on Trinity Sunday, a day which perhaps captures the imagination less than any other in the Christian year, and to a point that is understandable, for rather than historical events this date in the calendar is concerned with abstract doctrine which has perplexed theologians and ordinary believers alike across the centuries. Yet complex though the issues may be, we do well to reflect on them, for this should be a day which captures the imagination like no other, reminding us of the sheer breathtaking reality which we describe as God. We try to pin that reality down as best we can; to talk about our experience in terms of God the Father, the Son and the Holy Spirit, but we are always at best simply grasping at the truth, for, as the prophet Isaiah reminds us, God's ways are not our ways, neither are his thoughts our thoughts. Thank God for this day which reminds us of this simple inescapable fact, and use it to deepen your faith and enrich your experience of his living, loving, and transforming presence.

Hymn

Be still, for the presence of the Lord
The King is among us

Prayer

Almighty and everlasting God,
    we are here before you.
Grant us a glimpse of your awesome presence,
    and help us to worship you with reverent praise.
Father God,
    we are here before you.

Grant us a sense of your everlasting arms
   surrounding us,
      and help us to trust always in your loving
         purpose.
Lord Jesus Christ,
   we are here before you.
Grant us grace to hear your call,
   and help us to follow in your footsteps
      wherever that might lead.
Holy Spirit,
   we are here before you.
Grant us openness of heart, mind and spirit,
   and help us to know your peace and power.
Almighty and everlasting God,
   Father, Son and Holy Spirit,
   we are here before you.
Grant that we may know you better,
   and help us to live and work for you,
      this day and always.
Amen.

Slides and music   *The Mirror of the Trinity (Magnificat)* Praetorius
                       during which John 15:12-27 is read

Meditation 80   *I didn't know what he was on about at the time* – John

Silence

Slides and music   *He was despised and rejected (Messiah)* Handel
                       during which Matthew 13:54-58 is read

Meditation 36   *Do you know what they're saying about him?* –
                    Resident of Nazareth

Silence

Hymn   *All creatures of our God and King*
           Father, we adore you

Slides and music   *Cum Sancto Spiritu (Mass in B minor)* J. S. Bach
                       during which Acts 1:15-26 is read

Meditation 76	*Did it go to my head, becoming an apostle like that? –* Matthias
Silence	
Slides and music	*Salut d'Amour* Elgar during which 1 John 4:7-21 is read
Meditation 98	*Sentimental rubbish, that's what some will accuse me of –* John
Silence	

Prayer   Gracious God,
    there are some experiences
    which we cannot put into words
    however hard we try –
    moments of joy, love, awe, hope, beauty
    and so many more.
Yet though these may defy expression,
    they are no less real;
    on the contrary they are often more real
    and special than any.
So it is with our experience of you.
Together with your Church across the ages,
    we strive to articulate our faith,
    to describe somehow
    everything that you mean to us –
    your awesome sovereignty,
    your unfailing care,
    your intimate closeness,
    your presence within –
    yet the language we use
    seems hopelessly inadequate.
Father, Son and Holy Spirit,
    three in one and one in three.
It makes no sense according to human logic,
    yet we know it to be true,
    not in our minds but in our hearts.
And so we rejoice,
    and acknowledge you as our God
    in joyful worship,

one God, world without end.
Amen.

Hymn   *Father in heaven*
Father, we love you

Blessing

Music   *En Trinitatis Speculum (Magnificat)* Praetorius

QUIET DAY

New Beginnings

Suggested visual material	Jesus of Nazareth 2, 3, 4, 5 and 6 The Life of Christ IV St Paul The Story of Saint Paul In the Beginning

MORNING SESSION

Music	*Since by man came death (Messiah)* Handel
Introduction	How often have you wished you could have another go at something? When an opportunity is missed or a chance wasted there is nothing we would like more than to turn the clock back and have another bite of the cherry. Sadly, of course, that is impossible. We may, on occasions, be allowed a second crack at what we failed to capitalise on first time round, but the legacy of the past will always in some way be with us. Except, that is, when it comes to Christ, for in him the offer is always there of a fresh start, a clean break, a new beginning. That is a truth we see time and again throughout the Gospels, lives which had apparently come to the end of the road, people who had come to the end of their tether, suddenly finding a new chapter opening up before them full of promise. Whatever had happened before, it was over and done with, its power to tie them down broken for ever! Here in a nutshell is the good news of Jesus Christ, and it is that which we shall be exploring today through the experience of some of those who were touched by his ministry. But we start at perhaps the greatest new beginning of all – the birth of Jesus Christ, the Word made flesh, and the birth of life itself at the dawn of time which that same Word brought into being.

Prayer	Loving God,
	      we thank you for this new day,
	      rich with opportunity,
	      full of promise.
	Speak to us through it of the newness of life
	      you offer through Jesus Christ –
	      how, through him,
	      you are able to take any moment,
	      any situation,
	      any person,
	      and give the opportunity to begin again.
	Keep us looking to the future with confidence,
	      and so help us to greet this and every day
	      with a sense of anticipation,
	      inspired by the knowledge of your love,
	      and the assurance of your renewing power;
	      through Jesus Christ our Lord.
	Amen.

Slides and music	*Gloria (Missa Ouer natus est nobis)* Tallis during which John 1:1-5, 10-14 is read
Meditation 3	*'Where did it all start?'* – John the Apostle
Prayer	(See prayer following Meditation 3)
Silence	
Slides and music	*El Rorro* Traditional Mexican Carol during which Luke 2:1-7 is read
Meditation 10	*He looked so tiny lying there* – Mary
Prayer	(See prayer following Meditation 10)
Silence	
Slides and music	*Come to me (Fountain of Life)* Rizza during which Mark 5:21-24, 35-43 is read
Meditation 26	*I can't tell you how awful it felt* – Jairus

Prayer	(See prayer following Meditation 26)
Silence	
Slides and music	*Silent, surrendered (Fountain of Life)* Rizza during which Mark 5:25-34 is read
Meditation 27	*I was sick* – The woman who touched Jesus' cloak
Prayer	(See prayer following Meditation 27)
Silence	
Music	*Chanson de Matin* Elgar

AFTERNOON SESSION

Music	*Spring Song in A* Mendelssohn

Prayer	Lord Jesus Christ,
	    you are the same yesterday, today and tomorrow,
	    always loving,
	    always ready to show mercy,
	    always waiting to lead us forward.
	Because of your constancy
	    we know that you will be with us
	    in whatever we face,
	    for you are Lord of past, present and future.
	Take, then, what has been,
	    work in what is,
	    and direct what shall yet be,
	    to the glory of your name.
	Amen.

Slides and music	*Adagio (Piano Sonata K332)* Mozart during which Luke 7:1-10 is read
Meditation 30	*They thought I was mad* – The Roman centurion
Prayer	(See prayer following Meditation 30)
Silence	

Slides and music	*O Lord, my heart is not proud (Fountain of Life)* Rizza during which Luke 8:26-39 is read
Meditation 31	*You just can't imagine what it was like* – Legion
Prayer	(See prayer following Meditation 31)
Silence	
Slides and music	*Libera me Domine (Requiem)* Verdi during which John 8:2-11 is read
Meditation 32	*I expected him to condemn me like all the rest* – The woman caught in adultery
Prayer	(See prayer following Meditation 32)
Silence	
Slides and music	*Gloria (Coronation Mass)* Mozart during which Luke 24:36-43 is read
Meditation 67	*He was back!* – Peter
Prayer	(See prayer following Meditation 67)
Silence	
Slides and music	*Adagio (Cello Concerto)* Haydn during which Acts 15:36-41 is read
Meditation 86	*Was I hurt by Paul's attitude?* – Mark
Prayer	(See prayer following Meditation 86)
Silence	
Blessing	
Music	*Jesu, joy of man's desiring* J. S. Bach

QUIET DAY

The Cost of Discipleship

Suggested visual material	Jesus of Nazareth 3 and 4 The Life of Christ IV Man of the Cross

MORNING SESSION

Music	*Come to me (Fountain of Life)* Rizza
Introduction	'If any want to become my followers, let them deny themselves and take up their cross and follow me' (Mark 8:34b). Words of Jesus which, in the euphoria of Christian celebration, we can sometimes forget, yet which lie at the heart of Christian discipleship. The life of service involves cost as well as reward; a price to pay as well as a blessing to receive. Lose sight of that and we are in danger of presenting a lop-sided and ultimately false gospel. Alongside what we get out of faith we must always remember what Jesus asks us to put in; his call to deny ourselves and put others first, to seek treasures in heaven rather than riches on earth, to be last rather than first, to face trials now in order to help build his kingdom to come. If we expect the Christian life to be plain sailing, then we have not understood the call or listened to the words of the one who called us. Responding in faith will inevitably bring times of challenge, just as it has done to those before us, but, if we are willing to meet the cost, then, like them, we will find the price worth paying, for we will discover life as God intends it to be. 'Those who want to save their life will lose it, and those who lose their life for the sake of the gospel, will save it' (Mark 8:35).

Prayer	Lord Jesus Christ,
	   you gave your all so that we might have life.
	You counted yourself as nothing
	   so that we might rejoice
	   in the wonder of your love.
	You endured agony of body, mind and spirit,
	   so that we might receive mercy
	   and know the peace which only you can give.
	Help us today to recognise more clearly
	   everything you did for us,
	   and so inspire us
	   to give a little of ourselves in return.
	Teach us to walk the way of the cross,
	   and to bear the cost gladly
	   for the joy set before us,
	   knowing that you will be with us,
	   each step of the way,
	   whatever we may face.
	Amen.

Slides and music	*Canticle de Jean Racine* Fauré during which Luke 7:18b-19, 21-23 is read
Meditation 21	*Shall I tell you something strange?* – John the Baptist
Prayer	(See prayer following Meditation 21)
Silence	
Slides and music	*Adagietto from L'Arlésienne (Suite No. 1)* Bizet during which Luke 18:18-25 is read
Meditation 34	*It was a lot to ask, wasn't it?* – The rich ruler
Prayer	(See prayer following Meditation 34)
Silence	
Slides and music	*Kyrie eleison (Fountain of Life)* Rizza during which Luke 21:1-4 is read
Meditation 37	*I was ashamed, if I'm truthful –* The widow at the treasury

Prayer	(See prayer following Meditation 37)
Silence	
Slides and music	*Jesus, you are the way (Fountain of Life)* Rizza during which Mark 14:3-9 is read
Meditation 40	*Was it guilt that made them turn on me? –* The woman who anointed Jesus' head
Prayer	(See prayer following Meditation 40)
Silence	
Music	*Pié Jesu (Requiem)* Andrew Lloyd Weber

AFTERNOON SESSION

Music	*Adagio (Oboe Concerto)* Marcello
Prayer	Loving God, we talk of serving others but so often we live for ourselves, we speak of self-sacrifice but practise self-interest. Forgive us for failing to follow Jesus, and for distorting the Gospel to serve our own purposes. Remind us afresh of the great love you have shown in Christ. Inspire us through those who responded faithfully to his call, and so help us in turn to give as well as receive, to bear willingly the cost of discipleship, for his name's sake. Amen.
Slides and music	*Adagio un poco mosso (Piano Concerto No. 5)* Beethoven during which John 3:1-6; 19:38-42 is read
Meditation 24	*It was dark when I went to him* – Nicodemus

Prayer	(See prayer following Meditation 24)
Silence	
Slides and music	*Lesson 1 for Maundy Thursday* Palestrina during which Luke 22:39-46 is read
Meditation 50	*He was unsure of himself* – Peter
Prayer	(See prayer following Meditation 50)
Silence	
Slides and music	*Agnus Dei* J. S. Bach during which Mark 15:33-36, 40-41 is read
Meditation 59	*He was gasping* – Mary Magdalene
Prayer	(See prayer following Meditation 59)
Silence	
Slides and music	*Jesu, joy of man's desiring* J. S. Bach during which Philippians 4:4-7, 10-12 is read
Meditation 93	*Was I happy with my lot?* – Paul
Prayer	(See prayer following Meditation 93)
Silence	
Slides and music	*Pilgrims' Chorus (Tannhäuser)* Wagner during which Hebrews 11:32-12:2 is read
Meditation 96	*I was ready to give up, if I'm honest* – The writer to the Hebrews
Prayer	(See prayer following Meditation 96)
Silence	
Blessing	
Music	*Jesus, you are the way (Fountain of Life)* Rizza

QUIET DAY

Peter – Journey of Discovery

Suggested visual material	Jesus of Nazareth 5 and 6 The Life of Christ IV Man of the Cross

MORNING SESSION

Music	*Träumerei* Schumann
Introduction	For Simon Peter, the last days in the earthly ministry of Jesus must have looked very much as though they were the last days of his own discipleship. He had come far from the time when Jesus first called him, and going into that final week he believed his faith was able to face anything thrown at it, but, of course, events were to prove otherwise. Three times he was to deny the man he had so confidently promised to follow, and the experience was to all but break him. Yet the journey wasn't over; in fact, it had barely begun. Today, then, we begin with the events of that last week and we explore how Jesus was to take Peter forward into new horizons previously undreamt of. His story brings hope to us all, for it reminds us that no matter how hopeless the future may seem, the grace of God is always there, waiting to lead us forward.

Prayer	Lord Jesus Christ,
	    you have called us to faith
	    and we long to respond,
	    to live as your people
	    and offer our lives in joyful service,
	    but the reality is that all too often we fail,
	    the spirit willing but the flesh weak,
	    and it is hard at such times not to lose heart.
	Speak to us today

and assure us of your grace
which never gives up on us,
however weak our faith may be,
however often we may let you down.
Teach us to let go of the past
and to look forward to the future,
confident that your purpose continues
and that you are able to use us
in ways beyond our imagining,
In your name we pray.
Amen.

Slides and music   *Adagio (Oboe Concerto)* Marcello
during which Luke 22:7-13 is read

Meditation 46   *It was ready for us, just as he'd said it would be*

Prayer   (See prayer following Meditation 46)

Silence

Slides and music   *Lesson 1 for Maundy Thursday* Palestrina
during which Luke 22:39-46 is read

Meditation 50   *He was unsure of himself*

Prayer   (See prayer following Meditation 50)

Silence

Slides and music   *Gloria (Coronation Mass)* Mozart
during which Luke 24:36-43 is read

Meditation 67   *He was back!*

Prayer   (See prayer following Meditation 67)

Silence

Music   *On wings of song* Mendelssohn

AFTERNOON SESSION

Music   *Spring Song in A* Mendelssohn

Prayer   Loving God,
    you call us to a journey of faith,
    but sometimes that journey grinds to a halt.
We get stuck in a rut,
    closed to new directions,
    bogged down by the past,
    or reluctant to step into an unfamiliar future,
    preferring the view we know
    to horizons which may stretch and challenge us.
Move within us through your Holy Spirit,
    meet with us through the risen Christ,
    and so give light to our path
    that we may step forward in faith,
    and travel onwards wherever you might lead,
    through Jesus Christ our Lord.
Amen.

Slides and music   *Send forth your spirit, Lord (Fountain of Life)* Rizza
during which Acts 2:1-21 is read

Meditation 78   *I don't know who was the more surprised*

Prayer   (See prayer following Meditation 78)

Silence

Slides and music   *Gavotte (Holberg Suite)* Grieg
during which Acts 10:1-6, 9-20, 23a, 24-28, 34b-35, 44-48 is read

Meditation 83   *You must be joking, Lord!*

Prayer   (See prayer following Meditation 83)

Silence

Blessing

Music   *Jesu, joy of man's desiring* J. S. Bach

QUIET DAY

John the Apostle – Witness to the Light

Suggested visual material	In the Beginning Jesus of Nazareth 1, 3, 4 and 6 The Life of Christ IV

MORNING SESSION

Music	*Intermezzo* Mascagni
Introduction	'There was a man sent from God, whose name was John. He came as a witness to testify to the light, so that all might believe through him. He himself was not the light, but he came to testify to the light.' Words written by the Apostle John concerning his namesake John the Baptist, but they could just as well have been written about himself, for in the words of his Gospel we have one of the best-loved accounts of the life and ministry of Jesus, and a testimony of faith which over the years must have led countless others to a personal experience of the love of Christ. There is, of course, no way in a time as short as we have to do justice to either the extent or the depth of his writings, and we make no attempt in this Quiet Day to do so. The aim, rather, is to give us a flavour of the faith which sustained John, the convictions that he held, and the experience of Christ which lay behind it all. To do so, we dip briefly into his Gospel and the first of his epistles, supplementing this with a description of his preaching ministry taken from the book of Acts. Finally, we turn to the book of Revelation, a book which, according to some, was written by one of John's successors in the Church, carrying on the Apostle's ministry where he had left off. The voice of John has spoken powerfully to innumerable people across the years. What does it have to say to us today?

Prayer   Gracious God,
              we thank you for the testimony of Scripture
              to your love revealed in Christ;
              and, above all, we thank you today
              for all the experiences of your grace
              and goodness which lie behind the testimonies
              of the Evangelists.
          They wrote to preserve a record
              of his love and ministry,
              they wrote to set down their understanding
              of the story,
              but, most of all, they wrote to communicate
              their faith,
              so that others in turn might come to see
              and believe for themselves.
          Speak to us now as we share together,
              as we listen to your word,
              and reflect on the nature of Jesus.
          May all that we hear and see
              come alive in our hearts,
              so that our faith may grow
              and our love for you be enriched.
          In the name of Christ we pray.
          Amen.

Slides and music   *Gloria (Missa Ouer natus est nobis)* Tallis
                         during which John 1:1-5, 10-14 is read

Meditation 3   *'Where did it all start?'*

Prayer   (See prayer following Meditation 3)

Silence

Slides and music   *Alleluia (Exsultate, Jubilate)* Mozart
                         during which John 20:1-10 is read

Meditation 65   *One look, that's all it took!*

Prayer   (See prayer following Meditation 65)

Silence

Slides and music	*Veni, lumen cordium (Fountain of Life)* Rizza during which Acts 1:1-5, 8, 12-14 is read
Meditation 77	*'You will be my witnesses'*
Prayer	(See prayer following Meditation 77)
Silence	
Music	*Adagio sostenuto (Moonlight Sonata)* Beethoven

AFTERNOON SESSION

Music	*Grave/Allegro di molto e con brio (Pathétique Sonata)* Beethoven

Prayer	Lord Jesus Christ,
	    we have considered your ministry
	    during your earthly life,
	    from your birth to your death
	    to your resurrection.
	Now we think of your continuing ministry
	    through your Holy Spirit;
	    a Spirit and a ministry in which we share.
	Open again your word to us,
	    so that we may learn
	    from all who have gone before us,
	    and so live in such a way
	    as to be an example for those who will follow,
	    for your name's sake.
	Amen.

Slides and music	*The Mirror of the Trinity (Magnificat)* Praetorius during which John 15:12-27 is read
Meditation 80	*I didn't know what he was on about at the time*
Prayer	(See prayer following Meditation 80)
Silence	

Slides and music	*Salut d'Amour* Elgar during which 1 John 4:7-21 is read
Meditation 98	*Sentimental rubbish, that's what some will accuse me of*
Prayer	(See prayer following Meditation 98)
Silence	
Slides and music	*Come, Lord (Fountain of Life)* Rizza during which Revelation 21:1-4; 22:5 is read
Meditation 100	*I had a dream last night*
Prayer	(See prayer following Meditation 100)
Silence	
Blessing	
Music	*God so loved the world (The Crucifixion)* Stainer

QUIET DAY

Paul – the Man and the Message

Suggested visual material	In the Beginning Jesus of Nazareth 3, 4 and 6 The Life of Christ IV St Paul The Story of Saint Paul

MORNING SESSION

Music *Pilgrims' Chorus (Tannhäuser)* Wagner

Introduction Few people, besides Jesus himself, have had such an impact on the Church or the Christian faith as the Apostle Paul. It is to his vision, energy and enthusiasm that we owe the transformation of Christianity from a branch of Judaism to a world-wide faith which still today continues to grow. Yet few people could have seemed more unlikely candidates for such a job, given Paul's hatred for anything to do with Jesus, unparalleled in his time. Admittedly he had many ideally suited gifts which God was able to make use of, but there were equally as many characteristics totally unsuited to the demands of his calling, not least his poor health, his unimposing presence and his so-called 'thorn in the flesh', whatever that might have been. Yet not only was he used uniquely by God in those early days; he continues to speak equally powerfully today, his letters together making up a substantial portion of the New Testament. Today, then, we stop to consider both the man himself and the message he preached. What can we learn from the way Jesus changed Paul's life? What lessons can we draw from his experiences? And what does he have to say concerning our own faith and discipleship? If we are willing to explore such questions we will find the voice of Paul speaking to us here and now and, through that, the voice of God himself.

Prayer   Sovereign God,
     we thank you for the way
     you have spoken across the centuries,
     the way you have repeatedly changed people
     and transformed situations in a manner
     which, to human eyes, looked impossible.
Inspire us today
     as we reflect upon one such example
     of your renewing power,
     and help us through that
     to understand more clearly
     everything you are able to do in our own lives
     and the world today,
     through Jesus Christ our Lord.
Amen.

Slides and music   *First Movement (Holberg Suite)* Grieg
during which Acts 9:1-9 is read

Meditation 82   *Jesus? The very name filled me with fury*

Prayer   (See prayer following Meditation 82)

Silence

Slides and music   *The Swan (Carnival of the Animals)* Saint-Saens
during which Romans 7:14-25 is read

Meditation 87   *Have you ever tried turning over a new leaf?*

Prayer   (See prayer following Meditation 87)

Silence

Slides and music   *The trumpet shall sound (Messiah)* Handel
during which 1 Corinthians 15:12-22, 35-36, 42-44a,
50-57 is read

Meditation 89   *'What will it be like?' they ask me*

Prayer	(See prayer following Meditation 89)
Silence	
Music	*I know that my redeemer liveth (Messiah)* Handel

AFTERNOON SESSION

Music   *Pié Jesu (Requiem)* Andrew Lloyd Weber

Prayer

Gracious God,
  you are able to do in our lives
  far more than we can even begin to imagine.
Forgive us for losing sight of that fact –
  for being content to muddle along,
  frustrating your will and quenching your Spirit
  through the narrowness of our vision.
Give us today a new sense
  of all you want to achieve,
  and of the way you are able to use us
  in achieving it.
Stir our imaginations,
  and send us out renewed in faith,
  to live and work for your glory;
  through Jesus Christ our Lord.
Amen.

Slides and music   *Etude in E* Chopin
during which 2 Corinthians 12:7b-10 is read

Meditation 90   *I could think about nothing else at the time*

Prayer   (See prayer following Meditation 90)

Silence

Slides and music   *Jesu, joy of man's desiring* J. S. Bach
during which Philippians 4:4-7, 10-12 is read

Meditation 93   *Was I happy with my lot?*

Prayer   (See prayer following Meditation 93)

Silence

Slides and music   *Moderato (Serenade for strings in E minor)* Dvořák
during which Galatians 1:13-24 is read

Meditation 94   *It looked impossible at the beginning*

Prayer   (See prayer following Meditation 94)

Silence

Slides and music   *Nocturne No 2 in E flat* Chopin
during which Philippians 1:3-8 is read

Meditation 95   *It's been good to share with you*

Prayer   (See prayer following Meditation 95)

Silence

Blessing

Music   *Pilgrims' Chorus (Tannhäuser)* Wagner

QUIET DAY

Living with Doubt

Suggested visual material	Jesus of Nazareth 1, 2, 3, 4, 5 and 6 The Life of Christ IV Man of the Cross

MORNING SESSION

Music	*Credo in unum Deum (Mass in C minor)* Mozart
Introduction	'I believe in God, the Father Almighty, creator of heaven and earth. I believe in Jesus Christ, his only Son, our Lord.' The opening words of the Apostles' Creed, which across the centuries have been accepted and repeated as a summary of the faith of the Church, the essentials of Christian belief. And probably most of us most of the time would be happy to add our voices alongside those who have gone before us. Most, but not all, of the time – because for virtually every one of us there are times when we find ourselves wrestling with doubts; a multitude of questions which unexpectedly thrust themselves upon us, disturbing our peace and even threatening to undermine our faith completely. To make things worse, such moments are often compounded by a sense of guilt, a feeling that we are wrong and even sinful to entertain such thoughts. The result can be a lonely struggle in the wilderness, crushed by a sense of isolation, failure and shame. Yet if we look at the Scriptures we see there that doubt is not as uncommon as we might at first imagine. Alongside the glowing testimonies of faith, there are also several examples of those whose faith was tested to the limit; those who were not quite so sure and who found themselves struggling to keep going. Who can forget the words of the father who came to Jesus seeking help for his son: 'I believe; help my unbelief'; or the words of Thomas: 'Unless

I see the mark of the nails in his hands, and put my finger in the mark of the nails and my hand in his side, I will not believe.' Even Jesus himself apparently faced a time when for a moment he seemed to question his ability to continue: 'Father, if you are willing, remove this cup from me; yet, not my will but yours be done.' Doubt may come to us all, however secure in faith we appear to be. Do not fear it, for it is not something to be ashamed of. Believe, rather, that God is able to take and use your questions to lead you into a deeper understanding of his purpose and a richer sense of his love. Do that, and you will discover that doubt is not the opposite of faith, but for many of us an essential part of the journey of discipleship.

Prayer   Gracious God,
   we come today confessing our faith
   in your love,
   your goodness,
   your purpose.
We acknowledge your greatness,
   we rejoice in your mercy,
   and we thank you for the many blessings
   you have showered upon us.
But we come today also confessing our doubt –
   the many things we don't understand,
   the statements of faith which don't make sense,
   the events of life which seem to contradict
   everything we believe about you.
Gracious God,
   there are times when we are sure
   and times when we are uncertain;
   times when we feel ready to take on the world
   and times when faith hangs by a thread.
Give us sufficient trust in you
   to acknowledge all such feelings openly,
   and sufficient humility
   to offer each to you honestly in prayer.
Save us from taking refuge
   in hollow words or empty ritual,
   but teach us to face the challenges life brings

and to work through our faith
in the light of them,
so that, having been tested,
it may grow the stronger,
able to face all and still to stand,
through Jesus Christ our Lord.
Amen.

Slides and music   *Il riposo – per il Santissimo Natale
(Concerto for strings)* Vivaldi
during which Isaiah 9:2, 6-7 is read

Meditation 1   *'The people who walked in darkness'* –
Resident of Jerusalem

Prayer   (See prayer following Meditation 1)

Silence

Slides and music   *Ovysen and Kolyada Procession (Christmas Eve Suite)*
Rimsky-Korsakov
during which Luke 1:5-20 is read

Meditation 4   *I wanted to believe it, honestly!* – Zechariah

Prayer   (See prayer following Meditation 4)

Silence

Slides and music   *Intermezzo (Carmen, Suite No. 1)* Bizet
during which Matthew 6:31-33; 7:7-11 is read

Meditation 23   *'Ask,' he said, 'and you will receive'* –
Listener to the Sermon on the Mount

Prayer   (See prayer following meditation 23)

Silence

Slides and music   *Credo (Mass in B minor)* J. S. Bach
during which Mark 9:14-24 is read

Meditation 29   *Lord, I do believe* – Father of the epileptic boy

Prayer	(See prayer following Meditation 29)

Silence

Slides and music	*Lesson 1 for Maundy Thursday* Palestrina during which Luke 22:39-46 is read

Meditation 50	*He was unsure of himself* – Peter

Prayer	(See prayer following Meditation 50)

Silence

Music	*Silent, surrendered (Fountain of Life)* Rizza

AFTERNOON SESSION

Music	*O Lord, my heart is not proud (Fountain of Life)* Rizza

Prayer	Gracious God,

    we come to you just as we are,
    with all our strengths and weaknesses,
    our faith and our doubt.
Open your heart to us and respond to our need.
Nurture our faith,
    strengthen our love,
    and enrich our understanding of your grace.
Draw close to us so that we may draw closer to you,
    today and every day,
    through Jesus Christ our Lord.
Amen.

Slides and music	*Gloria (Mass in B minor)* J. S. Bach during which John 20:19-29 is read

Meditation 71	*I wanted to know, that's all* – Thomas

Prayer	(See prayer following Meditation 50)

Silence

Slides and music	*The Gadfly* Shostakovich during which Acts 12:1-17 is read
Meditation 85	*Our prayers were answered that night –* Mary, the mother of John Mark
Prayer	(See prayer following Meditation 85)
Silence	
Slides and music	*Etude in E* Chopin during which 2 Corinthians 12:7b-10 is read
Meditation 90	*I could think about nothing else at the time* – Paul
Prayer	(See prayer following Meditation 90)
Silence	
Slides and music	*Pilgrims' Chorus (Tannhäuser)* Wagner during which Hebrews 11:32-12:2 is read
Meditation 96	*I was ready to give up, if I'm honest –* Writer to the Hebrews
Prayer	(See prayer following Meditation 96)
Silence	
Slides and music	*Moderato (Serenade for strings in E minor)* Dvořák during which Galatians 1:13-24 is read
Meditation 94	*It looked impossible at the beginning* – Paul
Prayer	(See prayer following Meditation 94)
Silence	
Blessing	
Music	*Credo in unum Deum (Mass in C minor)* Mozart

APPENDIX 1

Suggestions for Accompanying Music

ADVENT

1   *Il riposo – per il Santissimo Natale (Concerto for strings)* – Vivaldi (3:49)
2   *Trumpet Voluntary* Clarke (2:45)
3   *Gloria (Missa Ouer natus est nobis)* Tallis (3:03)
4   *Ovysen and Kolyada Procession (Christmas Eve Suite)*
       Rimsky-Korsakov (4.08)
5   *Schlafe, mein Liebster (Christmas Oratorio)* J. S. Bach (4:01)
6   *Videntes stellam (Quatre motets pour le temps de Noël)* Poulenc (3:08)
7   *Cherry Tree Carol* Traditional (1:49)
8   *Ave Maria* Schubert (2:31)
9   *A Hymn to the Mother of God* Taverner (2:23)

CHRISTMAS

10   *El Rorro* Traditional Mexican carol (2:16)
11   *L'Enfance du Christ (The Shepherds' Farewell)* Berlioz (5.05)
12   *Jesu, Thou the virgin-born* Holtz (3:12)
13   *Earl of Salisbury* Byrd (arranged Graves) (3:20)
14   *Sleep, holy babe* Carol (3:23)
15   *The three kings* Carol (2:43)
16   *Sie Werden aus Saba alle kommen (Cantata No. 65: Epiphany)*
       J. S. Bach (4:28)
17   *Preter rerum serium à* Desprez (6:36)

LENT

18   *O Thou that tellest (Messiah)* Handel (5:27)
19   *Mars (The Planets)* Holst (7:46)
20   *And the glory of the Lord (Messiah)* Handel (2:59)
21   *Canticle de Jean Racine* Fauré (5:22)
22   *Träumerei* Schumann (3:20)
23   *Intermezzo (Carmen, Suite No. 1)* Bizet (2:40)
24   *Adagio un poco mosso (Piano Concerto No. 5)* Beethoven (7:15)
25   *Asturias (Suite Espanol)* Albéniz (6:44)
26   *Come to me (Fountain of Life)* Margaret Rizza (4:03)
27   *Silent, surrendered (Fountain of Life)* Margaret Rizza (4:22)

28   *Lord of my life (Fountain of Life)* Margaret Rizza (5:06)
29   *Credo (Mass in B minor)* J. S. Bach (1:54)
30   *Piano Sonata K332 (Adagio)* Mozart (5:17)
31   *O Lord, my heart is not proud (Fountain of Life)* Margaret Rizza (7.43)
32   *Libera me Domine (Requiem)* Verdi (3:43)
33   *Jeux d'enfants (Petite Suite)* (3:53)
34   *Adagietto (L'Arlésienne, Suite No. 1)* Bizet (3:14)
35   *Sicilienne* Fauré (3:40)
36   *He was despised and rejected (Messiah)* Handel (11:43)
37   *Kyrie eleison (Fountain of Life)* Margaret Rizza (7.15)
38   *Pié Jesu (Requiem)* Andrew Lloyd Webber (3:53)
39   *Nocturne in B flat minor* Chopin (6:03)
40   *Jesus, you are the way (Fountain of Life)* Margaret Rizza (5:02)
41   *Prelude in C sharp minor* Rachmaninov (4:29)
42   *Dies irae (Requiem)* Mozart (1:44)

HOLY WEEK

43   *Berceuse* Godard (5.27)
44   *Osanna in excelsis* J. S. Bach (2.50)
45   *Finlandia* Sibelius (8:32)
46   *Adagio (Oboe Concerto)* Marcello (4:43)
47   *Chanson Triste* Tchaikovsky (2:55)
48   *Cello Concerto in A major (Largo)* C. P. E. Bach (10.29)
49   *Behold the Lamb of God (Messiah)* Handel (4:14)
50   *Lesson 1 for Maundy Thursday* Palestrina (5:48)
51   *St Matthew's Passion (Final Chorus)* J. S. Bach (5:26)
52   *Prelude in A* Chopin (2:43)
53   *Prelude in E minor* Chopin (2:05)
54   *In Paradisum (Requiem)* Fauré (3:41)
55   *Death of Åse (Peer Gynt Suite)* Grieg (5:08)
56   *Valse Triste* Sibelius (4:58)
57   *Miserere mei* Allegri (10:10)
58   *Piano Concerto No. 4 (Andante)* Beethoven (5:36)
59   *Agnus Dei* J. S. Bach (5.45)
60   *Ave Verum* Mozart (2:49)
61   *Lacrymosa dies illa (Requiem)* Mozart (3:20)

EASTER

62   *Gloria in Excelsis Deo (Gloria)* Vivaldi (2:20)
63   *I know that my redeemer liveth (Messiah)* Handel (6:52)

64   *Ode to Joy* Beethoven (7:58)
65   *Alleluia (Exsultate, Jubilate)* Mozart (2:44)
66   *Hallelujah (Messiah)* Handel (4:07)
67   *Gloria (Coronation Mass)* (4:53)
68   *How beautiful are the feet (Messiah)* Handel (2:28)
69   *Why do the nations? (Messiah)* Handel (3:00)
70   *Gymnopédie No. 2* Satie (3:40)
71   *Gloria (Mass in B minor)* J. S. Bach (1:43)
72   *Since by man came death (Messiah)* Handel (2:12)
73   *Worthy is the lamb that was slain (Messiah)* Handel (3:37)
74   *Spring Song in A* Mendelssohn (2:15)
75   *On wings of song* Mendelssohn (4:33)

PENTECOST

76   *Cum Sancto Spiritu (Mass in B minor)* J. S. Bach (3:52)
77   *Veni, lumen cordium (Fountain of Life)* Margaret Rizza (5:22)
78   *Send forth your spirit, Lord (Fountain of Life)* Margaret Rizza (2:06)
79   *The ride of the Valkyries* Wagner (4:57)
80   *The mirror of the Trinity (Magnificat)* Praetorius (2:03)
81   *Have mercy, Lord (St Matthew's Passion)* J. S. Bach (7:19)
82   *Holberg Suite (First Movement)* Grieg (2:58)
83   *Gavotte (Holberg Suite)* Grieg (4:10)
84   *Gratias (Mass in C minor)* Mozart (1:36)
85   *The Gadfly* Shostakovich (5:53)
86   *Adagio (Cello Concerto)* Haydn (5:21)
87   *The Swan (Carnival of the Animals)* Saint-Saëns (3:28)
88   *Danse profane (Danses sacrée et profane)* Debussy (2:04)
89   *The trumpet shall sound (Messiah)* Handel (3:56)
90   *Etude in E* Chopin (4:29)
91   *The prophet bird* Schumann (2:02)
92   *The little bird* Grieg (2:53)
93   *Jesu, joy of man's desiring* J. S. Bach (3:22)
94   *Moderato (Serenade for strings in E minor)* Dvořák (4:12)
95   *Nocturne No. 2 in E flat* Chopin (4:54)
96   *Pilgrims' Chorus (Tannhäuser)* Wagner (6:23)
97   *Credo in unum Deum (Mass in C minor)* Mozart (3:34)
98   *Salut d'Amour* Elgar (2:46)
99   *Sleepers awake! (Choral Prelude)* J. S. Bach (4:55)
100 *Come, Lord (Fountain of Life)* Margaret Rizza (3:58)

APPENDIX 2

Visual Resources

The following collections of slides have all been used in conjunction with the meditations, readings and music offered in this book. Most powerful of all has been the pack of 144 slides in six sets based on the television series *Jesus of Nazareth* directed by Franco Zeffirelli, produced by the Bible Society.

Sadly, this and many of the other collections referred to here are no longer available from the producers, but the details given may be of help in tracing them, either through your local Diocesan Religious Studies Resource Centre if you have one or, perhaps, through a local library, school, college or university. Failing that, you might try:

Rickett Educational Media Ltd (formerly The Slide Centre Ltd)
Great Western House, Langport, Somerset TA10 9YU
Tel 01458 253636

As well as the collections mentioned, I have occasionally used slides of the Holy Land, particularly, for example, scenes of the wilderness to accompany meditations on Jesus' temptation or John the Baptist preaching in the desert.

(Note: An asterisk indicates that the resource is no longer commercially available)

ADVENT

1 *Jesus of Nazareth 1: Jesus – Birth and childhood**
   Jesus of Nazareth 2: Jesus – Begins his ministry*

   Colour transparencies from the TV series directed by Franco Zeffirelli. Was produced by The Bible Society.

2 *In the Beginning**

   A cartoon slideset produced in conjunction with a Ladybird Bible Book primarily aimed at children. Was produced by Scripture Union.

3 *The Life of Christ I*

Slides focusing on the annunciation, nativity, and childhood of Jesus, as 'seen through the eyes of the artist', produced by:

Visual Publications
The Green, Northleach, Cheltenham, Gloucestershire GL54 3EX
Tel 01451 860519

4 *Jesus, the Child**

A cartoon slideset produced in conjunction with a Ladybird Bible Book primarily aimed at children. Was produced by Scripture Union.

CHRISTMAS

1 *Jesus of Nazareth 1: Jesus – Birth and childhood**

2 *Come, let us adore**

A series of 27 slides on the nativity. Was produced by Audio Visual Productions UK.

LENT

1 *Jesus of Nazareth 3: Jesus – Heals**
   *Jesus of Nazareth 4: Jesus – Cares**

2 *The Life of Christ II*

Slides focusing on Christ's public ministry. See Advent for details.

3 *Jesus of Nazareth 5: Jesus – In the last week**

4 *The Parables of Jesus**

A slideset primarily aimed at children. Was produced by the National Christian Education Council.

HOLY WEEK

1 *Jesus of Nazareth 5: Jesus – In the last week**
   *Jesus of Nazareth 6: Jesus – Trial to Resurrection**

2 *Oberammergau 1990*

A sequence of 36 slides from the Oberammergau Passion Plays, produced by:

Huber
Drosselstraße 7, D-8100 Garmisch-Partenkirchen, Germany

3 *The Life of Christ III*

See Advent for details.

4 *Man of the Cross*

A slide-sound presentation (code: 70P326), also available as a set of 15 posters (code 73P262), using a variety of artistic media, including photography, vividly portraying the Way of the Cross. Produced by:

St Paul MultiMedia Productions
199 Kensington High Street, London W8 6BA
Tel 020 7937 9591

5 *He Carries Our Cross**

An audiovisual programme for liturgy, prayer and reflection, including slides of line-sketches, focusing on the events of the Passion under two subsections: (a) Journey to Jerusalem, and (b) Journey to the Cross. Was produced by St Paul MultiMedia Productions.

6 *Bread and Wine**

Pictures of the elements of the Eucharist, particularly suitable for meditations on the Last Supper. Was produced for the Church Pastoral Aid Society by Falcon Audio Visual Aids.

EASTER

1 *Jesus of Nazareth 6: Jesus – Trial to Resurrection**

2 *The Life of Christ IV*

See Advent for details.

PENTECOST

1 *St Paul**

A radiovision slideset consisting of 45 picture slides. Was produced by the BBC.

2 *The Story of St Paul**

A picture slideset produced in conjunction with a Ladybird Bible Book primarily aimed at children. Was produced by Ladybird Books.

3 *The Gospel: Life of Jesus**

A cartoon slideset. Was produced by St Paul MultiMedia Productions.

APPENDIX 3

Leading a Quiet Day/Reflective Event Practical Suggestions

The success of a reflective event, like that of any other, depends on the care taken beforehand in planning and preparation. Key points to consider are:

LOCATION

- If you are holding a Quiet Day, a tranquil location is essential, and preferably one with a chapel/quiet area and grounds/gardens to walk in. Make sure there will be enough parking for everyone.

- If slides are to be used, ensure that the room can be blacked out.

- Send all participants clear instructions instructions beforehand showing how to get to the venue.

PREPARATION

- Examine carefully the resources available and consider ways in which they might be used most effectively.

- A 'low-key' event among friends or a small invited group can be just as effective as a larger, more ambitious project.

- If possible, ascertain in advance the names of all those who will be attending the event.

- Prepare the seating beforehand, and ensure there are enough places for everyone plus a few spare, just in case!

- If you would like people to read during the event *always* contact them beforehand with the reading in question and a copy of the programme for the day. Anybody taking part will want to give their best, and will not thank you for springing a passage full of tongue-twisters on them at the last moment.

PRESENTATION

- Start each session informally, perhaps with tea and coffee. This helps people unwind and gives them the opportunity to get to know each other a little better.

- Prepare everything you will need for the event carefully. A last-minute panic will unsettle participants and could cause you considerable embarrassment.

- Depending on the type of event, consider opening with a short and simple ice-breaker.

- If you are allowing time for discussion, avoid becoming so side-tracked that the point of the event is lost completely. Equally, some freedom must be given for people to raise issues and thoughts which may arise, even if this might mean going off on a tangent for a time. It is your role as leader to encourage people to open up, whilst at the same time gently steering each session back to the key theme being covered.

- Never force people to read, or assume everyone is happy to take part in this way. Some will find any public participation purgatory, and the chances are that they will not come back to your next event.

- If you are using slides, ensure these are inserted in the right order and the right way up, or the atmosphere you have tried so hard to build will be destroyed at a stroke! Always arrive early and check through all slides on location. Make sure also that you have a spare bulb in case one should blow. A projector stand will also save you a lot of unnecessary trouble.

- If you are using recorded music, ensure that the tape is ready at the right place or that you know how to locate the correct track on the CD. The equipment you are using should be suitable for the location, and it is a good idea to come armed with an extension lead.

- Don't be afraid of silence. Times for quiet reflection are all too rare in our hectic world, so don't jump in the moment you feel the silence may have become a little awkward.

- Be sensitive to the needs and feelings of participants.

Most of the above points, though primarily concerned with reflective events, can be applied equally to leading any act of worship. Ultimately what participants get out of such events will depend on what you, with God's help, put into them.

Index of Bible Passages

References are to meditation numbers, not pages

Index of Bible Characters

References are to meditation numbers, not pages

INDEX OF PRINCIPAL SUBJECTS

References are to meditation numbers, not pages